"This exceedingly readable book goes well beyond mere calls for courageous behavior in the workplace; it provides us with a rich store of exemplars, insights, tools, and tactics that can serve to literally rewire our habitual responses to what's possible. Jim Detert's concept of 'competent courage' becomes less a matter of exceptional bravery and more a matter of choice."

 —**MARY C. GENTILE**, author, *Giving Voice to Values*; Professor of
  Practice, University of Virginia Darden School of Business

"Leaders should take note. It just shouldn't be so hard to speak truth to power; it's a leader's responsibility to create an environment where everyone can be courageous. As Professor Detert shows, that's both good for employees and good for the organization."

 —**DICK RAINES**, CEO, Carfax

"As we watch with great disappointment our current-day leaders' failures, *Choosing Courage* provides a road map for effectively demonstrating courage at all levels of leadership. This is a great read for leaders on the rise as well as those frustrated by the seemingly intractable polarization of many of today's challenges in both business and politics."

 —**MARK BERTOLINI**, retired Chairman and CEO, Aetna

"At no time has there been a greater need for the lessons and guidance that Jim Detert provides in this book. *Choosing Courage* has captured the secret for how leaders and organizations can have a greater impact—and that includes greater social impact, associate engagement, business performance, innovation, and personal growth."

 —**TOM POLEN**, CEO and President, Becton, Dickinson
  and Company

CHOOSING COURAGE

CHOOSING COURAGE

THE EVERYDAY GUIDE TO BEING BRAVE AT WORK

JIM DETERT

HARVARD BUSINESS REVIEW PRESS

BOSTON, MASSACHUSETTS

Library of Congress Cataloging-in-Publication Data

Names: Detert, James R., author.
Title: Choosing courage : the everyday guide to being brave at work / Jim Detert.
Description: Boston, MA : Harvard Business Review Press, [2021] | Includes index.
Identifiers: LCCN 2020050840 | ISBN 9781647820084 (hardcover) |
    ISBN 9781647820091 (ebook)
Subjects: LCSH: Courage. | Work environment—Moral and ethical aspects. |
    Employees—Attitudes. | Industrial relations.
Classification: LCC BJ1533.C8 D48 2021 | DDC 179/.6—dc23
LC record available at https://lccn.loc.gov/2020050840

ISBN: 978-1-64782-008-4
eISBN: 978-1-64782-009-1

To the Detert women

CONTENTS

PREFACE:
A TIME FOR COURAGE

We are living in an extraordinary time. As I write this, in October 2020, Covid-19 continues its global devastation of individual lives and entire communities, and protests about police brutality and systemic racial injustice are ongoing in cities across the United States and around the world. Amid this pain and despair, we're also witnessing acts of true courage, from health-care providers speaking out about unsafe or unacceptable working conditions, retail clerks trying to enforce safety standards that those above them won't, or people of color demanding change in their organizations and beyond.[1]

Though current events make the need for courage more obvious than ever, I committed to writing this book more than a decade ago. Around 2008, I began ending my courses with students and professionals with a short wrap-up lecture. Then I said: "If we had more time, there are many more tools I could have shared to add to your toolkit. But here's the thing: in the end, I don't believe the range of one's toolkit is the primary differentiator between better and worse leadership. What I think matters much more is the courage to use those tools when needed."

Then I'd give a few examples of workplace courage and share why I thought it was desperately needed for all of us to become examples for others. Not one student, then or since, said they worked in an environment where courageous behaviors weren't critical or that they always happened when they should. Aspire as we might, there are as of yet few (if any) truly "fearless organizations."[2] So I'd implore them to go out and make the world a better place, to do something courageous and report back so I could update my final speech with their stories.

Here's what has consistently happened since. People write me weeks, months, and even years after hearing these remarks to ask for resources on the topic because they need help preparing for a difficult conversation, engaging with an issue they've been avoiding, or pursuing what they know is important but fraught with risk.

That's why I've spent the last few years reading everything I could about courage—and courage in workplaces more specifically—and collecting my own data from thousands of people in different investigations of workplace courage. I didn't just want to add my voice to the cacophony of others just "encouraging courage" with no concrete road map or advice; I wanted to add something meaningful to the dialogue for those who know they should and would like to act more courageously. This book represents my attempt to distill everything I've learned into a research-based but highly accessible guide for those I've had the privilege of working with in person and the many more I've yet to meet. I was truly inspired by the incredible stories I've been told, and I want to share them with others.

Truth be told, I also needed these stories in a way I can only now articulate. I grew up in a relatively poor, single-parent family in a nondescript Midwestern city. I often felt impotent, knowing that my life wasn't what I wanted it to be but unable as a kid to do much about it. Perhaps most depressingly, when I looked around for inspiration, it was often lacking. Adults, too, including those in positions of authority, seemed too often to be (to use Thoreau's words) "living lives of quiet desperation" rather than competently and courageously charting a better future for themselves and others. All these years later, I'm still disheartened and angered by the lack of courageous action by leaders and non-leaders alike. I just can't stand the idea that we'd be so willing to give up our agency, authenticity, and moral calling for whatever it is we get in return.

We all have fairly regular opportunities to act in courageous ways, to undertake actions that we or others perceive to be worthy or noble *despite the risks the behavior entails.* Worker safety or working conditions certainly weren't perfect before Covid-19, and we were far from a world where people could expect the same treatment at work and elsewhere regardless of their skin color, gender, or other demographic or identity characteristics. What's so unfortunate is that we've largely accepted the notion that courageous action is only to be expected from extraordinary people in extraordinary situations.

This book presents a challenge to the idea that courage is the province and responsibility of the few. I'll share why I believe that courage, especially courageous acts done competently enough to create positive change, isn't innate. We don't believe that only some of us are born with the capacity to be virtuous in other ways—such as by being honest, fair, or prudent—or expect these kinds of behavior only once in a great while, so why would we expect that only some of us have the capacity for courageous action?

My goals in writing this are to urge you to accept the need for courageous action as your responsibility too and to understand that competent courage comes from the choices you can make to learn and repeatedly practice specific skills (just like competence in *any* domain does). And I want to help you more frequently choose to act during everyday opportunities to step up or speak out at work, rather than letting your fears hold you back.

I also want to help you understand that courage isn't just about the spectacular, rare acts that make headlines or get one labeled *Time*'s Person of the Year.[3] It's about all kinds of behaviors that are desperately needed in organizations if individuals and organizations are going to learn, be healthy, and thrive.

If you want to do more to *protect others* at work—whether colleagues, subordinates, or customers—who are powerless and often ignored, taken advantage of, or discriminated against, this book is for you.

If you want to do more to *solve important problems* at work, whether they be inefficiencies that waste time or money, internal processes that sap morale, or product or service choices that lead to dissatisfaction among current customers and inability to attract new ones, this book is for you.

If you want to *pursue opportunities* more frequently, whether that means taking "stretch assignments" that might increase your impact and satisfaction or pursuing work in a different organization that better fits your talents and values, this book is for you. Likewise, this book is for you if you want to be the person bold enough to lead your organization into new markets or new lines of business or to make other decisions that allow your organization to better fulfill its mission.

And if you want to get better at *innovating*, whether that be conducting and implementing small experiments in parts of an organization, developing and launching new products, or creating new processes that allow your organization to radically improve, this book is for you.

We know that we desperately need more of these behaviors. When we don't step up to protect others, we allow continued abuse and discrimination toward our colleagues and harm to our customers (think of Wells Fargo or Volkswagen).[4] When we don't step up to solve problems or pursue opportunities, we contribute to the likelihood of organizational failures and the statistics showing that only about one-third of American employees are highly engaged at work.[5] And when we don't have the courage to innovate, we increase the odds that we and our organizations will join the millions that have been leapfrogged by nimbler upstarts and those more prepared to thrive in a rapidly evolving digital world. Thus, the question isn't whether these everyday opportunities for courage are important. The question is whether you'll embrace more of them.

But to be clear, this book is not a call to organizational martyrdom. I'm not encouraging everyone who reads it to be prepared to lose their job, their friends, or their health every time they spot a problem or an opportunity at work. It's not a call to shoot from the hip or make yourself vulnerable the second you have a strong emotion or an idea. Instead, I'm encouraging you to consider courageous action as something that can be done more or less competently, where competence means you increase the chances of actually accomplishing something positive and decrease the likelihood of negative personal consequences.

The people whose stories I share throughout this book have chosen courage. Their accounts provide inspiration, but also clarify that competent courage is about perspiration. To choose competent courage is to accept not just the responsibility to act, but the obligation to learn and continuously practice the skills that increase your chance of creating positive outcomes for yourself and others.

If you're ready to choose that path and be inspired along the way by the incredible people you'll meet, then this book is for you.

CHAPTER 1

Choosing Courage

Stuart Scott will always be remembered as a trailblazer. As the first Black anchor on SportsCenter, ESPN's flagship program, Scott's use of slang, his references to Black music and culture, and his clever catchphrases helped ESPN appeal to younger viewers—especially younger Black Americans.

Scott's style was influential. "African Americans throughout the history of this country have been told that we needed to conform, to assimilate. That we needed to be less street, be less hip-hop, be less hood. Just be *less*," recalled Michael Smith, a sports journalist and former ESPN commentator who grew up watching Scott on television. "We had to be less of ourselves in order to make the majority feel comfortable. For Stuart to come along and be every bit as good and professional, as sharp, as polished as any broadcaster doing it, but yet still be able to be as authentic and connected and representative of the culture as he was—it was just incredible."[1]

Beyond his on-air brilliance, Scott fought a well-documented, multiyear battle against terminal cancer and became an inspiration to many beyond his sports viewers. Upon his death at age forty-nine, he was universally praised by fans, colleagues, athletes, and journalists;

in a written statement, President Barack Obama commended Scott for being a pioneer: "Stuart Scott helped usher in a new way to talk about our favorite teams and the day's best plays."

That's the part of Scott's story many of us know. Keith Olberman, his longtime colleague, shared another part few people knew. "I cannot think of anybody I worked with in sports whose professional courage I have admired more," he said in a heartfelt tribute.[2]

Olberman was referring to Scott's behind-the-scenes struggles at ESPN. Though he is praised today, Scott received strong pushback from some viewers, media critics, and an ESPN executive. He was told to stop using language that most of the audience—meaning "white viewers"—didn't understand or he'd be taken off SportsCenter. "It was awful," recalled his wife, Susan. "People really don't know how awful it was. . . . Stuart was desperately frustrated."

Scott's response to this pressure, said Olberman, "was the single most impressive thing I've ever seen a television sportscaster do."

Faced with two apparent choices—to back down and tone down his style to protect himself and his career or to lash out—Scott decided on a more creative option: he defied the directive from above but did so in a way that made it nearly impossible for the executive to carry out his threat.

Scott went on air and *publicly congratulated* ESPN on its willingness to accept crucial aspects of American culture that had traditionally not been adequately represented on TV. This brilliant, gutsy act neutralized the executive, who now had little choice but to let Scott carry on or be seen as explicitly against tolerance and respect for Black culture.

That, Keith Olberman wants us all to remember, was a brilliant act of workplace courage.

What Is Workplace Courage?

Throughout my career, I've heard hundreds of stories of people like Stuart Scott who've acted courageously at work.

Take Chris, a medical student, who pushed a supervising psychiatrist to order a simple diagnostic test before sending a suicidal patient in the ER to the psych ward. Because of Chris's courage to challenge authority, the medical team discovered that the patient's unremitting pain was caused by a vascular disease, which was resolved with surgery.[3]

Or consider Jackie, who launched a marketing and sales campaign that her organization's president was against. "If you want to do this, your job is on the line," he told her. "If it works, you stay. If it doesn't, you can find something else to do." Jackie, after a few days of intense deliberation, decided to go for it. Though the campaign was a success—she's told it was the most successful one in the company's history—and she kept her job, she was never thanked for her work.

Though these examples may not fit into the traditional view of courage, which, historically, has focused on physical acts, Stuart Scott's, Chris's, and Jackie's feats are surely courageous.[4] Each faced a choice to act or not, and—despite the threat in all three cases, of recrimination from their superiors—each chose to step up when most people wouldn't.

In scholar-speak, I define workplace courage as *work-domain-relevant acts done for a worthy cause despite significant risks perceivable in the moment to the actor.*[5] But put more simply, workplace courage is taking action at work because it feels right and important to stand for a principle, a cause, or a group of others, despite the potential for serious career, social, psychological, and even physical repercussions for doing so.

Workplace courage comes in many forms. It is speaking truth to power—and to peers, subordinates, and other stakeholders whose behavior is causing problems or falling short of what's possible. And it includes acts aimed at personal and organizational growth, such as taking on stretch assignments, owning bold initiatives, and innovating within or beyond one's current organization.

You'll notice that these acts represent "everyday" opportunities for courage—the kinds of things we might hope we'd do routinely. When it comes to courage, we need not go looking for special occasions or wait for a single big moment. We need only decide to act when the chances come, which they do for all of us.

This runs counter to how many people view courage—as a rare trait that's practiced only by exceptional people. In fact, thinking of it this way is counterproductive and an excuse for our own inaction. As educator and social activist Parker Palmer has written, if examples like Rosa Parks's unwillingness to move to the back of the bus in the 1950's South are going to inspire us to our own action, rather than merely be something we passively admire, "we must see her as the ordinary person she is. That will be difficult to do because we have made her into superwoman—and we have done it to protect ourselves."[6] As Palmer correctly notes, we have to take her, and others, off the pedestals we've placed them on to avoid holding ourselves to the same standard of virtuous action when the opportunities arise.

I've had the privilege of meeting some amazing people as I've studied workplace courage, and I can assure you that they range across gender, ethnicity, nationality, physical appearance, political orientation, religious commitment, education level, and so many other dimensions we use to categorize people. A few are rich or high-status, but the vast majority are not. Unless we normalize acting courageously, seeing it as a possibility and responsibility for everyone, too many of us will keep waiting for others to do it, hiding (uncomfortably) behind assertions like "We can't all be Mandela or Gandhi" or that we're going to do it later when we have more power.

You'll always have something to lose, and there's no credible evidence that says an abundance of courage in others is right around the corner to save us. If you want to make things better at work, for yourself and for others, the only thing you control with certainty is your own willingness to take action.

As I'll detail in this book, courage is about skills that can be learned and developed: there are specific things you can do before, during, and even after a courageous act to increase the odds that the risk you take isn't for naught. And there are plenty of opportunities to practice everyday courage, building your "courage muscle" a little at a time by starting with relatively safer, more manageable acts from which you can learn.[7] It's these skills, honed through practice, that differentiate those who act—and act competently—from the rest who don't.[8]

Why Courage Is in Short Supply

We know in the abstract that courage is valuable (even if we wish someone else would be the one to act). Winston Churchill said courage was the first of human qualities because it guarantees all the rest.[9] Writer C. S. Lewis likewise claimed courage wasn't merely *a* virtue, but "the form of every virtue at the testing point, which means at the highest point of reality."[10] The leadership literature is also rife with claims about courage as a virtue, attribute, trait, or behavior pattern needed for effective leadership. My own students certainly believe that courage differentiates those leaders who succeed from those who fail over the long run.[11]

Protecting and inspiring others. Solving problems. Pursuing opportunities. Growing and innovating. Put that way, it seems clear that we should want and be motivated to be more courageous. So, why aren't we?

We're Programmed to Avoid Unnecessary Risks

Because humans have evolved to (subconsciously) prioritize perpetuating their genes, it's quite logical to worry about not doing grave harm to ourselves in all types of social settings. We've also spent most of our time as a species living in small groups or clans, and so making sacrifices for those not very closely related to us—such as risking one's family's well-being to do what is right for a large group of employees or citizens scattered around the globe—probably isn't instinctive for most of us. It's a conscious choice we have to make against these very primal instincts.

Our instincts are often reinforced by vicarious learning. Sadly, we see too many cases of people getting ahead at work—at least in the short run—despite, or even because of, their lack of courage. While it may eventually catch up to you, there are certainly enough examples of "getting ahead by going along" for people to believe that courage might be for naive losers. When I asked a sample of my MBA students to think of someone highly successful in a leadership position over the course of an entire career, and then rate that leader on a set of characteristics, courage scored highest—higher than technical knowledge or skills, intelligence, and work ethic. But when I asked them to think of and rate another leader who has been highly successful in a leadership position for just a short period of time, courage rated last (with work ethic at the top). So, in the eyes of these ambitious young people, courage is clearly a hallmark of those who have had highly admirable careers. They don't, however, think it's as important as other things when one is getting started. The question, of course, is when courage will kick in for those who spend years rationalizing that "it's just not time yet." In my experience, the answer is too often "never."

Our language has also evolved to remind us of the benefits of conformity and risks of challenging the status quo: phrases like "Be a team player," "Be loyal," "Don't rock the boat," "Don't risk your career over this," "We've always done it this way," "Everybody does it," and "Let it go" are abundant, whereas those pointing to the value of speaking up and persisting in change efforts are few in comparison and suggest significant hardship (e.g., "Fight tooth and nail" or "Stick to your guns").[12]

There's also the fact that, whether or not we are willing to admit it, most of us want to be *liked*. And given the intense pain that social rejection can bring, we certainly don't want to be *dis*liked. Hence, it's natural to view life, and leadership in particular, as an extended popularity contest. Consciously or not, we avoid doing things that might anger or alienate the people whose approval we seek so they'll continue to like and endorse us. If you doubt that, check out the behavior of posters on Twitter, Facebook, or any other social media platform.[13]

There Are Real Risks

Beyond the instinctual and culturally reinforced bases for frequent conformity and conflict avoidance, it's undeniably true that courage is in short supply because it is inherently risky. People *do* sometimes see their promotion prospects vanish, some *do* lose their jobs, and some *do* suffer broken relationships and deeply bruised egos as a result of courageous action at work.

In most modern work organizations, there are plenty of risks. Even in places like the United States, where the First Amendment of the Constitution protects free speech, most employees with at-will contracts (and that's the vast majority these days) can't say what they want without potential repercussions. Want to publicly criticize public officials in the United States? Go for it. Want to criticize your organization's leaders? Tread carefully.

Fortunately, many fewer of us face *physical risks* at work today than at any time in history, though firefighters, police officers, oil rig workers, and miners, among others, still routinely put themselves in harm's way. And, to a surprising degree, so do those who deal with angry customers or former employees.[14]

Most of us do, however, face potential *career risks*.[15] Despite all the talk about flatter organizations with more shared leadership, most people still have bosses and are still wage dependent in one way or another.[16] If we push the envelope too far, we could get fired, blackballed, held back, or otherwise negatively impacted financially.[17] As William Deresiewicz noted in his book *Excellent Sheep*, people don't like it when you challenge the consensus because you're forcing them to question it as well.[18] You're trying to surface for clear consideration the doubts that others are working hard to keep below the surface. Numerous former Wells Fargo employees, for example, reported being fired for minor violations like slight tardiness shortly after speaking up internally against the illegal sales tactics that eventually led to hundreds of millions of dollars in penalties and a congressional investigation.[19] Career risks for speaking up loom large even in environments like the military where physical courage is expected. The most decorated military leaders sometimes still feel "afraid to paint the true picture" to those above them, and some certainly face career consequences for going against their boss's wishes.[20]

Social risks also loom large. For most of humans' time on earth, being ostracized by those around you wasn't just psychologically unpleasant—it was life-threatening. You courted death if you were left alone to face violent predators and harsh environmental conditions. While today you're unlikely to actually die if your coworkers shun you, that doesn't mean we don't have horrible fears of "social death."[21] Indeed, some research suggests that "social rejection is perceived by the brain and other mechanisms as similar to physical injury."[22] Consider the social consequences Edwin Raymond, a New York City police officer, has faced for trying to change routine practices in the police department, such as how arrest statistics are used. He's been called "crybaby," "rat," "zero," and worse on anonymous officer message boards. Even his friends have told him he's nuts for continuously trying to do what's right against such significant pushback.[23]

Often, acts of courage court both social and career risks. Sam Polk, a former hedge fund trader in New York, described how difficult it was to speak out against the "bro talk"—the belittling, sexist banter—that made it hard for women to advance on Wall Street. "It feels really good to be in the in-crowd," he acknowledged, and to protest typical male behavior would have "been embarrassing and emasculating" and "bad for my career." As a result, he "stood silent hundreds of times as men objectified and degraded women."[24] While it's easy to be the armchair critic about rich Wall Streeters, it's more useful to acknowledge that it's hard for any of us to go against the grain of strong norms and, as Polk noted, "even harder when doing so means jeopardizing millions of dollars in future earnings" for challenging a "culture of brutal conformity."

Standing out also poses *psychological risks*. No one wants to feel stupid or impotent. Taking on high-visibility projects or stretch assignments beyond one's current competence courts public embarrassment. When you show vulnerability in facilitating the work or well-being of others, you risk being seen as weak or incompetent. Implementing a truly innovative product or process you developed could cast you as the champion of a failed experiment. Sure, these behaviors sometimes also expose you to career and social risks. But they expose you to psychological risks every time. You're your own judge and juror, and when you're really pushing boundaries, there's a real chance you'll take at least a temporary hit to how you feel about yourself. "Looking stupid" or "feeling incompetent" or "being a failure" are often self-imposed labels and, hence, represent the psychological risks of workplace courage.

In our studies of thirty-five acts of workplace courage, Evan Bruno and I have consistently found a strongly negative correlation between the level of risk (and courage) attributed to a behavior and the frequency with which the behavior happens when it could. Put simply, when perceived career, social, psychological, and physical risks for doing something go up, the willingness to do that thing goes way down.[25]

And, unfortunately, these risks suppress courage even among the most powerful. I've had countless senior leaders tell me that they don't tell their bosses or boards what's really going on for fear of career repercussions, and just as many tell me they pass up opportunities for courageous action to avoid social or psychological consequences. Others similarly note that too many of today's CEOs "wait for public opinion to tell them what to do."[26] The same is true in politics—too many politicians putting their own interests above principled stands has led to an "unprecedented deficit" of courage in the halls of Congress today, says Eliot Cohen, the dean of the School of Advanced International Studies at Johns Hopkins.[27]

Why Courage Matters

Given all these risks, you might be ready to put this book down now. If I've validated your fears about workplace courage, why is it worth reading on? Are there really enough upsides to counteract all these risks?

The truth is, we don't have nearly enough strong, systematic evidence about the conditions under which courageous workplace acts produce good and bad outcomes for both the actor and others or the organization itself.

Still, a core premise of this book, and the focus of several subsequent chapters, is that how we engage in workplace courage can make a big difference in whether we bring success or harm to ourselves and others. That is, we can be more or less *competent* in our courageous action. Assuming for now that a courageous act is performed competently, what are some reasons to expect that good things might happen?

Your Courage Matters for Others

Let's start with the chance to directly affect important outcomes. As I argued in the preface, courage at work can protect others, solve problems and avert disasters, and lead to opportunities seized and various forms of innovation and growth. Stuart Scott paved the way for more diversity in sports broadcasting, Chris saved a patient from intense physical and emotional suffering, and Jackie spearheaded the most successful campaign in her company's history. This is undoubtedly why people at the top of organizations, and those charged with overseeing them on behalf of others, claim to value courage so much.[28]

Conversely, the costs when employees fail to demonstrate courage can be immense, in both human and financial terms. Volkswagen shareholders have lost billions of dollars (already) following the revelation that the automaker sold millions of cars worldwide with software used to cheat on emissions tests. According to one commenter who had worked on emissions software for one of the Big Three US automakers, "There was simply no way this didn't involve a concerted effort by many individuals." Surely some of them had the sense to know that this fraud was not just wrong, but eventually going to be detected and to lead to great harm to the company's many key stakeholders.[29]

Courageous acts, or their absence, can also have more indirect effects on performance through their impact on how others feel and behave. A single act of courage, particularly by those in leadership roles, can inspire others to be more committed, to work harder, to do things of benefit to the organization that they can't be made to do (scholars call these "citizenship" or "extra-role" behaviors), and even to perform their own courageous acts. When I asked a group of executive MBA students to describe the impact on them and others of a courageous behavior by a leader, they used words like "great sense of pride," "motivated to work harder and be more creative," and "energized." "It has been a career-defining moment for me, as it taught me and others how to be courageous and accountable," said one. "It reinvigorated our sense of purpose and commitment," said another, adding that it "strengthened our resolve and confidence in each other that we were prepared to face any challenge and be successful."

In contrast, the responses I received from another group of executive students who described the impact of a leader's failure to act with courage in a specific situation show the incredibly negative effects that can result from being seen as having failed the courage test. Respondents said they "felt angry and undercut," "lost confidence in, and respect for, the leader," and "lost faith in the competency and ability of the department manager from that day forth." Another said that he was "disgusted and saddened that I was being overseen by such a cowardly individual with low moral fiber." I doubt any of these individuals were going the extra mile for those bosses anymore. Those with options were probably looking to get out.

In this final commencement speech to US Naval Academy graduates in 2011, former defense secretary Robert Gates summed up nicely just how important courageous action is. Not just physical courage, he clarified, but "the courage to chart a new course, the courage to do what is right and not just what is popular, the courage to stand alone, the courage to act, the courage as a military officer to 'speak truth to power.'" For those who will become leaders, he told the young men and women, "the time will inevitably come when you must stand alone. When alone you must say, 'This is wrong' or 'I disagree with you and, because I have the responsibility, this is what we will do.'"[30] Being courageous is, in short, how we fulfill our obligations to others under difficult circumstances.

Your Courage Matters for Yourself

I'll also offer you two broader reasons to choose courage: legacy and regret. Our legacy is what endures after we're gone. Beyond tangible things like money or buildings, it's what people say about us, how they remember us, and what they do or don't do because of the impact we had on them. And legacies tend to be about what we *did*—at least if we're talking about a positive legacy. Research shows that regrets, in contrast, tend to be about the things we *didn't do*, but wish we had. This links opportunities for courage inextricably with the shaping of our legacy and our regrets.

Let's look a bit more at regret first. Admonitions to avoid regret are commonplace throughout history, be it President Teddy Roosevelt reminding us that "it is hard to fail, but it is worse never to have tried to succeed," or poet John Greenleaf Whittier's warning that, "for all sad words of tongue and pen, the saddest are these, 'It might have been.'" And, indeed, research does suggest that "regret" is a major theme among those who look back on their life as they age, with that regret stemming more from things not done than from trying things and not succeeding.[31] John Izzo interviewed 235 people between ages 59 and 105, and found "Leave no regrets" to be one of the five secrets to a great life. To do this, he argued, "We must live with courage, moving toward what we want rather than away from what we fear."[32] When we don't, suggests the research of Australian nurse Bronnie Ware on patients in their last twelve weeks of life, we live not just with a psychological burden, but physical illnesses related to bitterness, resentment, and regret.[33]

It doesn't take until the end of life to have regrets haunt us. Sam Polk, the hedge fund trader mentioned above, is middle-aged. He lives with deep regret about what he didn't do during his eight years on Wall Street, and with sadness and fear for the world his daughter will enter as an adult. He's used those feelings to make major changes in his life: he left the trading environment, owned up to his part in perpetuating a sexist culture, and has started Everytable, an organization whose mission is to bring healthy food to low-income communities at affordable prices.[34]

For all of us who have screwed up an attempt to do something bold, it sure may feel like we're more likely to regret actions taken and gone wrong. Over the longer term, though, research shows it's regret for inaction that tends to linger.[35] The enduring potency of "I should have" regrets probably stems from it being harder to tell ourselves a convincing story about why we didn't do something. That's why courage matters, why it's so important to push beyond your fears, to embrace actions outside your comfort zone before it's too late. Not just because you can do a lot of good for others by daring to stand up and speak out—though I think that's the main and most important reason—but also because when you don't, you live with regret.

As for our legacy—whether we'll be remembered much at all after we've left a job, an organization, or the Earth and, if so, for what—that depends on what we do now. While our preferred legacy is deeply personal, I've learned about a number of common aspirations by surveying people anywhere from thirty-five to eighty-five years old. Interestingly, whether they were just a decade or two into their careers, or well into retirement, what people hoped their legacy would be was pretty similar. They wanted to be remembered as people of high integrity, people who'd served others well, people who'd made a positive difference in the lives of those they'd worked with and on their organizations. Most of all, they wanted to be remembered as good to, and role models for, those closest to them. In explaining these aspirations, they didn't talk about the wealth or titles or awards they'd accumulated. They talked about acts of service, of taking risks on behalf of others. They talked, in short, about times they'd been willing to show courage rather than take the easy or more comfortable path.

Sometimes they suffered personal consequences, but they didn't report regret. They reported hope that these acts would lead to them being remembered as they desired.

. . .

I've collected far too many workplace courage stories done by people like you and me to believe it's impossible to hope for more. There is much we can learn from the collective experience of those I've studied that can help tip the balance in favor of competent courage. We can understand how to set the stage via our ongoing actions so that we'll be more likely to succeed when the time for courage arises; we can improve our clarity about our key values and purpose, and hone our sense of the best timing for a bold move; we can learn all kinds of techniques for managing ourselves and others more skillfully in the heat of the moment; and we can learn what to do after our big moments to keep the ball rolling or contain any damage. Perhaps most importantly, we can choose to see courage as a skill and not a natural endowment. When we do, we can commit to the kind of practice needed to make courageous acts seem less daunting and more likely to go well.

To be clear, there's no magic bullet for eliminating the risks or guaranteeing good outcomes. If there's no risk at all, we're not talking about courage. It's precisely the riskiness of the kind of acts I'll talk about in this book that makes courageous action the truest test of virtue. As the philosopher Alasdair MacIntyre reminds us, "If someone says that he cares for some individual, community, or cause, but is unwilling to risk harm or dangers on his, her, or its own behalf, he puts into question the genuineness of his care and concern."[36] I think most of us do genuinely care. We just need a healthy dose of instruction and inspiration to help us take productive steps forward. That's what I hope this book provides you.

What's Next

In the chapters that follow, I'll use findings from years of my own research and insights from many others' work to systematically explore these ideas. My aim isn't just to inspire you to act, but also to provide useful diagnostics, frameworks, and tools that increase your chances of having maximum impact when you do.

In chapter 2, we'll look closely at *truth to power*—the category of behaviors most closely connected to people's conception of workplace courage. Truth to power behaviors include confronting or challenging direct bosses or other higher-ups, acting with more autonomy than you technically have, protecting or promoting others, and owning (rather than hiding or denying) your mistakes.

Chapter 3 is all about *candid conversations and bold actions*, other common types of behavior that require courage at work: difficult conversations and actions involving peers, subordinates, and other important stakeholders like customers or external partners. We'll also look at other bold actions, like taking stretch assignments or personal responsibility for major initiatives, starting a new venture, or making principled stands. While some of these may seem like, and technically are, everyday learning behaviors or part of people's jobs, they're done with surprising and disappointing infrequency due to their perceived riskiness.

Once we're on the same page about what workplace courage looks like, and you've done some initial self-assessment using the Workplace Courage Acts Index as a guide, you'll start your personal journey toward more frequent and competent courage by *building your courage ladder* in chapter 4. Choosing courage is about committing to practice—to taking small and specific action steps that will help you slowly but surely improve how you feel, think, and behave during situations that feel risky but also important. I'll encourage you to choose an action from the bottom of your courage ladder, so your initial steps feel more manageable and likely to lead to some early wins and motivation to keep climbing.

To increase the odds that your courageous acts actually change something for the better, I'll describe in part 2—chapters 5 through 9—what, collectively, differentiates courageous acts that seem to have the largest and most enduring positive effects, and fewest negative effects, from those that fail to have the intended influence or keep the actor from undue harm. Drawing from hundreds of experiences shared with me and a host of related studies I and others have done, I'll share how people from all walks of life enacted multiple aspects of what I call the Competent Courage framework to increase their odds of successful action.

In chapter 5, I'll first talk about *creating the right conditions* for successful courageous action. The focus here isn't on a particular courageous act, but rather on how we behave *over time* to enhance the odds that we succeed when we do step up and to minimize downside risks. We'll delve into the importance of a strong internal reputation, which involves being seen as emotionally intelligent, humble, kind, and generous, and also as a consistent high performer. We'll also look at ways to optimize one's own autonomy to act with less fear of retribution. This includes keeping your job mobility high and taking steps to be less financially dependent on your specific employer.

Chapter 6 focuses on *choosing your battles*—deciding which specific acts to undertake. You'll learn about developing the discipline to both know what matters most to you, and also what things automatically set you off even if they're not that important. While your emotions are an important guide, for sure, competent courage is also about understanding what your ultimate objectives are and being in control of when you act and when you hold back in the service of longer-term success.

Choosing your battles is also about timing. The competently courageous avoid pushing an issue too early, when those they must influence aren't ready or able to pay attention; conversely, they don't wait until it's too late to matter. The saying "A crisis is a terrible thing to waste" also applies here. Challenging the status quo is a lot harder when you're seen as the sole impetus than when you're acting amid some other obvious source of internal or external pressure for change.

No matter how well you set the stage and choose your battles and their timing, you've also got to be skilled at managing the moment itself when it comes. That's the focus of chapters 7 and 8. In chapter 7, we'll focus on *managing the message*, which is fundamentally about understanding the targets of your action—how *they* see the issue, what *they* care about, and what kinds of data and solutions *they* are most likely to find compelling. Knowing this allows you to make many important decisions, including those involving the *framing* of your message. It helps you know, for example, whether to present something as an opportunity with an upside or a necessary response to a threat. It also helps you decide to paint your picture in primarily economic or cultural terms, and to find ways to connect your issue to their priorities.

In chapter 8, we'll turn to the importance of successfully *managing emotions*—both yours and those you seek to influence—during critical moments. Shaking in your boots while talking, going silent, or literally fleeing the situation because you're so scared at the first sign of resistance aren't hallmarks of effective courage acts. And, while being angry might fuel your action, failure to control your anger undermines success. Failed communication happens in part because when you're being overwhelmed by your own emotions, it's darn near impossible to focus on managing others' emotions. Thus, we'll also focus on some strategies for harnessing, rather than being hijacked by, the emotions involved during courage opportunities.

Chapter 9 examines the importance of *taking action after the act*. Though we don't spend as much time thinking about it—perhaps because we're just relieved to have finally done something or are busy licking our wounds—what we do *after* a bold act can also be vitally important. This chapter delves into the importance of following up, whether to clarify your target's position and solidify next steps, or to check in and address lingering negative emotions. We'll learn the importance of thanking those who have helped you and sharing credit for any wins. And we'll look at the importance of persistence—accepting that meaningful change requires multiple, sustained efforts—and the choice to see setbacks as data to learn from rather than reasons to give up.

Having reviewed the principles of competent courage, we turn, in part 3, to putting them into action. Chapter 10 invites you to decide on and commit to your next steps. Then we'll return to the courage ladder you started in chapter 4 and walk through some specific tools for managing the cognitive, emotional, and behavioral responses that can help you start *cultivating courage* one step at a time. I'll share some strategies for turning your goals into routine practice, such as using implementation intentions and public commitments to override our tendency to fail at developing new habits.

In chapter 11, I'll end by encouraging you to get clear about your "must dos." No matter how skilled you become, how much you increase your "can do" based on the ideas and tools in this book—you also need to understand what you want your life to stand for. Why? Because no amount of skill eliminates all risk. So if you want to increase the chances you push past that risk and act anyway, you need to keep front and center what you consider your responsibility to do, either merely so you can look yourself in the mirror without shame, or because you want to avoid long-term regrets while building a legacy you and others will feel good about. *It's up to you.*

One Final Note

Before moving on, let me address one question you may already have: "Do you think everything you're saying here is universally applicable?" My answer, in short: No. I'd be skeptical of any social science book that claimed to be presenting something that applied perfectly in any context, and you should be too.

Given my data sources and my own cultural embeddedness, this book speaks most directly to the situation in the United States. There are many cultures where the behaviors described in this book would be even more risky due to political environments and judicial processes that offer no guarantees against severe punishment for speaking up or acting against the rules. For example, Omeleye Soworo, who runs a website providing online news to Nigerians, has succinctly described the reality in Nigeria: "It is not so much a problem of free-dom of speech, but freedom after speech."[37] There are many other places around the world where speaking up may be legally allowable and not likely to get you jailed or killed, but nonetheless remains very difficult due to cultural norms. In its report on the Fukushima nu-clear accident, for example, the Independent Investigation Commis-sion concluded that the accident was a "disaster 'Made in Japan.' Its fundamental causes are to be found in the ingrained conventions of Japanese culture: our reflexive obedience; our reluctance to question authority; our devotion to 'sticking with the program.'"[38]

This said, many of the phenomena described in this book are really a function of natural *human* tendencies in the face of common oppor-tunities for courage. So while the risks may be different around the world due to varying physical, social, and economic circumstances, I'm pretty sure that in almost any culture, humans—especially those organized in social hierarchies—will find the behaviors examined in this book to at least sometimes reflect courageous action.

In the end, part of being competently courageous involves adopt-ing and tailoring the general principles that can work *in your context.* On that front, your expertise certainly exceeds mine.

Remember

- Workplace courage is about taking action at work on behalf of a principle, a cause, or a group of others, even though one knows there could be serious career, social, psychological, and even physical risks for doing so.

- Courage is risky, but it's also hugely important for ourselves and for others. Choosing courage in key moments helps us build the legacy we want and avoid the regrets we don't want. Acts of courage at work can protect others, help solve problems and avert disasters, and lead to opportunities seized and to various forms of innovation and growth. Courage acts also impact how others feel and behave. They can inspire commitment, bolster trust, and lead others to act more courageously.

- The lack of courage permeates all levels of organizations, but so do positive examples from people who differ on every conceivable characteristic. Thus, thinking about courage as constituting specific *acts*, not an innate characteristic of a limited number of people, helps us recognize that we all share responsibility for being courageous and that skill comes from preparation and practice.

- We can all improve our competence, and hence the likelihood of positive outcomes when we act courageously, by studying what others do well before, during, and after their acts of courage, and by committing to practice those kinds of behaviors.

PART ONE

THE NATURE OF WORKPLACE COURAGE

CHAPTER 2

Truth to Power

As adults, we know what we'd like to do when it matters most at work: we hope we'd tell the truth, stand up for ourselves or others, and say "no" when going along would be wrong.

For example, if you were Rebecca, who works at a New York investment firm, and realized you were making only a fraction of what your male colleagues were making despite significantly outperforming them, you'd like to think you'd confront the male founders on behalf of yourself and other women facing this systemic inequity. Or that if you (like too many accountants, sales managers, and safety experts) got told to "make the numbers look better" or "downplay the severity of the risks," you'd push back and refuse to do something that's misleading and possibly illegal or dangerous.

Sadly, people face similar choices every day and often don't speak up or push back. Feeling scared, unclear how to voice their concerns effectively, and trapped, they instead carry on silently and hope for the best. They lose respect for those above them and perhaps for themselves for their complicity. Over time, they're likely to start giving less and less of their best selves to their work and struggle to feel committed or engaged. They "quit before leaving."[1]

Why We Fear Power

The fact that we're highly attuned to, and hesitant to offend, those above us in any hierarchy—those with power over us—isn't news to anybody. We depend on powerful people for all sorts of resources, and we need to stay on their good side to avoid negative consequences.

Our fear of power is deep-seated. We've been socialized since childhood to listen to those above us, whether that means our parents, teachers, religious figures, or other group leaders. Whether it's "Eat your peas," "Be quiet in class," or "Listen to the minister," we're surrounded by instructions to conform to the wishes of those in authority if we want to have our social and material needs met and avoid rejection or expulsion.[2] Indeed, as Professors Herbert Kelman and V. Lee Hamilton remind us, "the duty to obey is inherent in the very concept of authority."[3]

Evolution has most likely played a role in our tendency to organize ourselves into hierarchies and be deferential to those above us. Our nearest relatives (as a species) are the great apes, and they are . . . *not* egalitarian. The alpha males abuse rivals, while the beta males bully everyone besides the alpha (to whom they are deferential).[4] Likewise, signs of rank ordering in humans goes back thousands of years.[5] Higher-rank individuals slept in the safest part of the house (the rear), while those of lowest rank (slaves) slept inside the front door in case of a raid. Humans too have evolved all sorts of dominance and submission signals and behaviors that tend to keep the hierarchy intact. Fortunately, these days we tend to stop short (in the United States, anyway) of physical altercations, imprisonment, or murder as hierarchy enforcement mechanisms.[6] But we still make it clear who's in charge, whether that's reflected by the size or location of an office, how people dress, where they sit in meetings, and lots of rules that make it more likely that the challenger of authority, not the challenged, faces formal or informal sanctions in the case of disagreement.[7]

The truth is, when we fear challenging authority, we don't know with certainty how likely or severe any negative consequences might be. If your job is to jump out of airplanes, there's objective risk. But when we're talking about disagreeing with a boss, taking a problem to a higher-up, or admitting a mistake, we almost never know for sure what's going to happen. The person you confront might be 100 percent OK with what you say or do, and 0 percent likely to retaliate. Or the odds might be 50/50. Even if you'd argue with me that you do know with some certainty, I'd simply reply: "That doesn't really matter. It's your *belief* that doing something is risky that affects your decision to do it." Similarly, others' *belief* that you did something worthwhile despite it being risky is what leads them to label it courageous. They don't know how risky it was, objectively or from your perspective—they are calling you courageous based only on their perception of the situation.

One last thing about our perception of workplace risks: if we had a perfect way of measuring actual risk levels (that is, determining after the fact exactly what happened across a huge range of situations), it's quite likely we'd find that most people overestimate them. It's only natural, literally. If you think you see a poisonous snake ten times and automatically jump back and run away, your flight instinct has kept you alive even if, all ten times, the "snake" was actually a stick. But if you fail to perceive the snake that is actually there even a single time, you might be in serious trouble. In short, evolution favors self-protection.[8] We have primitive brain components that help us start to protect ourselves before we even consciously perceive danger (or use more recently evolved parts of our brain to process whether it's real) and memory and behavior activation systems that favor "bad" over "good" and "false positives" (you think there's a snake when there's not) over "false negatives" (you fail to perceive an actual snake).[9] False positives lead us to waste some energy (e.g., jumping back, starting to run), but we're still alive; false negatives could mean death (that stick actually was a poisonous snake that bit you when you got too close).[10]

In short, courage is often in short supply not just because the world of work is filled with objective risk, but also because we're hardwired to overestimate it. We're also not very good at testing those estimates or updating them over time.

One manufacturing operator I interviewed told me he no longer speaks up because he's sure there will be trouble. This seemed unusual, since the reason I was visiting his plant was that it had been identified in a recent all-employee survey as one of the safest environments for speaking up in the whole company. And he acknowledged that the current plant manager and his direct boss were very open and approachable. I pressed him—why was he nonetheless sure it wasn't safe? Because he "got threatened with retaliation after speaking up *twelve years ago*" by the plant manager who was "*three plant managers ago.*" So was it really professionally risky for him to speak up at the time I was talking to him? Probably not. But he was still using the incident to justify his silence, even though he recognized in telling me that this wasn't a very rational basis for his current fear or behavior.

So we've got lots of real reasons to be afraid of challenging those above us, and a natural tendency to automatically overestimate that risk on top of it.[11] Put that all together, and it's no surprise that we often see silence and inaction. Whether in my own or others' research, the data is clear: people routinely forgo opportunities to speak truth to power.[12]

What Truth to Power Looks Like

Despite the risks of challenging or otherwise upsetting those with the power to harm us, not everyone stays silent or chooses inaction. Some people do defy expectations for conformity and deference to authority, becoming what author Ira Chaleff calls "courageous followers."[13] In fact, if authority structures can lead to what Kelman and Hamilton called "crimes of obedience," my research has revealed that they also set the stage for what I call the *courage of disobedience*.

When I started studying workplace courage, I interviewed people in all kinds of jobs and simply asked them to tell me about a specific example where they or someone around them did (or didn't do) something they considered courageous. As these examples accumulated into the hundreds, and my research assistants and I started to categorize them by type of behavior, one thing immediately stood out: acts involving, and usually directed at, those higher up the organizational chain of command were by far the most common. While only about one-third of the questions on the Workplace Courage Acts Index (WCAI) Evan Bruno and I created directly involve "truth to power" behaviors, about half of all the workplace courage stories I've been told (well over a thousand at this point) are of this type. In many ways, challenging, confronting, defying, or in other ways making oneself vulnerable to those with more formal power is the prototype of a courageous work act in a world where most of us need the pay, benefits, and various forms of social and psychological identity afforded by jobs in structured hierarchies. Put simply, angering those above us in an economy where so much is tied to our ongoing employment and most of us can be easily fired involves real risk, even when we're acting for quite legitimate purposes.

The Workplace Courage Acts Index

Below is a list of eleven behaviors that collectively represent a fairly comprehensive set of ways that people with less power can do worthy things that are risky (primarily because they might incur the anger or disappointment of those with more power at work). These are, in short, behaviors that are often considered courageous by the actors themselves or by others who observe the behavior. Remember: I consider workplace courage to be *an act* done for a worthy cause despite significant potential risks. Thus, the WCAI assesses specific *behaviors* that people engage in on identifiable occasions, not some kind of personality disposition or stable character assessment of a person.

On the WCAI, respondents first rate how courageous the behavior would be in the environment directly around them, from "not at all" to "extremely." They then estimate how often that kind of behavior actually happens around them when opportunities for it exist, from 0 percent to 100 percent. Jarrod, for example, might report that challenging a direct boss about strategic or operating policies or practices is "extremely" courageous in his environment, and therefore happens only about 20 percent of the time it could. Quinetta, who works in a

TRUTH TO POWER

Challenging authority figures

- Challenging/pushing back on direct boss about strategic or operating policies or practices

- Confronting direct boss about their disrespectful, hurtful, unprofessional, or inappropriate behavior

- Speaking up or standing up to a boss about their unethical or illegal behavior

- Challenging/pushing back on a leader above one's direct supervisor about strategic or operating policies or practices

- Speaking up to a leader above one's direct supervisor about others' unacceptable behavior

- Reporting unethical or illegal behavior to a leader above one's direct supervisor or other internal authorities

Demonstrating agency

- Operating with more autonomy than currently granted by job description/internal authorities

- Explicitly defying, saying no to, or refusing to go along with a direct boss's problematic orders, expectations, or decisions

- Advocating for subordinates or peers

- Taking the hit for subordinates or peers (for their mistakes, efforts, decisions)

- Admitting one's significant mistake to a boss or higher-ups

---

different environment, might report that the same behavior is only "moderately" courageous and happens about 50 percent of the time it could.

Across all respondents to date—and this represents people in all kinds of work environments—the behaviors shown above are seen on the whole as requiring significant courage and not happening nearly as frequently as we'd like. For example, about 75 percent of all WCAI respondents say it's at least moderately courageous to challenge a direct boss about strategic or operating policies or practices in their proximal environment; more than a quarter say it's "very much" or "extremely" courageous to do this. As a result, this type of honest upward input happens only about 40 percent of the time when it could. When the challenge becomes more personal or about more intense matters—as captured by some of the other questions—the percentages become even more discouraging. For example, when it comes to confronting their boss about his or her disrespectful, hurtful, unprofessional, or inappropriate interpersonal behavior, 84 percent of all respondents say it's at least moderately courageous to do so; 45 percent say very much or extremely so. The percentage of time this behavior is said to happen when it could drops to less than one-third of the time.

So we know that these kinds of behaviors are often seen as quite courageous and that they don't happen as much as we need them to. But clearly some people are doing them. Who are these people? What kind of people accept the potential risks involved in doing the kinds of things described above? The short answer: *All kinds of people.*

If you look for patterns in the WCAI or in other courage data I and others have collected, there are no strong "those kind of people" results to share.[14] Risking the wrath of higher-ups isn't easier or more likely to happen based on any obvious individual differences. On the WCAI, for example, there are no consistent differences in how these behaviors are rated across demographic categories like respondents' gender or place in their organization's hierarchy. Being in a formal managerial position doesn't systematically change views, nor does being closer to the top or bottom of one's organizational hierarchy. Nor are there stark differences in responses from people in different industries.

In short, if you're looking for a reason to conclude that these behaviors are important, but should come from other kinds of people, I can't help you out with that rationalization. These courageous acts toward those with more power come from men and women, from people with PhDs and people who have not completed a high school education, from people in higher- and lower-level jobs, from people in huge bureaucracies and smaller, newer organizations. People of all types take on power, whether or not they've got strong job security.

For sure, sometimes things don't turn out well for those who undertake these actions. Sometimes, though, they absolutely do. People who speak truth to power can—and often do—survive and thrive, and things can and do get better for others and organizations as a result. Let's take a closer look.

Challenging Authority Figures

Authority figures are by far the most common targets for behaviors deemed courageous in workplaces. Whether you're challenging your direct boss, addressing those even higher-up, or otherwise taking stands that involve those with more power than you, there's a good chance it feels—or actually is—at least somewhat risky.

Challenging the Boss

Sometimes you might need to tell your boss that they are off track or just plain wrong: "This policy is not working." "The way we're doing this is inefficient." "That isn't fair." "This is dishonest." Speaking truth to power takes many specific forms, but often involves the same basic reality—you'll risk upsetting someone above you to try to make something better.

It might seem that pushing back against an operating policy or practice or strategic direction isn't that risky because you're critiquing those *things*, not the boss's character or overall competence. Still, we all become identified with things we've put a lot of energy into, things we've supported or stood behind, or things for which we're accountable. So no matter how politely you say, "Boss, our marketing campaign is flawed" or "Boss, our planning process is flawed," it's not at all rare for the boss to hear that as, "Boss, *you're* flawed."

Sometimes challenging bosses about a policy or practice is the only way we can take care of those around us. For example, due to budgetary restrictions, Becky wasn't allowed to hire more people to keep up with an ever-increasing workload. As a result, some of her direct reports had to take on more and more. Realizing that this had become fundamentally unfair, she challenged management to reclassify her employees, going back and forth for nearly nine months until they received the significant raises they deserved.

Confronting a boss's disrespectful, hurtful, or otherwise inappropriate interpersonal behavior is often even harder, and less common. It's no easy feat to step in when a boss makes rude or offensive comments or shows blatant favoritism. Still, some people do take a stand to put a stop to this kind of behavior. Hugh, for example, was a new manager doing everything he could to keep things on track on a day when his restaurant was slammed with about twenty-five hundred guests. When his district manager came in and started screaming at him about dirty sections, Hugh requested that they continue the conversation in the back. Sternly, but respectfully, he told his boss, "Don't ever talk to me in that demeaning tone and fashion. I can explain the situation, but don't ever talk to me like that again." Hugh knew what he was doing was risky, but felt he had to set the tone for how they were going to interact. Fortunately, his manager took it well—he cooled down, and later called to apologize. There was no retribution.

Speaking truth to power can involve defending or shielding those who've done nothing wrong but are nonetheless being mistreated. Pedro was presenting some results at a board meeting when the managing director started insisting he was wrong in a derogatory way. While everyone else sat mute, looking at their shoes, Pedro's direct boss firmly said, "No, I'm supporting these figures, and I'm supporting Pedro because he's right. And we'll prove it if you want." It seems even more admirable when someone speaks up on behalf of a person not in the room whose work or character is being demeaned. While others sit silently, these people challenge power to defend those who can't defend themselves.

Challenging someone above you might be hardest of all when you're implicating their ethics. It can be downright terrifying to confront a boss about accounting or safety violations, discriminatory or harassing behavior, or broken promises to employees or clients. Perhaps not surprisingly, but quite disturbingly, WCAI respondents say these conversations happen in only one-third of the cases where they could. Said a different way, that means people don't confront unethical or illegal behavior by those above them in two out of every three opportunities. Think of all the major damage done because people remain silent.

Fortunately, some people *do* speak up about their boss's unethical or illegal behavior. Meredith, for example, was reviewing a presentation to be made to a customer and noticed that her boss had made adjustments to the numbers. When she confronted him in the doorway of his office, he asked her to manipulate the data to suggest that the product was performing better than it was. Loudly enough for everyone around to hear, she said that she would not do so. In another instance, when a downturn was making it hard to hit sales numbers, Marcelo's boss decided to respond by selling personally identifiable customer data to larger companies—a move that would have harmed customers. In a meeting with the entire leadership team, Marcelo challenged his boss, stating that he believed it was unethical to do this without written permission from every customer. His boss was irate, and the conversations that followed were not pleasant. But the company did not sell the customer data.

Taking It to Higher-Ups

Perhaps your boss won't clean up his act, and even starts to retaliate because you spoke up. Perhaps it's too dangerous to even try confronting them. Perhaps they just don't get it. Or perhaps they agree with you but don't have the power or willpower to tackle the issue. In all of these cases, you have to take it to higher-ups if you want something to change. This can be just as hard, or even harder, than confronting someone you know better; therefore it's done too infrequently, according to our survey respondents and others' research.[15] Fortunately, some people do engage higher-ups.

Alana was relatively new when her boss drove a company vehicle to a bank appointment despite having a suspended license for drunk driving. The boss had an accident on the way back to work and, to save himself, tried to get Alana to say she'd been driving. When she refused, he conned a friend into taking the blame. Alana didn't want to be an internal whistleblower, and she tried to forget about the whole thing. But when her boss continued to be aggressive and to be derelict in his duties, she knew could no longer stay silent. She arranged a meeting with the company's chief operating officer and, despite her fear, told him the truth.

When she told her story, Alana reiterated that she knew she was the only one standing between the truth and a permanent cover-up. So why'd she do it? Because, she said, "I have more integrity than that. In the end, being labeled a whistleblower or anything else wasn't as important as being honest and truthful." She felt she owed it to herself and to the other people who were dealing with her manager at the time.

Sometimes the reason to challenge skip-level authorities is because they're the ones with control over resources or policies. Michelle, for instance, knew that patients were having trouble opening their medications because of the excessive amount of packaging. Local quality control personnel were uninterested in making changes, so she took the data about drug safety and stability—which suggested no reason for all the packaging—directly to the operations director and company president. Her goal? To lessen the burden on patients, not make life easier for a set of employees.

In other cases, it's the skip-level authorities themselves who have to be confronted by someone two or more levels below them. Richard, for example, was among the employees hosting some higher-ups from corporate who were visiting their warehouse. One of the blue-suiters kept referring to a female office employee as "doll." Despite her visible discomfort, she and everyone around her remained silent. Except Richard, who in a nonaggressive manner quietly said to the senior manager, "Hey, she has a name." As reported by a colleague, "We were the peons of the company and yet Richard said that to someone who could have easily fired him or had him fired." Said the colleague, "The guy apologized, and that was that." And perhaps more importantly, it left him and others feeling closer to each other, "as if we all watched out for each other."

Demonstrating Agency

Not all acts that risk the wrath of those above you require direct, challenging communication. Sometimes you can do other things that demonstrate your agency—your willingness to decide for yourself what to do and whom to take responsibility for—in ways that might anger your bosses. You might act beyond your scope of formal authority to do what seems right, you might choose to ignore your boss's decisions or orders that seem wrong-headed, or you might own your mistakes or those of others you care about when you might have stayed silent.

Deciding for Oneself

Sometimes you can't wait around for instructions or to propose a policy change. You either do what seems right in the moment or you live with the regret that you didn't. Clay, a restaurant manager, faced this situation when a young customer went into cardiac arrest. He knew that it was a firing offense for a manager to leave the restaurant for any reason. He also knew that an ambulance would take twenty minutes to arrive and that the hospital was only two hundred yards away. He therefore quickly told other employees how to hold the fort in his absence, then drove the customer to the emergency room in his own car. Why? Because, he said, "In that moment, it's my principles, not the policy, that guides me."

Ben, a construction engineer, likewise put his customers above company policy at his own risk. His company was paid on a time-and-materials basis, so that the company got paid for any time it spent correcting its own mistakes. Feeling this to be wrong, he unilaterally decided to offer a client a required rework free of charge.

In other cases, people refuse to follow the orders of someone above them. Alan, a research manager in a pharmaceutical company, was told by the R&D president that one of his research teams was wasting time. Shut it down, he ordered Alan, and move the resources to higher-potential areas. Knowing the president's point of view was not consistent with the most current science, Alan consciously chose to ignore the mandate. "Carry on," he told his team. This kind of defiance is not easy, and it's risky for sure.

Protecting or Promoting Others

Defying an order, as Alan did, is one way to protect or promote others' interests. Sometimes this type of courage explicitly requires taking the hit for someone who has in fact made a mistake or is in the wrong in other ways. Nate, for example, violated a requirement to clear new marketing approaches or expenditures with corporate leadership. Knowing that Nate had done so only to avoid losing out on a key advertising space, his boss took the responsibility and shielded Nate from repercussions.

Amanda, a general manager in a retail chain, faced pressure to fire a supervisor after a stint of underperformance led to a poor store inspection. Believing in her employee's ability to improve, she shouldered the blame from corporate and refused to fire the supervisor. In these cases and others like them, people defend others whom they could easily allow to take responsibility for their own choices.

Owning Your Mistakes

Sometimes you demonstrate agency by owning up to *your* mistakes, rather than compounding matters by trying to hide them or letting others shoulder the blame. This is the courage of accepting responsibility or fault, of saying, "I'm sorry, I made a mistake. I admit it."[16] It's the courage of telling the whole truth without sugarcoating what happened, so people can get on with making it right before more damage is done by a cover-up.

Alicia, an R&D scientist at a global pharmaceutical company, noted that it can be daunting for project leaders to admit flaws in their research design or results even though it's obvious that acknowledging mistakes is important when patient health is what's potentially at stake. "People don't like to see failure," she told me. "Sometimes you just get tunnel vision into what you're trying to achieve." This makes it hard, and scary, to say, "We've wasted our time. We should just drop this." Likewise, in another R&D environment, Paul realized that his lab's data was compromised because of a procedural mistake. No one was aware of the mistake, so he could have easily kept it quiet. Instead, he told his supervisor the truth. The result? He ended up with "more work, but a clear conscience."

What Happens When You Speak Truth to Power

"Fine," you might be thinking, "you've given some nice examples. Inspiring even. But that doesn't mean it's still not stupid, on the whole, to engage those in power in the ways you've described. Aren't these more likely to be career-enders than happy endings?"

If you require precise statistics as an answer to this question, I can't give you any. To my knowledge, no one can. And certainly, bad things do sometimes happen to people who challenge those with more power. People do sometimes get chewed out, dinged on performance evaluations, held back from exciting opportunities or promotions, or, in the worst cases, fired for standing up to those above them.[17] If you take your concerns outside the organization, you're probably even more likely to get harassed, demoted, or otherwise reprimanded for daring to challenge powerful others. I've talked with and know personally people who've had these things happen to them, so I'm no Pollyanna about the risks people take when speaking their truth to power or refusing to give up their agency in other ways.

But here's the flip side to those instances where bad things happen: people engage in these behaviors all the time without ruining their careers or suffering other negative outcomes. And they accomplish the changes they were hoping to make for others or their organizations. Problems do get solved, people do get protected, possibilities do get exploited, and people do start to behave more appropriately or effectively.[18]

Sometimes those who act courageously actually see *positive* career benefits, though few would say that's what motivated them to act.[19] And, whether these good things happen or not, those who act often walk away with a heightened sense of self-respect and self-confidence.[20] They've stood up for what they believe is right, and they've survived. They have no lingering regret about what they "should have done."[21] Colin, for example, worked for a boss who "kissed up but kicked down." His boss was pleasant to the president but cruel and impatient with her staff. And she'd admitted to others that she loathed Colin. After silently taking the abuse while his own and others' drive and passion waned, Colin had finally had enough. He first went to her and told her directly how her behavior was impacting the team and his own morale. Then he went above her to the CEO to report on everything that had been happening.

The results? Unfortunately, the CEO didn't take visible action against Colin's boss, and morale in the unit stayed low. But the manager stopped harassing Colin and no longer speaks about him behind his back to his colleagues. Colin has no regrets. He's put it behind him, still believing it was the right thing to do and feeling pleased with himself for standing up and facing the issue directly. Here's how he explained why, in his own mind, this was clearly a win: "Having been on the receiving end of much bullying as a child, I had never once mustered up the courage to confront my aggressor and fight back. For once in my life, I didn't turtle. I didn't just choose the easiest path where I simply endure being disrespected by someone simply because of their position."

Beyond how you'll feel about yourself when you know you "didn't turtle," there's also a chance you'll inspire others to follow suit and be courageous themselves.[22] Watching someone else step up reminds others of what's possible, and can create emotional "elevation"—"the awed and inspired feeling we get when we witness a moral act."[23]

Consider this example. After having watched his manager, who was known for being "over-the-top and cruel," yet again berate a fellow employee about his appearance and life outside of work, Vic finally stood up. He told the abusive manager he planned to report him to higher-ups and do whatever he could to make sure he never worked another day at the company. Following Vic's lead, the person who told me this story and the rest of his coworkers banded together, went to corporate, and indeed got the manager fired within a week. Vic's act, this coworker told me, "empowered the rest of us to take his side and fight back" after being "too scared prior to this." "It inspired me, and maybe others," he continued, "to act out in the future rather than worrying about only ourselves. It taught me that no job was worth compromising your ideals or putting up with an abusive manager, even if you're not directly in the path of abuse."

It Depends on Others

Here's the biggest reason no one can tell you with certainty what will happen after you demonstrate truth to power: *It depends on others.* Remember, courage is an *attribution* about a behavior. It's a subjective judgment applied by whomever is labeling the behavior, not an objective description of a behavior. Imagine an employee town hall where a senior leader says the sales team is letting the company down with its lower-than-expected numbers. Mary, a sales manager who knows her team has been working incredibly hard but faces a terrible overall market, stands up and says to the senior leader in front of everyone, "That's unfair. It is not the team's fault that the country is in a recession. Frankly, it's only due to their incredible skill and hard work that we're not in a much worse situation, like some of our competitors." The "facts" here are the words Mary has spoken and the context in which she has spoken them. That many around Mary, and perhaps Mary herself, would call her behavior an instance of workplace courage is an attribution—a label that adds special, positive meaning to the behavior itself.

Why does the attributional nature of workplace courage matter? Because people don't see the world the same way. Some will see Mary's act of speaking up as a laudable attempt to defend her team; others will see it as an inappropriate public rebuke of a superior. Neither side is objectively (in)correct—we're not arguing about real versus fake facts here. Courage is, and always will be, in the eye of the beholder, and those with opposite perspectives often disagree vehemently.

Therein lies the problem: the people we are challenging are generally the least likely to consider our actions "courageous" or respond positively. Consider the results from a simple study I ran.[24] All participants read about a scientist at a large pharmaceutical company:

> Wayne, like other chief research scientists, oversaw a large number of research teams trying to make basic scientific discoveries in therapeutic areas like diabetes, cancer, and heart disease. At a recent research review meeting, the president of R&D listened to the various updates from Wayne's teams and Wayne's colleagues' teams and then stated forcefully, "I'm pleased with our progress in the cancer and heart disease areas, but I see little to be hopeful about in the diabetes area. Wayne, I want you to immediately start shifting major resources from diabetes research to the other more promising areas."
>
> Wayne composed himself for a minute, thinking about what he might say. Then he pointed out, summarizing several different arguments and studies, that he believed all the evidence from the labs pointed in the opposite direction. He stated that his diabetes teams were working as hard as any others in the company, and that they were as close to breakthroughs in diabetes as in other areas, and as close to diabetes breakthroughs as any competitor company. "You heard me," blasted the R&D president, and then turned to the next agenda item.

The next day, Wayne met with his diabetes research teams. He explained to them what had happened, told them that he believed in them, and that he would continue to defend them and allocate the same level of resources as before. He then met with the CEO and laid out the case for continuing with the diabetes research efforts at the same level, noting that he disagreed strongly with the R&D president's conclusions. When the CEO said it was ultimately the R&D president's call, Wayne replied, "I disagree. You're the CEO. The buck ultimately stops with you. I'm asking you to do your job by listening to the people most intimately connected to the science at hand, rather than just deferring to someone else because it's easier for you."

Participants were then told to imagine they were one of five different roles (assigned randomly): Wayne (the actor), a subordinate on Wayne's diabetes team, a peer (another chief research scientist), the R&D president (Wayne's boss, and the target of his act), or the CEO (Wayne's skip-level boss). Taking that person's perspective, they then rated Wayne's act on several questions designed to assess how courageous the act was and, to keep it simple here, how "dumb" (e.g., foolish, insubordinate, careless, wrong) the act was.

Here's what I found. Those taking every perspective *except* that of the target—Wayne's boss, the R&D president—saw the act as highly (and roughly equally) courageous. Only those assigned the view of Wayne's boss, the person being challenged and defied, saw the act as significantly less courageous. Those taking this perspective also saw the act as significantly more foolish, insubordinate, and inappropriate than those viewing Wayne's act from every other perspective. In sum, just asking people to imagine themselves being the one who was challenged and defied led them to view this act as less courageous and more defiant and wrong. Clearly, courage is a matter of perspective, not fact. Acts are considered courageous by some precisely because there's a good chance that others will *not* appreciate what's been done.

It Depends on You

While it's undeniable that how your courageous acts turn out depends in part on others' reaction, it's also a cop-out to conclude that others are the sole reason why courage might come with too high a price. In many, if not most, instances, how *we* act also determines what happens next. We can confront, challenge, or disagree with powerful people in ways that evoke more or less threat, anger, and defensiveness simply by changing the how, where, or when of what we say or do.

Though the coming chapters will explore extensively what we can do to tip the odds that our courageous act will have positive outcomes, let me give just a simple example here. Imagine that the team you lead has taken on extra work for months and performed extraordinarily well. Despite strong profits, you've just been told that there will be no promotions and only minimal raises for your team members this year. You talk to your boss, and while she agrees with you, she says she doesn't have any more control over this than you do. You therefore request a meeting with a more senior leader to discuss the issue. Assuming you've already shared what the meeting is about, you could dig in by saying:

> This concerns me because I know many on my team often get overtures from other companies. I'm worried that if they see a limited future here, we're at risk of losing incredible talent. This would be bad for us all. I know they love this place, but they also see themselves spending more time here at the same time their kids are growing up and their expenses are rising. Do you think we could try to work together on ways to show them how much we value them, including at least some form of additional raise or bonus? I want to help.

Or, you could say:

> This is fundamentally unfair, and I'm sick of trying to defend a pay policy that says there's no more for us at the same time we

all see the huge compensation packages at the top. My people are getting overtures from other companies and, knowing what I know about things around here, how am I supposed to tell them with a straight face that this is a better place for them?! If you don't do something now, I guarantee a bunch of your best people are going to bail next year and that'll be on you. So, what are you going to do?

While both statements might represent your truth, it's pretty obvious that these two options are unlikely to lead to the same response from that senior leader and, hence, to the same outcomes. If you said something like the first statement, you might have a chance of working toward something that benefits your team. And you'd be unlikely to suffer any negative personal repercussions. If you said something like the second statement, the odds are lower you'll get what you want for your team and much higher that you'd have caused yourself a problem.

In short, the outcomes of challenging power aren't dictated solely by the situation. They also depend on how *you* behave.

Is It Worth It?

No matter how skillfully you behave, there are still risks. People do suffer negative consequences some of the time or we wouldn't associate truth to power behaviors so strongly with courage. That doesn't mean there aren't also positive outcomes, or that the act isn't hugely valuable for others. For example, Xavier, a military officer, told me about his experience speaking up three levels on behalf of a soldier who felt isolated and further victimized after filing a sexual harassment claim. His courage got the soldier transferred to a better environment and led to the soldier's direct boss being severely reprimanded. It also got Xavier labeled a troublemaker.

Rebecca, the investment manager mentioned at the beginning of this chapter who realized that she was being paid way less than her male peers despite outperforming them, confronted the male founders—her bosses—head on. In the meeting, she presented data about her performance as well as what she had pieced together about her compensation relative to others. She then laid it on the line, saying: "If the difference in pay is not based on objective metrics, there must be another reason. Is it because I'm a woman?"

When the dust settled and a new agreement had been reached, Rebecca's compensation was doubled effective immediately. Less positively, her pay had now been pegged to a specific metric over which she had little direct control in her role. In the year after the new agreement took effect, she did not see her role expand or compensation increase even as the firm's business increased overall. And, unfortunately, no broader effort was made to explore or correct gender-based pay inequities throughout the organization.

Both Xavier and Rebecca created some positive change by speaking truth to power, but they also clearly experienced some negative repercussions. Were these consequences worth it to them? Absolutely, say both. Xavier remains proud of what he did, knowing he "allowed this soldier to escape rather than be forever ostracized." Rebecca was disappointed in her firm's reaction, but it clarified the path forward for her. She concluded that the only way to fix the problem to her satisfaction—both for herself personally and for other women in their male-dominated industry—would be to start her own firm. Shortly after she told me her story, that's exactly what she did.

I can (and will) tell you many more stories about folks like Xavier and Rebecca who feel that their actions—despite coming with a mix of bad and good outcomes—were worth it. I can also tell you what my research suggests about just how inspirational these kinds of courageous acts are for others who witness or hear about them, especially if you're in a position of leadership. For example, Evan Bruno and I had respondents rate the types of workplace courage behaviors discussed in this chapter, varying whether they reported on the positive effects of seeing each behavior done or the negative effects of seeing the behavior not done when opportunities arise. We also varied whether people reported on the effects when the behaviors were done or not done by either their direct boss or a peer.

We found that for almost every behavior rated, the motivational impact of a boss doing or not doing something was far larger than when a peer did or didn't do the same behavior. This is consistent with all sorts of research showing that we attend more to those with more power, expect more of them, and see their behavior as more symbolic of the organization's culture. Our data shows that we're most inspired when we see our own boss stand up to his or her own boss(es), be it about unacceptable interpersonal behavior or unethical or illegal behavior. We're also highly impressed when our boss goes to bat for us to those above him or her or defends or takes the hit for us with higher-ups in order to protect our well-being.

On the flip side, when do bosses do the greatest motivational harm by not acting? When they don't speak up or take other action about the most egregious types of behavior. If you want to lose your subordinates' trust, respect, and willingness to work hard on your behalf, let them see you stay silent in the face of illegal or unethical conduct or disrespectful, unprofessional, or hurtful behavior by others. If you think people don't notice your inaction or aren't bothered because they know it's really hard to do these things, our data suggests you should think again.

If you're not in a managerial role, does that mean your opportunities to inspire others are more limited? Not at all. In fact, our findings suggest that peers are positively influenced by seeing us tackle all sorts of difficult conversations. Stand up to the boss about his or her unethical or illegal behavior, and your peers are going to be impressed; likewise if they see you go to skip-level bosses about big problems. You'll also inspire your peers by advocating upward on behalf of others.

The overall message here? No one is free from judgment—flattering or harsh—when they face opportunities for courageous action. But does knowing this make it worth it to you? That's for you to decide. Only you can evaluate what's most important to you, what you want your life to stand for, and how much you're willing to risk in pursuit of those objectives.

What about You?

Being the change you want to see, as Gandhi encouraged, starts with an honest assessment of where you are. How courageous do each of the behaviors discussed in this chapter feel to you? How often do you actually do them when the opportunity arises? To find out, take the "Truth to Power" portion of the free Workplace Courage Acts Index (www.workplacecai.com) now.

When you're done, study the results. What's your fear, or pain, around the behaviors covered in this chapter? How do your responses compare to those of everyone else who has taken the survey?

The coming chapters will address the strategies for choosing your actions carefully and a method for building a specific action plan to do them more skillfully. For now, set aside any embarrassment or shame about your current truth, and don't waste time rationalizing where you're at. What you see as really hard may be easier for others, but I assure you that the reverse is true too: some things you find easier are the hardest for others. Remember, too, that context matters a lot in determining how risky or worthy something is perceived to be. A highly courageous act in your context could be pretty safe in another and even cowardly in others. Most of all, remember that if the behaviors discussed in this chapter were easy and everyone else were consistently doing them, I wouldn't be writing this book.

Remember

- Fear of speaking up and engaging in other acts that might anger those with more power than us is widespread, for both real and imagined reasons. That's why truth to power is the prototypical form of workplace courage.

- People of all types nonetheless do demonstrate these courageous behaviors in all kinds of workplaces. They speak truth to direct bosses and skip-level leaders, they use their own judgment in ways that might anger authorities, they defend others from those in power, and they admit mistakes despite the potential for trouble.

- While bad things do sometimes happen as a result of challenging power, good things also happen. Outcomes depend not just on how those in power react, but also on how you do what you do.

- While others will likely be appreciative, and maybe even inspired to act, only you can decide if and when it's worth it to you to speak truth to power. Only you can choose courage for yourself.

CHAPTER 3

Candid Conversations and Bold Actions

While "truth to power" acts might be the prototypical type of workplace courage, this chapter covers other behaviors that consistently earn the label. These include handling difficult, uncomfortable situations with peers and subordinates, customers, and various external partners. They also include a number of bold moves that people sometimes make, ranging from stretching and holding oneself accountable via starting a new job, taking a major new assignment, or deviating from established practice. We'll explore choices to make oneself vulnerable in the service of a greater good, to quit on principle, and to blow the whistle outside the organization as a last resort.

At first blush, you might think that behaviors directed toward peers or subordinates, or those involving our own personal integrity and growth, are nowhere near as difficult as those involving truth to power. That's true sometimes, but not always.

Consider Zeb, a white regional manager of a national hospitality chain, who was at a bar with five of his peers, all of whom were also white. After several drinks, one of Zeb's peers went on a rant about their Black boss, Darnell. Included in his peer's racist tirade were the words "porch monkey" and the n-word. Zeb, who highly respected Darnell for his professionalism, expertise, and dedication, was shocked—so shocked that he didn't confront his peer, but instead just quickly changed the subject and left as soon as he could.

The next day, Zeb and two colleagues told Darnell what had been said behind his back by a subordinate. They said they wanted Darnell to fire this person. Darnell appreciated this sentiment. He felt the same. He also knew how hard it was to fire anyone at his organization, and how hard the conversations with HR and then this employee would be.

From a distance, it's easy to say that Zeb and his coworkers should have confronted their racist peer on the spot, and it's easy to say Darnell should fire his racist subordinate. The statements were clearly appalling, and since the speaker was Zeb's peer and Darnell's subordinate, there are no obvious career risks to responding definitively. But, as we'll see in this chapter, people fear a lot more than economic or career derailment. And that's why there are many work-related behaviors beyond speaking truth to power that are seen as requiring courage.

Social, Psychological, and Physical Risks at Work

When we face situations like the one above, where the target of what we must do is someone with equal or lower formal power than us, the risks often shift from career-related ones to social, psychological, and even physical ones. While Zeb couldn't have been fired by his drunk, racist peer if he'd confronted him, he could have been physically assaulted. He also could have faced social isolation and perhaps even personal doubts about how he'd responded if his peers hadn't stood by him when he confronted the racist remarks or went to their boss the next day. As we'll explore below, the fears associated with these kinds of risks can be just as crippling as career-related risk.

Courting "Social Death"

In the early 1990s, management professor James Barker wrote an account of the shift from traditional control (i.e., supervision by bosses with formal power) to self-managing teams in a small manufacturing company. You might think workers experienced this as a huge relief in terms of pressure and stress, but you'd be wrong. Barker described the even stronger "iron cage" that trapped workers who had to exercise *social* control over each other's behavior: breaking rules or norms became less about the fear of formal consequences and more about the risks of social disapproval and group rejection.[1]

Barker's ethnography is a nice example of a simple fact: humans are social animals. We need social acceptance nearly as much as we need food and water, and the isolation that comes from being ostracized feels like "social death." It's no surprise, then, that we're pretty careful about doing things that might lead to rejection by the pack.[2] That's why taking a stance at odds with the views or wishes of those around us at work often involves sufficient perceived risk to make it an act of workplace courage. Indeed, numerous definitions of moral courage involve overcoming the fear of social rejection, of standing tall despite the discomfort of dissension or disapproval.[3]

Sadly, all too often, we don't overcome our fear of social ostracism, and silence prevails. For example, even among members of airline cockpit and cabin crews, where we'd hope people always speak up, researchers Nadine Bienefeld and Gudela Grote found plenty of instances where the opposite was true. Among the major reasons for holding back was fear of damaging relationships, reported by frightening percentages of study participants—53 percent of captains, 43 percent of first officers, and 42 percent of flight attendants.[4]

And to be clear, we don't have to be explicitly denounced or rejected to be affected by this kind of pressure. Just watching others being ridiculed can be enough to stoke our own fears.[5] And merely being ignored has been shown to be a painful form of social ostracism.[6]

Jeopardizing Psychological Well-Being

Sometimes the risk involved in courageous acts is primarily psychological: "Can I do this?" "Am I good enough?" "Will I fail? Humiliate myself?" Think about agreeing to try a real stretch assignment or adding a new responsibility or activity to your job. Perhaps you're being asked to do this because it's critical to the organization, even though you're not sure you're quite ready or going to be able to succeed. You might not get into trouble if it doesn't go well—after all, you were just trying to help—but that doesn't mean it wouldn't be a hit to your self-esteem to fail, and perhaps fail publicly.

During one consulting engagement, I was trying to figure out why a high percentage of a group of scientists had reported feeling afraid to speak up in "blue sky" research meetings. During our interviews, their explanations weren't primarily about possible career consequences or peer retaliation. They were mostly worried about looking stupid in front of other people. Here were brilliant, accomplished people from the world's best universities who nonetheless felt emotionally uncomfortable presenting or discussing ideas that extended beyond their zone of complete expertise. It takes courage, I realized that day, to make ourselves vulnerable.

Facing Physical Threat

We tend to think that physical bravery in work environments is restricted to those whose job description includes it—police officers, firefighters, and military personnel, for example. And, not surprisingly, the vast majority of WCAI respondents think that jumping in to absorb or prevent imminent physical danger is indeed a very courageous act. Here's what is surprising and, frankly, a bit scary: a lot more people sometimes face physical harm at work than we think. Ours is a world with many weapons and lots of angry or mentally ill people.

Consider the challenges facing those who work in hospitality or other customer-service businesses. They handle guests who are irate, drunk, or abusive in language or behavior, and even customers who brandish weapons to get what they want. Employees, too, sometimes create physical risks. In one restaurant I studied, a manager had to jump in when a buffet employee started screaming and waving his vicious carving knife at a customer who had insulted the employee for not giving him a large enough portion. In the same chain, a supervisor described how her boss rushed in to help when an employee she had just suspended for using drugs at work jumped over the table and started physically assaulting her. The boss broke his leg in the process of subduing the employee before the police arrived, but the supervisor was unharmed.

The risks of physical harm, unfortunately, are in all kinds of workplaces at all levels. Executives, journalists, and many others get death threats, and others actually experience violence directly. I was told, for example, about a receptionist who had a knife put to her throat by a deranged person who entered her workplace spouting conspiracy theories that implicated the company. No matter how safe we like to think we are, the truth is that these things can happen to any of us.

Overcoming the Risks

Fortunately, people *do* sometimes act courageously in these challenging situations. They accept physical or psychological risks to protect others or pursue growth. They confront peers who are out of line. They make tough calls and have difficult conversations involving subordinates or external stakeholders. Some of these acts—disciplining, demoting, or firing subordinates, terminating relationships with external partners or suppliers, etc.—represent what Joshua Margolis and Andy Molinsky have called "necessary evils," the kinds of tasks in which we do something that might hurt others in the service of a perceived greater good or purpose.[7]

Sometimes these people pay a price, but often it's not nearly as bad as we, or they, anticipate. And they seldom regret what they did, because they know it was the right thing to do based on their values, whether they're defending someone else, doing what's best for the organization, or simply being able to sleep well at night.

Let's take a closer look at these types of courageous acts, starting with those involving peers.

Facing Difficult Peer Situations

Sometimes you've got to confront or risk upsetting your peers. (See the box "Courageous Acts Involving Peers.") Not because you're formally expected to do so—you're not their boss, after all—but because they're doing something sufficiently wrong or hurtful that you feel obliged on principle to do something. Your goal isn't to boss them around, it's simply to get them to stop or start doing something that has significant repercussions on you, others, or the organization.

Maybe you confront a colleague who continuously shows up unprepared for meetings or who doesn't do his fair share of group work, or maybe you tell a colleague that her skills have deteriorated or that you think her behavior is unethical. Maybe you escalate a problem with a peer to higher-ups.

Though the racist comments in the story reported at the beginning of this chapter are starker than usual, there are myriad ways in which people need to confront hurtful terms or stereotypes in work settings. Bonnie, for example, talked about the positive difference a peer on her management team made by standing up to say the use of the word "retarded" was an unacceptable way to talk about people with disabilities. Many had cringed, but only one spoke up and gave clear reasons for why and how that word makes other people feel. The next day, a companywide email was sent out reminding everyone that words are powerful, that what may seem meaningless to one person can have a huge impact on other people. This marked what Bonnie described as a "major turning point in our company."

COURAGEOUS ACTS INVOLVING PEERS

- Confronting peer(s) about their inadequate work quality, quantity, or timeliness

- Confronting peer(s) about their disrespectful, hurtful, unprofessional, or inappropriate interpersonal behavior

- Confronting peer(s) about their unethical or illegal behavior

- Sharing bad or hard-to-hear news or point of view with peer(s)

- Reporting peer(s) to direct boss for problematic behavior

- Actively or publicly disagreeing with a broadly shared view or popular position held by peer(s)

It's even easier to appreciate that people struggle to confront their peers about behavior that is explicitly unethical. Now you're not just asserting that their behavior is unacceptable, you're running the risk of them thinking you're calling them a bad or immoral *person*. Imagine a colleague takes credit for your work, and your only choices are to confront him or swallow it and let the idea theft go unnoticed by those above you. What about a colleague who repeatedly pads her budget to get resources to create a discretionary slush fund or distorts other accounting numbers to make things look better?

We might think that confronting unethical peers is relatively low risk, because surely everyone except the person doing something wrong will be grateful to you. Unfortunately, not necessarily. In research by professors Linda Trevino and Bart Victor, respondents who evaluated a peer as highly ethical also evaluated him or her as unlikable.[8] It could be that norms against disrupting group cohesiveness are so strong that doing so even to call out an obvious wrong comes with social consequences. Or—and perhaps more likely—it may be that our own standing up against a wrong makes others (probably unconsciously) feel bad about themselves for not doing so. Faced with the implicit choice of considering themselves bad or weak for not standing up first, it's understandable that others often make harsh judgments about those who do.

Sometimes it's hard to threaten the comfortable (if potentially dangerous) space created by "groupthink." Gregory, for example, worked in his company's toy division. Late in the design process, he stood up to protest the fact that 90 percent of their toy lines were male, and that female characters tended toward the scantily clad or outright sexualized. In the face of serious opposition from all of his colleagues, he asserted that this sort of implicit sexism was wrong and should be immediately addressed.

Other times, it takes courage to overcome what Kim Scott calls "ruinous empathy"—failing to tell the truth because we don't want to hurt the recipient in the short run. For example, imagine telling a peer that the career path she's exploring just isn't a good fit for her. Or telling a colleague who has just been offered his dream position as general manager for a restaurant that he shouldn't take it because that venue is in trouble and only going to get worse based on its location. Said Keith, whose colleague did tell him that, "It was courageous not just because it went against the advice and request of the area director (their boss), but because I was thinking it'd be a good choice and was excited about it. It was hard for him to burst my bubble by telling me this."

Some find particularly brilliant ways to confront their peers. Arica was the VP of customer experience at a large telecommunications company. For four years, she was frustrated with her colleagues' response to key problems, feeling that they consistently resorted to oversimplified, isolated tactics rather than a holistic approach. As she prepared for yet another review with the top team, one colleague suggested that she use the company's preferred format. She replied that she'd done that three years in a row, and each time gotten nodding heads and commitments to be different but then little actual change.

So, when she arrived at the review meeting the next day, she started by reading an executive summary that said, in a nutshell, "Despite undertaking a number of tactics, customer expectations have grown faster than we've improved, our competition has outpaced us, and we need to take a more holistic approach." She again saw the nodding heads. Then she handed out her presentation and asked them to turn to a slide that showed that the executive summary she'd just read was the one the group had received two years ago. She acknowledged that hers was a difficult message, but said it wasn't an attempt to be critical for criticism's sake but rather a plea for them to all learn from past mistakes and truly take a different approach.

It was a very risky move—publicly confronting others with direct evidence that they were repeating the same unproductive behavior year after year. She expected to be met with defensiveness and denials and feared she'd be criticized for being "too emotional" by the male-dominated group. Instead, she was pleasantly surprised that her bold statements, backed by incontrovertible data, led to a more honest dialogue and more genuine interest in taking a different approach.

Tackling Tough Subordinate Situations

If you're a manager, you already know that disagreeing with or giving bad news to one or more subordinates can feel risky. (See the box "Courageous Acts Involving Subordinates" for example behaviors.) Sure, you're their boss, so they can't directly retaliate or punish you economically. That doesn't mean they can't start excluding you socially or harm you indirectly by working less hard or looking for ways to get you in trouble. And it doesn't mean they can't make you doubt yourself or, on occasion, even present physical risk.

Still, sometimes disagreeing with the majority view and making tough decisions is exactly why you've been put in charge. David, for example, was the officer in charge in a hostile environment in Afghanistan. Most in his platoon, who were hungry for action, were continuously pressuring him to authorize combat operations against lower-level terrorists. Knowing that this could result in grave risk for little reward, he forcefully told the group—with whom he lived 24/7 and literally needed to have his back—that this wasn't going to happen. Martin, in a completely different context, took the same kind of

COURAGEOUS ACTS INVOLVING SUBORDINATES

- Actively or publicly disagreeing with a broadly shared view or popular position held by subordinate(s)

- Confronting subordinate(s) about disrespectful, hurtful, unprofessional, or inappropriate interpersonal behavior

- Providing informal negative feedback to subordinate(s) about current or desired work or role

- Providing subordinate(s) with formal negative feedback, a negative evaluation, or discipline

- Demoting or laying off or firing subordinate(s)

---

unpopular stand. His subordinates were a tightknit group of manufacturing operators with whom he had worked and socialized for a long time. But when they began to slack off in an effort to extract new benefits that he believed weren't reasonable, he stood up to his subordinates and let them know he was happy to fight this with the union if they didn't shape up.

If you're a proactive manager, you can probably handle most uncomfortable employee situations with just *informal* negative feedback—something that's clearly part of your job anyway. Still, it's surprisingly rare and inconsistently done. Indeed, Stone and Heen reported that 63 percent of the executives who responded to a survey said that their biggest challenge to effective performance management is managers who lack the courage and skill to have difficult feedback discussions.[9] That's unfortunate, because the literature on giving feedback is clear on the benefits to employees and organizations—better direction, better motivation, earlier correction of mistakes, and so on.[10]

It's obvious that we avoid giving feedback that we think will make people angry. People don't like being confronted about their hurtful or inappropriate behavior, whether it's gossiping, disrespecting peers, or coming to work with the wrong attitude. It's also true, though, that we avoid conversations that will make people feel bad. Especially when we like the people to whom we're showing that "tough love." That doesn't mean they don't need to hear it, or that they won't (eventually) come to appreciate it. Felipe, a young restaurant manager, got told by his boss, Tim, that he didn't yet know how to handle his team appropriately, that he was being too nice and letting them take advantage of him in a competitive environment where this would cause business failure. "At the time," he admitted later, "I hated him. I wanted to punch him." But it helped him realize that if he didn't start to hold people accountable—to run the restaurant more like it was his own business—he would not succeed. Now at a new company, he still asks himself, "What would Tim do in this situation?" Said a senior manager in another context, when you "chicken out" and don't give honest feedback, you create trouble for the company and *for that person* because your unwillingness to tell the truth denies them a chance to grow, and may even leave them feeling you don't actually care about their development.

Providing *formal* negative feedback to subordinates, whether in the form of a job evaluation or disciplinary action or anything else involving official documentation, tends to be even harder. Jaila, for example, had a mandate to standardize a set of operational procedures at one of the world's largest nonprofits. While most got on board with the training and new requirements, one of her subordinates continued to resist all changes despite several months of patient guidance and coaching. The situation finally came to a head when the subordinate again disagreed to do things the new way and made a scene on her way out of Jaila's office. Jaila went to HR, documented the pattern of insubordination, and began working to find the employee a new role. Soon thereafter, the employee was demoted to a nonmanagerial role where she was unable to negatively influence others who were on board with the unit's new mandate.

Sometimes no amount of formal or informal feedback prevents the need to lay off or fire someone. These are among the most painful, least pleasant things a manager has to do, and also seen as substantially courageous by 70 percent of those we've surveyed.

One reason it can feel daunting to fire someone is because he's a great performer in other respects, or someone who you know it will be very difficult to function without in the short run. For example, Warren was told that Charlie, a member of his team, had behaved in an extremely inappropriate manner at a sponsored work event. Most of the organization's employees were there, so many knew about Charlie's behavior. But Charlie was a key player at a pivotal moment in the company's growth—someone Warren and others knew was vital to preparing for the company's sale both because of his specific skills and his credentials. Nonetheless, Warren fired Charlie, concluding that the firm's integrity was ultimately what made it worth significant value to any would-be buyer.

Here's another reason it can be hard to fire someone—it might actually present physical risk. Harvey fired a service employee for performance reasons. The next day, the fired employee's cousin showed up demanding an explanation and warning Harvey that he'd better reconsider the decision. When Harvey said that wasn't going to happen, the cousin flashed open his sports coat, revealing a gun, and said to Harvey, "I'll be waiting for you outside" before walking out. Thankfully, this turned out to be an empty threat.

If it's hard to lay off or fire one person, think about having to do it en masse. Kealy, for example, had just joined a large utility company when a major accident led to significant financial losses. As a result, rather than being able to focus on building subordinates' trust in her as their new leader, one of the first steps she had to take was to eliminate about two hundred jobs. This was anything but easy for her, but she did it to try to secure the company's long-term viability and, hence, the well-being of those who remained.

Engaging External Stakeholders in Sticky Situations

Most external stakeholders—whether customers or clients, suppliers or contractors—don't have formal power over you. That doesn't mean they can't create ugly confrontations, challenge your psychological mettle, or otherwise cause you trouble for standing up to or walking

COURAGEOUS ACTS INVOLVING EXTERNAL STAKEHOLDERS

- Engaging in a difficult or unpleasant confrontation or conversation with a customer or client

- Making a decision or changing a policy that might anger customers or clients

- Engaging in a difficult or unpleasant confrontation or conversation with an external partner or stakeholder

---

away from them. (See the box "Courageous Acts Involving External Stakeholders.") That's why upward of 75 percent of respondents to the WCAI say decisions or confrontations involving these groups can be courageous, and why they also say they're avoided a whole lot of the time.

Consider decisions or difficult conversations with customers or clients. While we can all recall conversations where we're the one who is angry or upset with perceived mistreatment by some organization, we're less likely to think about the cases where it's courageous for a company representative to calmly stand his or her ground because the customer is in the wrong. In some cases, confrontations with clients or other external partners risk not just their short-term ire but also the loss of business. Imagine being a consultant and reaching the conclusion that your client has a department that is overstaffed by 30 percent. You present this to the unit head, who nearly bites your head off and refuses to accept your analysis. Eventually, you have no choice but to take it above him to a senior leader who is more able to hear your difficult message. Or imagine being charged with telling a management team that a necessary IT solution is going to be significantly more expensive than they expected and standing firm in your opposition to their suggestion of a cheaper "Band-Aid approach."

The courage to push back on key stakeholders, despite potential consequences, is a requirement at every level in organizations. It's true for waiters, salesclerks, and customer service reps, and it's true for high-level professionals, senior managers, and even CEOs. When Howard Schultz was CEO of Starbucks for the first time, he came under a lot of pressure during a major economic downturn from shareholders who wanted him to cut costs by reducing the company's generous health-care benefits. "You'll never have more cover to do this than you do now," they told him. Feeling it was wrong—morally and for the company itself because of the commitment these benefits had engendered—he said, "There is no way I will do it, and if that's what you want us to do, you should sell your stock."[11]

Accepting Vulnerability to Facilitate Growth and Innovation

In some types of workplace courage (see the box "Opportunities to Grow" for examples), the "challenge" or "confrontation" we face is largely with ourselves. Will we voluntarily make ourselves vulnerable? Will we court potential failure that could be psychologically painful or economically costly?

Like it or not, creating opportunities for growth—whether for ourselves or for others—often entails psychological risk. While nearly everyone says they're open to learning and claims it's an organizational imperative, the truth is that many of us work pretty hard to avoid doing things that could leave others thinking we're weak, overly emotional, or perhaps just plain incompetent. That's a shame, because our willingness to say and do things that reveal our imperfections or desire to grow can be what ultimately makes us and others stronger. Alex Karras, a former NFL player and actor, argued in his biography that it takes "more courage to reveal insecurities than to hide them, more strength to relate to people than to dominate them."[12] Indeed, a demonstration of vulnerability might humanize you—especially if you're a man, someone with a highly assertive personality, or someone who always appears to "be rational"—in ways that further inspire respect and loyalty.[13]

That's how Jeffrey described his feelings about the actions of his company's executive vice president. Their company had suffered a

OPPORTUNITIES TO GROW

- Showing vulnerability to facilitate workplace performance or well-being of others

- Taking/trying a stretch assignment or additional responsibility, a new activity, or a new behavior in current organization

- Owning/accepting responsibility for a bold/novel deviation from organizational or industry norms or practices

- Voluntarily starting a new job in a different organization

- Creating a new business/engaging in an entrepreneurial act

workplace fatality, and the EVP was the one in charge of the response. He spent hours with the family, canceled numerous meetings, deferred a leadership conference with over six hundred leaders from across the business, and assigned a full-time worker to help the family sort out paperwork and finances. Even more impressive to Jeffrey was how the EVP made himself vulnerable by truly leaning into the family's pain in a public way. Rather than hide how he felt, he talked openly about how much the loss had rattled him and let others see him being quite emotional amid all the concrete actions he took to be helpful.

Owning the responsibility for charting a new course for oneself or one's organization isn't always just psychologically risky. It can also come with significant potential career consequences. Philippe, for example, took the initiative to propose a set of improvements that he believed would increase his facility's results significantly. As they exited the meeting with senior management, his boss put it bluntly: "I hope you get this right, because if you don't, they're going to break your legs."

Now consider the decision to start a new business. While we glorify entrepreneurs and can easily name high-profile success stories, the more complete picture is that entrepreneurship is fraught with risk of failure. One study covering startups over more than thirty years found a five-year survival rate of just about 50 percent.[14] That's right—the odds of a new business staying around for even a few years is about the same as the odds of getting heads in a coin flip.

Though most of us don't know these specific statistics, we seem to nonetheless understand the risks of putting it all on the line. Nearly 80 percent of WCAI respondents rate starting a new venture as very courageous, even though few are likely to have ever done so. Among nascent and actual entrepreneurs, according to a recent study, "nearly every interviewee regarded courage as important in starting a new business."[15] Lia, who started her business when her child was just seven months old and her husband still in school, certainly felt this way. But she believed the timing was right, so, "in spite of the fear of failing, and inconveniences to family, I went ahead and started the business."

Rashida, similarly, took the plunge and cofounded a company. Despite having no experience as an entrepreneur, she set aside the much safer path she was on and became president of the fledgling organization. She wrote business plans, outlined a clear strategy, and learned-while-doing all the other steps needed to raise funds and get the organization off the ground. She was excited about the idea of running a state-of-the-art manufacturing facility and bringing good jobs to a small town that desperately needed them. The job, though, was hugely stressful for her. She got physically sick from the fear she felt before and during certain events (e.g., pitches to potential investors) and was emotionally plagued by what psychologists call the "imposter syndrome"—the belief that she wasn't smart or talented enough and that she'd soon be found out for the fraud she was.[16] Still, she persevered, guided by the saying, "If not now, when? If not me, who?"

You don't have to start or run an entrepreneurial venture to put a lot at stake by pursuing a new career path. You might, for example, just choose to leave a perfectly stable, safe job to start a new job in a different organization, or even to pursue a whole new line of work. This is something I see a lot in my work with adult students who acknowledge they aren't truly happy or fulfilled where they're at and thus use their time in a graduate program or extended executive education course as an impetus to make major career shifts. If your first inclination is that this is easy, think again. For many, this choice means putting at risk a good part of the social and political capital they've spent decades accruing, as well as possibly forfeiting significant pay or benefits. "Starting over" in pursuit of growth is both worthy and risky—the defining features of a courageous behavior.

Taking the Toughest Stands

We've examined a lot of difficult behaviors in this chapter and the last. Before moving on, let's cover a few more that are among the very toughest. These involve choices to jeopardize, limit, or end important relationships or benefits to defend one's principles, knowing full well that these actions involve significant personal sacrifices and risks. (See the box "Taking Tough Stands.")

Sometimes you have to put your money where your mouth is if you want to embody rather than just espouse certain values. Consider Gina's experience as the only female, and one of only two technical experts, in a startup. During a meeting with potential investors who could have provided her firm with the funds for almost a year of ramp-up time, one of the investors walked down the aisle of the

TAKING TOUGH STANDS

- Refusing on principle to accept or continue to accept money, business, a contract, or an association with customer or external partner

- Taking reduced pay or role or refusing to accept increased pay or role on the basis of one's principles

- Quitting as a principled stand

- Reporting illegal or unethical acts to someone or some entity outside the organization as a last resort company's offices during a break and, for no apparent reason other than her gender, stopped at her desk and asked her to get him a coffee from Starbucks. Hearing this, Gina's CEO stepped in, explained that this was not her role, and offered to go get the coffee himself. Subsequently, the top team at Gina's company turned down the investment that was offered. For her, that decision to walk away from funds at such a risky time for the entire venture was "profound." "They chose to turn down money in order to create an organization where any employee would be valued, protected, and represented," she told me.

In another organization, Connie tendered her resignation because she was tired of being harassed by clients. As the first female account manager in a male-dominated industry, she had simply had enough. Instead of letting her go, management stepped in and canceled the contract with the client. Then they not only provided professional support to help Connie move past the abuse she'd endured, they also instituted costly harassment training for all employees. One of the results: in just a few years, many of Connie's colleagues were also female.

Sometimes no amount of skill or patience allows us to successfully defend our principles or those we care about at work. In those cases, the only courageous path left is to walk away and not look back. Consider this sacrifice. Karim led the regional luxury segment for a hotel chain during a time when his department was operating at "unheard-of profit levels" in that segment and far exceeding anticipated revenue and profit targets. Yet he was nonetheless given a directive to cut management positions by 30 percent. "No questions—just do it!" was the mandate from above. Karim saw the decision as unjust for a group performing as extraordinarily as his team was, and he wrote a letter saying the downsizing process would begin with his resignation. "If you insist on making even more," he essentially told his bosses, "you can start your cost savings with my salary." In the end, Karim's principled decision to quit saved the jobs of eleven of the eighteen managers he was told to fire.

Terry Sue Barnett, the sheriff of Nowata County, Oklahoma, also quit when she could no longer abide the conditions of continuing in her role. Barnett had moved inmates out of the local jail when she concluded it was not safe for them (or staff) to be there following a carbon monoxide leak that registered at a level of 18 (20 being the lethal level). "I cannot," she said at the time, "morally or legally endanger the prisoners' lives."[17] When the cause had still not been determined but a judge nonetheless ordered her to reopen the jail, she, five of her deputies, and several other staff members resigned in protest rather than follow the order. Beyond the carbon monoxide issue, she pointed to other problems that had not been adequately addressed— exposed wiring in shower and other areas giving inmates electrical shocks while showering, mold throughout the jail, and improperly installed sewer lines that occasionally caused methane gas to permeate the facility. In explaining her decision to walk away, Barnett pointed to her pledge when elected to "do the right thing" and her unwillingness to accept "hope and pray that nothing will happen" as an acceptable attitude about a dangerous, morally offensive situation.[18]

Quitting your job isn't the only way, of course, to make a major personal sacrifice on behalf of your principles or others' needs: you might take reduced income or a lower-status role, or you might refuse to accept an increase in pay or a higher-status role. Jared, for instance, praised his CEO's behavior amid a significant business downturn. Rather than implement a very strict austerity plan for all, the CEO "made a selfless and sacrificial decision and decided not to take his bonus for the next two years." He also encouraged (but didn't require) his direct reports to forgo their bonuses. Other senior leaders hated the idea, and even petitioned the board of directors to replace the CEO. The CEO merely reiterated that his decision was made for the greater good of the company, and specifically out of consideration for the lowest-paid employees (like the warehouse staff). The CEO kept his job—and garnered intense loyalty and an improvement in both employee morale and performance.

Let's end with a workplace behavior that's widely seen as among the most courageous—blowing the whistle about illegal or unethical behavior to someone or some entity outside one's organization. While this can sometimes be the only path left to try to prevent harm to others (nine out of ten whistleblowers first report to internal authorities) or to be able to look yourself in the mirror, there's no way to sugar-coat the risks.[19] Once you take something serious outside an organization, you'll be seen as disloyal or a traitor by many in power. In short, if you get perceived as a foreign antigen—a virus attacking the system—the organization's immune response is likely to try to expel you if it can.

Though hard to get precise statistics, available evidence suggests that retaliation against whistleblowers is still fairly common (despite laws being strengthened in recent years to protect against it).[20] There's a significant chance you'll lose your job, and if you don't, a good chance you'll face other types of serious retribution.[21] That includes the cold shoulder or actual verbal abuse from supervisors and peers, the withholding of opportunities, reassignment or demotion, and numerous other forms of harassment or unfair treatment.[22] Consider what happened to Courland Kelley, who eventually sued GM after finding and reporting serious flaws in GM's Chevrolet Cavalier and repeatedly failing to impel sufficient corrective action. When his case was dismissed on procedural grounds, Kelley's career in the company derailed. He was transferred to a job with no meaningful responsibilities and has struggled with his health in the years since.[23]

Still, he believes his choice was the only ethical thing to do. That's what's both interesting and inspiring about whistleblowers: even when things don't go well at all, most remain convinced that what they did was important and necessary.[24] They've tried to save lives, prevent massive fraud, and accomplish other highly noble objectives. Despite dealing with all sorts of loss, they have psychological peace of mind. For some, the only regret that lingers is that they didn't publicly disclose the wrongs earlier.[25]

Putting It on the Line for Your Values

Let's not pretend that the acts described in this chapter aren't hard. Like any behaviors worthy of the label "courageous," the behaviors we've covered don't always leave the actor in the best position. People do sometimes face backlash when they confront peers or subordinates, especially when the situation involves calling out highly inappropriate or unethical behavior.[26] Think about the situation faced by Zeb when his colleague made racist comments at the bar. Is it really hard to believe that more than half of us would have a hard time confronting something like this in real time? Standing up to bad behavior or a bully doesn't automatically stop the problem; it could even make you a target too.[27]

People also sometimes lose customers for taking a stand. One sports journalist, for example, told me her newspaper (located in a conservative part of the country) lost subscriptions when she started to publish articles about gay athletes coming out. And, as we've discussed, people do sometimes feel embarrassed when they step out of their comfort zone emotionally and behaviorally and do suffer materially when attempts to own bold decisions, start new jobs, or create new ventures don't go well.

So why do these things? Because, if you're a manager, there's a significant downside to *not* doing these things. For example, if you consistently fail to confront an underperforming subordinate with informal rebuke or formal sanctions, you'll lose a ton of respect in your subordinates' eyes. They'll conclude you're a wimp, not a good boss. Even if you're not in a managerial role, the failure to do the things discussed in this chapter costs you something. Others notice, and they think you're either complicit ("He never stands up to their gossiping either; he's just like them") or too insecure or conflict averse to act ("I can't believe she lets people treat her that way"). Consider the following two stories.

Joseph Reiman, a police officer, was recorded pummeling a teenager following a traffic incident.[28] It turns out that Reiman had racked up a long record of use of force in his short time on the job and a reputation for using excessive force, according to dozens of people interviewed by NJ Advance Media. Three fellow officers were recorded talking candidly about Reiman's behavior, saying things like, "This is indefensible." But did they, or other colleagues, take any action to get Reiman off the street? Nope. It took a lawsuit, journalists, witnesses, and a dashcam video to make that happen. Would it be very difficult for cops to report on other cops, given the culture of loyalty they operate in, where doing so risks being ostracized as a rat and potentially subject to physical harm? Absolutely. It would be a courageous act. None of them did it. If this sounds too familiar, it's because it is largely the same as what happened in the killing of George Floyd by an officer who had amassed a long record of prior complaints but faced no meaningful discipline and remained on the street.[29]

In contrast, consider this story about Mark Herzlich, a linebacker for the New York Giants NFL team. The world of pro football is a testosterone-driven one where a kind of violence is required and celebrated. It's also one in which fitting in with peers in the culture of locker room is about as important as it is in any work context. Yet when Herzlich heard jokes or other denigrating comments about women, he spoke up, telling his teammates what they said wasn't funny or appropriate. Having learned about the physical and emotional abuse his wife had suffered in childhood, Herzlich has become one of the NFL's most forceful advocates in raising players' awareness about domestic abuse. His core message: "Men overall need to stand up to other men." It's not just about how men behave toward women, he believes; it's about the courage to "hold others accountable to treat women how they deserve to be treated."[30]

In both of these stories, people faced risks of social rejection, and even possible physical harm, if those they confronted at work became less willing to have their back. But is there any question about whom you consider more courageous—those who stood silently by as a coworker engaged in and bragged about excessive violence, or the guy who confronted his peers about their degrading language toward women? Any question about whom you'd rather be compared to?

Let's end by returning to where we started this chapter—with the choices facing Darnell immediately after being told that one of his employees had said disgusting, racist things about him. Hurt and angry, Darnell talked to and got an ambivalent response from HR. While not defending the employee's racist remarks, the HR manager made comments like, "It's tricky, because it was off-site, off-hours, and he was spending his own money." The HR manager also pointed out that this employee had been a solid performer for nearly two decades.

After listening to this for a while, Darnell replied, "Either he goes or I go." The HR manager said he understood and would get back in touch soon.

One day later, Darnell was told by HR that it was fine to fire the offender, which he did. When Darnell told that employee he was being let go immediately, he was totally shocked but neither denied what he'd said nor apologized.

In reflecting years later on his ultimatum to HR, Darnell said, "Beyond how I felt personally, I thought I had an obligation to do something for the three who came to me. If I hadn't fired that guy, I would have let my other subordinates down." His reflections exemplify the essence of courageous action—the willingness to take significant risks to stand for your values. He explained:

> Having done very well in business now, others might think this was easy for me. But at the time, I was a young man from an extremely poor background. I had only been at the company for a few years and planned to stay at least a few more as I built my career. It would have been a serious blow if, instead of agreeing to let me fire him, they had said, "Bye, Darnell." But that's what it means to "put it on the line for your values." Are you willing to take risks when they are very real, not just when you already have the financial means to make it easier?

What about You?

In this chapter, we've again seen lots of inspirational examples of workplace courage. Admiring others, though, isn't enough. It's just the starting point in realizing we all can—and probably should—do more of these behaviors more often. It can't always be "someone else's job" to do these things. After all, if everyone thought that way, these actions would literally never happen!

If you haven't already, I urge you to take the Workplace Courage Acts Index survey before moving on. When you've finished, study the results for the behaviors covered in this chapter. How courageous do you find these to be in your current work environment? How hard are each for you personally? How often do you actually do them when opportunities arise? Do you struggle with these because you focus on being "nice" rather than truly honest? Or, conversely, do you do some of the things covered in the chapter but in ways that come off as so harsh or uncaring that people reject your message, no matter how valid?

Be honest with yourself—your results will be useful in your subsequent decision making only if they paint the real picture. And don't worry about admitting that these things are hard for you, whether that's because you hate confrontation, you don't know quite what to say or how to say it skillfully in these situations, you worry about tarnishing relationships, or any other reasons. I've not yet met a single person who claims all the behaviors we're discussing are easy for them to do, and do well.

Remember

- Opportunities for workplace courage don't present just economic or other career risks. They also raise social, psychological, or physical risks.

- Interactions with all kinds of stakeholders sometimes present opportunities for courage. Even when we'd just be "doing our job," decisions and conversations involving subordinates, peers, clients, and others are often deemed sufficiently risky and difficult that they don't happen with regularity.

- While nearly everyone espouses the value of personal growth and organizational innovation, the behaviors that lead to these are often seen as requiring significant courage and therefore often left undone. For those who embrace the challenge, there tend to be few long-term regrets.

- Opportunities for workplace courage are often chances to put your values on the line or, as Patrick Lencioni says, "make your values mean something." If you won't accept the pain or loss that may be associated with defending your values, they're just espoused or aspirational values, not core or in-use values.[31]

CHAPTER 4

Building *Your* Courage Ladder

I f you've come this far, and you accept that we need more courageous acts, including from people like you and me, and you've done some initial self-assessment, it's time to start thinking seriously about your own next steps.

Critical to this journey is your acceptance of the fact that skilled action in stressful situations requires practice—lots of it. You're going to have to expose yourself to the risks you've been avoiding, because the only way I know to the other side of your fears is straight through them.

To start making this tangible and concrete, I'll encourage you to build your own courage ladder—a personal road map of sorts that helps you think about where you want to start and get to on this journey. I'll talk about setting an initial goal for starting at the bottom of your ladder so your first steps are more likely to happen, and more likely to lead to increased self-efficacy and the motivation to keep climbing.

Habituation through Planned Exposure

I've noted that the ability to act courageously doesn't come from an exceptional trait that only a few possess. It's a capacity we can all develop by committing to learn and practice relevant skills. Your first courageous step might be to choose to make that commitment now.

Practice, Practice, Practice

Aristotle argued that courage is a moral virtue developed through habit, and psychologist Stanley Rachman's careful research in military settings nearly two thousand years later proved him right. Rachman and his colleagues demonstrated that aspiring paratroopers learn both to act with less fear and to act successfully despite their fear through repeated practice under skilled instruction in a supportive environment. In a nutshell, said Rachman, his studies "point to the powerful influence of adequate training."[1] That's similar to the conclusion subsequently reached by moral psychologist Kurt Gray in describing those who do extraordinary things in the service of others: the very act of doing good is self-reinforcing because it helps us feel more willing and able to withstand discomfort along the way.[2]

On the one hand, this is hopeful news; on the other, it means none of us is off the hook. We can't claim we lost some genetic lottery and leave it to others to stand up and speak out. In fact, even when someone's courage appears to be innate, it's probably not. For example, as told by historian Doris Kearns Goodwin, when (future US president) Teddy Roosevelt first spent time in the untamed West of the late 1800s, he was afraid of all sorts of things, from wild animals to gunfighters. Only by "forcing himself to do the most difficult or even dangerous thing" was he able to cultivate courage in himself "as a matter of habit, in the sense of repeated effort and repeated exercise of will-power."[3] Later observers referred to his "indomitable courage" as apparently "ingrained in his being," clearly not understanding how hard he had worked to "become fearless by sheer dint of practicing fearlessness."[4] Roosevelt's own goal had not been to deceive others about his own character; indeed, he hoped to inspire others to practice being courageous by his own example of facing his fears head-on.

It's easier, though, to simply put people like that on a pedestal as a way of excusing our own inaction. This tendency to underestimate how hard people have worked to achieve their competence in any domain is quite general. Psychologist Anders Ericsson and colleagues have studied "peak performers" for decades, finding that what actually differentiates them is their years of practice. The mental representations and associated skills of experts aren't developed by thinking about doing something, explain Ericsson and science writer Robert Pool, but rather "by trying to do something, failing, revising, and trying again, over and over."[5] Justin Stone, the great American tai chi instructor, likewise used the Chinese saying "You cannot appease the hunger by reading a menu" to remind followers that they couldn't improve their own relaxation skills by thinking or reading about doing so.[6] You have to practice, he said. Every day.

Practice Requires Exposure

The late John Lewis and his colleagues weren't born ready to demonstrate nonviolent resistance to hate and discrimination. Long before their marches, sit-ins, and freedom walks, they started practicing, over and over, the nonviolent techniques they wanted to employ in response to the verbal and physical assaults they knew would come their way. Their desired responses had to be learned and internalized. "We were taught not to strike back," recalled Lewis. "We studied. We had role playing. We had social drama. We were committed to the philosophy and the discipline of nonviolence as a way of life, as a way of living."[7] So they practiced.

What John Lewis and his colleagues did is consistent with decades of "exposure therapy" research. The concept (if not the practice itself!) is simple: the way to reduce the emotional hold of something frightening is to gradually expose ourselves to that same threat, over and over, so that we can practice handling it and thereby reduce its power over us. Exposure therapy is the most widely used and effective treatment in psychologists' toolkit for treating fear and anxiety across a host of different domains.[8] It's been shown to be helpful in reducing all sorts of persistent, crippling fears—from fear of snakes to fear of public speaking.

The ultimate purpose of exposure is habituation—a decreased physiological or emotional response to the situation that was once highly arousing. For example, imagine that you're terrified of speaking up to your boss. Maybe your father was a yeller, and you've seen leaders at your organization tear into people who challenge them. Your current boss hasn't been nasty to you, but you just can't shake the fear that grips you when you contemplate disagreeing with him. Your brain currently associates "being honest with powerful people" with "danger," and unless you manage to be honest with those above you in ways that lessen that automatic physiological fear response, or show you that you can survive just fine despite them, it's not going to get easier for you. To repeat an uncomfortable but important truth: there's no way it will get easier to speak truth to power unless you start doing it and prove to yourself that it's not as awful as you feared.

Of course, if you have a terrible experience when you do speak up, that's only going to reinforce your fear. That's why it's important to take small, controlled steps to reduce physiological and psychological arousal. You don't just charge into a room and pick up the snake you fear. Your first step might be only to enter the room and do some deep breathing from ten feet away from the caged snake. Fairly soon that would become downright boring, and you'd be ready to get a bit closer. Before doing so, you might learn some cognitive techniques to further help you beat back the fear that threatens to overtake the rest of your brain.

The same is true with overcoming fear of speaking up or screwing it up when you do: you start very small and work your way toward more challenging situations. Since it wouldn't be productive to keep moving to those more challenging situations if you didn't add new skills along the way, we'll focus extensively on those in the coming chapters. Some of these are methods for managing your automatic *physiological responses*, some involve how you *think* about stressful situations, and many involve your *behavioral repertoire*. The latter—your behavior toolkit—is particularly important because skillfully handling difficult conversations or decisions at work usually requires a broader range of behaviors than approaching a snake does (stepping forward; putting your hand in the cage; and so on). As we'll see, many of the behaviors you'll want to learn and practice are those we don't even know how to do skillfully in lower-stress situations.

While simply avoiding something is just fine when we don't care about its outcomes (for example, nothing I care about rests on me overcoming my fear of bats), purposefully "escaping" situations with consequences we do care about is actually worse than we already intuitively know. It's not just that we allow the problem to persist and that we feel disappointment or shame for again avoiding an important action. It's also that we are actually *reinforcing* our fear. Why? Because the good feeling we get from avoidance may only strengthen our belief that the situation we avoided was indeed too terrible to approach. Though we don't usually consciously note it when it happens, our sense of "I feel calm now" can heighten the contrast with "that terrible, scary situation" we just avoided. Explains psychiatrist Joseph Strayhorn, "Escape from a feared situation tends to reinforce fear, whereas prolonged exposure (especially with the practice of handling the situation courageously) tends to reduce fear."[9]

So, imagine that you sit in your boss's office wanting to tell her something but then are so scared that you don't. Instead, you end the meeting quickly, return to your office, and do something that relaxes you. What you've done is further strengthen two associations in your brain: (1) my boss in her office = scary; (2) alone in my office = safe. Sadly, you've reinforced your belief that you aren't able to handle an honest conversation with your boss *and* your tendency to retreat.

Build *Your* Courage Ladder

I suggest you start by building a courage ladder like the one shown in figure 4-1. On the bottom rungs, put things that currently feel

FIGURE 4-1

_My_ courage ladder

somewhat risky and difficult but that you can imagine starting to practice in at least some small way relatively soon. At the higher rungs, put
things that you'd love to be able to do more frequently or skillfully,
but that feel really risky or beyond you right now.

This exercise is for all of us, because every normal person feels
afraid or intimidated by the prospect of doing some things some of
the time. I think M. Scott Peck said it perfectly: "The absence of fear is
not courage; the absence of fear is some kind of brain damage. Courage is the capacity to go ahead in spite of the fear, or in spite of the
pain."[10] So let go of any negative self-judgment, put aside your worry
that you're uniquely vulnerable (you're not!), and get started.

Don't worry about how easy or hard the steps on your ladder might be for anyone else. It's your ladder. Feeling ashamed or embarrassed because you think what feels hard for you might be easier for others isn't going to help you move forward. There's a reasonable chance you're wrong about your assumptions anyway. If there's anything I've learned about the fears and lack of skills that inhibit the behaviors discussed in this book, it's that they're pretty widely shared. For any behavior you might put on your ladder, I can assure you there are tons of other people who have it on theirs too.

It's also true that except for a couple of extremely difficult behaviors—like putting ourselves at major physical risk or publicly revealing the illegal or unethical behavior of higher-power individuals—the order of the things on people's ladders varies quite a lot. A few years ago, I asked a group of business school students at Cornell to rate the level of courage for a series of work-related behaviors. The responses for every single behavior (there were about twenty of them) ranged from "no courage" to "extreme courage." That's why you've got to build a *personal* courage ladder. While I can assert that you have one, I can't possibly tell you what's on which of the rungs *for you*.

The two courage ladders shown in figure 4-2 provide a more tangible illustration of this. Adam has had very competent, supportive bosses and he's relatively young, so his fears about authority are more about doing things that show disrespect for their seniority and expertise than about challenging them for doing things that are wrong or inappropriate. Thus, for him, it feels a little courageous to step beyond the technical boundaries of his role. It feels a bit more courageous for Adam to challenge his boss about operating policies or practices because his assumption is that he probably doesn't have the same breadth or depth of expertise as his boss does. Similarly, it feels even more difficult for Adam to have to admit he's made a mistake to someone above him, because he's a perfectionist who hates to disappoint others and can't stand the thought of looking stupid. But because Adam has a strong need to be liked—and because he considers his colleagues the best and most important part of his work environment—the thought of having to confront *peers* about something they're doing wrong terrifies him. It's at the top of the ladder he's made for himself.

In contrast, confronting peers is at the lowest rung of Marty's courage ladder. He doesn't relish the idea, and he knows that without being careful in how he approaches peers (who can easily say "You're not the boss of me" in less nice terms), it can easily go badly. Still, he thinks of peer confrontations as mildly unsettling, not terrifying. In contrast, Marty dreads difficult interactions with *his boss* and others above him. He knows that these fears started in childhood; he can't remember a time that his father took a confrontation in stride. And he's had enough self-serving and insecure bosses that his body

FIGURE 4-2

Two sample courage ladders

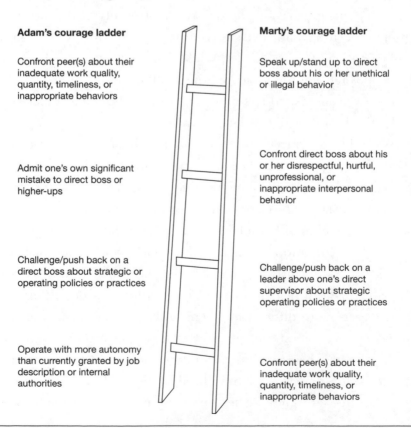

Adam's courage ladder

Confront peer(s) about their inadequate work quality, quantity, timeliness, or inappropriate behaviors

Admit one's own significant mistake to direct boss or higher-ups

Challenge/push back on a direct boss about strategic or operating policies or practices

Operate with more autonomy than currently granted by job description or internal authorities

Marty's courage ladder

Speak up/stand up to direct boss about his or her unethical or illegal behavior

Confront direct boss about his or her disrespectful, hurtful, unprofessional, or inappropriate interpersonal behavior

Challenge/push back on a leader above one's direct supervisor about strategic operating policies or practices

Confront peer(s) about their inadequate work quality, quantity, timeliness, or inappropriate behaviors screams "danger" when he thinks of almost any type of challenging interaction with higher-ups. He thinks his current boss might be able to handle a conversation about strategy or operating policies because those things aren't so personal. But when he thinks about confronting his boss about the inappropriate things she sometimes says or does, especially the couple of things Marty thinks cross ethical or possibly even legal lines, the immediate physiological signs of fear that appear make those behaviors feel out of reach.

To stimulate your thinking about what belongs on your ladder, you might go back to your results from the Workplace Courage Acts Index. What items—for you personally—would take a lot of courage? Or simply take some time to recall the last few irritations or complaints you've had at work that you talked about with peers or family members, but not the person involved or others who could actually help. Our "talked behind their back" list usually has good material for our courage ladder.

To be actionable, the final version of your courage ladder needs to be *specific*, because we don't take action on a type of behavior, but on specific instances of it. For example, if you feel that "confronting peers about inadequate work" is courageous, jot down both the name of a specific peer and the specific type or instance of his inadequate work. For example, to guide actual next steps, Marty's initial courage ladder has to be converted to one like that shown in figure 4-3.

To be sure you've got the behaviors in the right order and, more importantly, that you've got some things toward the bottom of the ladder that you can really imagine yourself doing in the near term, it can be helpful to give each behavior on your ladder a number indicating how hard it would be for you right now. You might use what psychiatrist Joseph Strayhorn calls a "SUD score"—that is, a rating from 1 to 10 of the "subjective units of distress" you currently associate with each act.[11] Don't worry about precision here—these are just your estimates and are for your use only.

Marty, for example, might consider talking to his peer John about shoddy reports to have a SUD score of 4, and those involving his bosses a 7, 9, and 10, respectively. This may lead Marty to add a few others to the list—perhaps a behavior even lower than a 4 so he's willing to

FIGURE 4-3

Marty's *specific* courage ladder

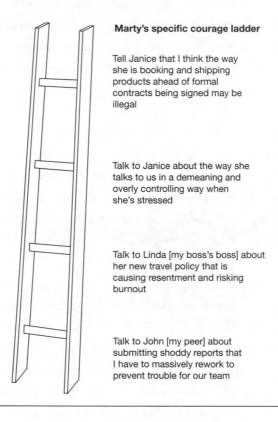

Marty's specific courage ladder

Tell Janice that I think the way she is booking and shipping products ahead of formal contracts being signed may be illegal

Talk to Janice about the way she talks to us in a demeaning and overly controlling way when she's stressed

Talk to Linda [my boss's boss] about her new travel policy that is causing resentment and risking burnout

Talk to John [my peer] about submitting shoddy reports that I have to massively rework to prevent trouble for our team

commit to doing it soon and perhaps something between the 4 and 7 so he can work his way up his ladder without taking such a leap after talking to his peer. He might ask himself "What is the easiest conversation I can think of having with Janice that is still intimidating for me?" to generate a boss-directed behavior that has lower than a 7 SUD score.

Assigning SUD scores to these behaviors now also allows you to track progress. In a few months, for example, with the experience of talking to John about the shoddy reports and a few others like this under his belt, Marty might decide this behavior now only feels like a 2. And maybe the ones involving his boss that he initially put on his ladder have come to feel less difficult for him, too.

Take a First Step

You've got your ladder. Now what? My advice is to start climbing from the bottom, just as you would on a real ladder. It's worth remembering that just like in physical training the most effective long-term strategy is to start with small, manageable steps.[12] Start with very short "courage workouts" and slowly build your capacity. Of course, you want the first steps to involve *some* (di)stress or they're not even courageous acts and you won't be practicing under conditions that sufficiently mimic the stresses involved with the things higher on your ladder. If your starting point is too easy, you might also have picked battles that, in the words of education activist Jonathan Kozol, are small enough to win but not big enough to matter.[13] You want activities with SUD scores of 2 or 3, not 0.

Say, for example, that you want to stop being a silent bystander when one of your colleagues gossips about the appearance of another coworker. Taking a forceful, public stand to rebuke this behavior the next time it occurs might feel like a very big deal. But, as Sharyn Potter (the codirector of the Prevention Innovations Research Center at the University of New Hampshire) reminds us, you don't need to "fly in with [your] Superman cape."[14] As a first step, you could commit to yourself to saying something in private next time it happens. Advises Linda Tropp, a psychology professor at the University of Massachusetts at Amherst, it could be as simple as "I don't appreciate that comment" or "That's not cool," said in a calm manner that doesn't demonize the speaker.[15] You don't need to give him a lecture about why you don't appreciate it, or why it's not cool. Just make the simple statement. Your colleague may not like it and may let you know that. But you'll survive, and he might be more careful about what he says going forward.

There are at multiple reasons to start at the bottom and take small steps when you first start climbing your courage ladder. For one, you're more likely to have some success—to get some "small wins" that help you begin to build self-efficacy (that sense that "I can do this"). You're trying to change your "can do" beliefs about the behaviors on your ladder, and the way to do that is to have some things go well (or at least OK) so you begin to lessen the association in your head between "behavior X" and "bad outcomes." You are trying, as Bryan said long ago (and as psychologists have confirmed), to develop self-confidence by doing the things you fear and getting a record of successful experiences behind you.[16]

Practice also helps you get comfortable with the discomfort that accompanies courageous actions. Small steps teach us that we can survive and move on, even if we're miserable in the moment. In recent decades, much has been written about "resilience," and the simple message is this: difficult experiences don't automatically doom us; they present opportunities to emerge on the other side even stronger and more capable of handling what life throws our way.[17]

For example, say you speak up with a new idea in a staff meeting and the boss shoots it down. You feel terrible that night, telling whomever will listen what a jerk your boss is, how you're never listened to or respected, etc. The next morning, you're still stewing over it. It stinks, for sure. But what we often forget when recalling experiences like this is that *we got past them.* We didn't suffer irreparable harm, and the pain wasn't so intense we couldn't move forward. In fact, viewed as a learning experience, we now know two things more clearly: (1) what *doesn't* work as well as we'd like it to in that kind of situation and, (2) that we are capable of living with and moving past some degree of emotional pain. So pat yourself on the back for speaking up, and choose to imprint this as a moment of strength and growth, not as a failure. Remind yourself that the differences we see between people who went through the same setback or hardship often has more to do with the post hoc story they told themselves than what they both objectively experienced.

Taking a small step now also reduces the chance that you'll have to take a much bigger step later because the situation has escalated due to your earlier inaction. For example, auditors routinely find relatively small deviations from accepted accounting practice. If they don't speak up about these minor indiscretions because it's uncomfortable, they might later need to be truly heroic in the face of what has become a much larger problem.[18]

Letting problems get bigger before taking action makes it harder to succeed for two reasons. First, having to confront, report, or admit something that is now much more serious increases the likelihood that others will react negatively. If you think someone won't like being told that they've just started to do something outside accepted accounting standards that could cause a problem if not stopped now, think how they're going to react if you wait six months and then have to tell them that they've got a major accounting problem that puts the organization at significant financial, legal, or reputational risk.

Second, when we don't take smaller steps earlier, our emotions often build up in ways that limit our ability to behave skillfully when we finally act. We've all seen people (and probably done it ourselves—I certainly have) who tell themselves "It's no big deal" or "It's fine" the first, second, and third time something problematic happens, and then later overreact unproductively when that same thing happens yet again. The truth is, it never really was OK to us, but we told ourselves that story to avoid doing something about it. Now, when we simply can't tolerate it anymore, we're stuck trying to confront the issue skillfully with our emotions at a 10 rather than the 2 or 3 they started at.

Small steps and small wins. They increase our confidence to take bigger steps. They show us it is possible to act where we used to think it was too hard or too dangerous. They reveal that we're not as incompetent or impotent as we thought we were.

And here's one more thing—what starts small can become something bigger. As organizational theorist Kark Weick has written, your small wins might start drawing others to your position, and openness to a bigger change might increase.[19] You might also see that what appeared to be little or no change was actually change happening out of sight. Many years ago, I was feeling frustrated that the changes I'd been working to make didn't appear to be bearing any fruit. A wise counselor suggested more was likely happening than I realized. "Imagine you're trying to knock down a cinder block wall," he said, "and you're swinging at the wall with a sledgehammer. Day after day, you hit the wall, and nothing appears to be happening. You're just about to give up, when suddenly the entire wall crumbles. Turns out, for quite some time small pieces were cracking off the back of the wall, hit after hit. You *were* making progress, but you couldn't see it until you literally broke through."

Remember

- You develop the skills to act competently in courageous situations by *practicing* those skills regularly, not by reading or thinking about them.

- Regular practice—with small increases in the level of difficulty in actions—can help you habituate to the situations you fear, thereby reducing their emotional grip and increasing your ability to act in desired ways.

- Everyone's courage ladder is different because the specific situations we fear and skills we need to develop to tackle them successfully vary significantly across individuals. But all of us have things we can identify and order by degree of risk and difficulty on a courage ladder. Pretending this isn't the case is only an excuse to keep from getting started.

- Taking small steps from the bottom rungs of your courage ladder increases the odds you'll have some success, thereby building self-efficacy and sustaining your motivation to keep tackling tougher situations. Even if things don't go well, you'll learn, you'll get more comfortable with discomfort, and you'll increase your resilience.

PART TWO

HOW TO BE COMPETENTLY COURAGEOUS

CHAPTER 5

Creating the Right Conditions

As her team's new leader, Janet wanted to address some problems and incon-sistencies she'd noticed in some of her former peers: shirking committee work, not responding promptly (or at all) to emails, and not being team players. Worse, the biggest offenders were also the ones who squawked if any decision got made without their chance to approve or veto it. They seemed to want the privileges that came from being high-status members of the organization with-out consistently taking on some of the less fun, but necessary, responsibilities.

Janet decided to bring up these issues at her first meeting with her team in polite, example-laden terms. This was necessary, she believed, to start making positive change.

What do you think about Janet's decision? Her willingness to talk about these issues with her team is certainly courageous. Since her direct reports were her former peers, she'd be sticking her neck out to confront them so directly. They'll probably be offended and angry. So, is Janet being smart raising these issues in her first meeting as the team's new leader? Do you think she'll produce her desired outcomes?

In this chapter, we'll focus on things you can do *ahead of time* to increase the likelihood that your courageous act goes well. This in-cludes building a strong reputation and coming across as warm and competent as well as emotionally intelligent, fair, and balanced. This gives you what psychologists call *idiosyncrasy credits*—a stock of good-will earned through sufficient conformity and trustworthy behavior over time that allows you to subsequently challenge norms with less personal risk and more credibility.[1] We'll also talk about optimizing your autonomy to act in risky circumstances without suffering consequences that feel unacceptable to you. These choices can help you feel less concerned about the fallout that could come from your courageous behavior at work.

Following my advice will not guarantee success; but it will increase your odds. For example, I found in one study that people who reported having created at least some of the conditions discussed in this chapter before doing a specific courageous act were more than twice as likely to report better outcomes for themselves and six times more likely to report positive outcomes for others and their organization.

Let's take a closer look.

Build Your Internal Reputation

Getting others to respond positively when you raise difficult issues isn't easy. It helps, though, to have already established your identity as someone who can be trusted to act—and act wisely—on behalf of others' interests.

Demonstrate Warmth *and* Competence

Social scientists have identified *warmth* and *competence* as the two key impressions we form when meeting and interacting with others.

When people assess our warmth, they're (often unconsciously) asking: "How trustworthy and moral is this person?" When they judge our competence, they ask, "Can she succeed at carrying out her intentions?" Across hundreds of studies, it's been repeatedly shown that people's answers to these two questions are a very strong predictor of how they perceive our specific behaviors.[2] For example, if you're seen as warm but incompetent, your behaviors might evoke pity (up to the point where your incompetence is creating harm, at which point anger also appears). In contrast, if you're highly competent but low in warmth, your actions might evoke anger, envy, or fear. In short, being seen as low on either (and certainly both) of these core dimensions is not a recipe for inspiring others' respect.

So, if you want to know whether your behavior will be perceived as courageous and worth doing something about, a good starting point is to get clear on whether you've established your warmth *and* competence in the minds of others—especially your targets.

Warmth

I can't overstate how much warmth affects your ability to get things done. Sure, if you've got power over a group of people, you can boss them around because they're afraid of the consequences of not doing what you say. But most managers don't want to behave this way; and if they're smart, they know that doing so only sets them up for subtle undermining and retaliation. Of course, not all of us are in positions of power, and even those who are often need the support of others not under their own chain of command. In these cases, your success depends on your *influence*—your ability to get people to freely do what you want them to do.[3] To be influential, people need to think that you won't intentionally hurt them if they listen to you or do what you suggest. That's why warmth is so critical.

Warmth engenders trust, and trust takes time to build up. It comes from seemingly small, but consistent, acts of goodness that show people that you really do care about them. A bar owner, for example, builds trust by regularly staying past closing so he can personally make sure all employees get to their cars safely. So does an advertising manager who continuously provides support and encouragement for the members of her team and shows meaningful compassion by memorializing a team member who passed away, organizing Secret Santa exchanges for employees' children, and other similar acts.

If you're a leader, these small acts of warmth and kindness can have a big impact. After Zak's baby was born earlier than expected, his boss

Tina provided consistent support and protection. Even though Zak was dealing with a demanding and inflexible client, Tina insisted that Zak immediately take time off to be with his wife and newborn. Later, when Zak returned to work, he learned that the client had sharply criticized Tina for the delay.

Tina's compassion, which Zak labeled courageous because of the pushback she faced, earned her Zak's and his colleagues' trust and loyalty; in turn, they were more willing to accept her decisions and feedback on other occasions when her message was harder to hear.

Sometimes you won't have time to build trust over a sustained period of time. For example, you want to speak up to the CEO, whom you hardly know, in a companywide meeting or, like Janet at the beginning of this chapter, you want to make a good first impression with a group of people you're just starting to lead. Here, your success depends on helping people form an almost immediate—and largely intuitive—sense that you mean no harm.

In these cases, nonverbal behaviors are likely your best bet for making a positive quick impression.[4] Leaning forward or into the conversation, nodding affirmation, using nonthreatening hand gestures, and being sure your body is oriented directly toward the person you're speaking to convey warmth. Keeping your posture open, rather than hunched or with arms crossed, signals trust and affection. Subtly copying the nonverbals of the person you're speaking to might also make them feel more comfortable with you. And by all means, make sure your face looks as happy as possible because truly natural smiling (what psychologists call a "Duchenne" smile) elicits positive responses.

I've learned to use the power of first impressions to positive effect when I work with any new audience. It turns out that my natural expression is quite intense, and my face looks even fiercer when I'm listening intently. I can come across as scary or angry to people I've just met—especially students. So I now start almost every group interaction with a lighthearted moment. "I have a medical condition that won't get in the way of our time together but I want you to know about. . . . I suffer from an incurable case of 'resting bitch face.' It will make you think I want to hurt somebody, when I'm really quite interested in what you're saying. Please don't let it stop you from being candid." It's funny, yes, but this initial revelation—a moment of vulnerability, if you will—really helps create a more intimate, safer environment right from the start.

Competence

Though warmth is important, in an organizational context it usually isn't enough. You also have to be seen as *competent*—as someone who has consistently performed at a high level and is therefore worth listening to. After all, you can't spend those idiosyncrasy credits if you haven't earned them in the first place.

In her excellent book *Rocking the Boat*, Stanford professor Debra Meyerson makes no bones about this. "Tempered radicals [people who are committed to their organizations but also to a cause or ideology that leads them to take courageous actions at work]," she tells us, would have "little hope of surviving, let alone succeeding" if they were not also excellent at their jobs.[5] Think about it. Would you, after all, be willing to assume the risks of being vulnerable, doing something differently, or putting resources on the line if you didn't trust the competence of the person asking you to do so?[6]

Consider Gretchen Morgenson, a Pulitzer Prize–winning business journalist (for the *New York Times* and *Wall Street Journal*, among others), who for decades has survived at the highest level while continuing to reveal the self-serving, foolish, or even corrupt. How has she done it? Put simply: her extreme competence.

Take, for example, the well-known *New York Times* article Morgenson wrote just after the bailout of insurance giant AIG in late September 2008. Her story was about how a unit within AIG had insured so many mortgage-based products that eventually the company couldn't cover the costs of all the collateral it was required to put up.

In the same piece, Morgenson also exposed Goldman Sachs, which would lose up to $20 billion if AIG failed. In conversations prior to publication, a Goldman representative had insisted the company was fully hedged, and that the risk was minimal. Morgenson reported this in the piece. She also reported on a meeting at the New York Federal Reserve Bank, then headed by Tim Geithner, to discuss what to do about AIG's potential failure and its effect on the economy should it happen. She implicitly questioned why Lloyd Blankfein, the Goldman Sachs CEO at the time, was in attendance at that meeting, given the potential conflict of interest.

Upset by the article, Tim Geithner—who subsequently was appointed secretary of the treasury under President Obama—called Morgenson at home the same Sunday the article ran. He said she'd misled readers: Blankfein's presence posed no problem, contrary to what she had intimated, because Goldman Sachs was fully hedged. "When the largest insurance company in the world goes off the cliff, those hedges will not hold," Morgenson responded, and then asked him if he'd even checked whom the hedges were with. After Geithner admitted that he had just taken Goldman's word for it, she told him in that case they'd have to "agree to disagree" on the Goldman Sachs situation, and the conversation ended. Geithner subsequently called the editor of the paper's business section to complain, and Goldman also contacted the paper's "public editor." Other than running a minor correction about others who had or hadn't attended the Fed meetings (Blankfein had, as stated), no action was taken by the *Times*. Morgenson later learned that Geithner had been contacted that Sunday morning by the angry chief financial officer of Goldman Sachs. She figures that explains Geithner's calls to her and others at the paper.

Why did the paper's editors and business leaders stand by her on that occasion, as they had many other times? The business folks— those who can't win Pulitzers for doing tough stories but instead face accountability for the loss of advertising or subscriptions—could have lobbied strongly to have Morgenson reined in or released. Her editors, or the *Times*'s lawyers, could have refused to stand with her. Surely, they, and others inside the paper, could have avoided recurring social and economic pressures by telling her to tone it down. Even among fellow business journalists at the *Times*, there were people who weren't unreserved Morgenson cheerleaders. She clearly used her platform to promote accountability, whereas others preferred to stick more to explanation without what they saw as a "point of view" that infuriated many in power or played to the stereotype that the *Times* is too liberal or antibusiness.

Put simply, the paper's leaders supported Morgenson time and again because they trusted that she knew what she was talking about. She understands so well the complicated reality of modern finance that befuddles most that she couldn't be easily dismissed as a jealous, clueless crackpot taking cheap shots. Has the *Times* been sued for her stories, and has Morgenson been personally attacked and slandered? Yes on both counts—multiple times. Have the lawsuits or attacks been found to have merit, and led to Morgenson's silencing? Never. Morgenson is too competent and conscientious. She focuses every day, in every story she writes, on being "very, very careful."[7]

As the stories above illustrate, it generally takes time to establish and reinforce your warmth and competence. Sure, you can arrive in a new organization or new job with a stellar reputation, but people are still going to want to see you operate in person before deciding whether to trust you and take you seriously. They're going to want to see you build new relationships and build your credibility *with them*.[8]

Jane experienced this reality, and adjusted skillfully, when she switched jobs from a tech company where speaking up with ideas and suggestions was welcome to one where she found managers at her new company acting as "door guards" who blocked her ability to add value. Realizing this, she didn't continue to push issues right away. Instead, she took those managers to lunch, listened and learned from them, and stepped in to help them address things that were going off the rails. She attended largely unneeded training classes to show she was a team player and went to lots of evening events where she could focus on getting to know her colleagues. She learned, in her words, the "cultural taproot" of the place, figuring out "how to align around others' 'why'" and frame what she was doing in ways that allowed others to perceive her intent as genuine and for the greater good. She studied their "buzzword actions and buttons" to figure out why they seemed reluctant, uninterested, or afraid of change. Over time, she started challenging norms again—such as going directly to senior managers in the largest target companies to offer her firm's services rather than using much slower, more circuitous routes. Now, rather than responding negatively to these moves, people at her firm cite these actions as courageous and accept the rationale that motivates them.

Show Emotional Intelligence

Emotional intelligence—the array of abilities that reflect how well we accurately recognize and skillfully manage our own and others' emotions—is equally, if not more important than, book smarts.[9]

If you haven't routinely demonstrated emotional ability and stability, people aren't likely to respond well to your courageous act. Beth, for example, described a colleague whom no one listens to anymore, even though the colleague is understood by peers to have others' best interest at heart. Why? "Because her credibility is already shot." Whenever she talks, Beth said, "she yells, and she cannot be calmed down." As a result, nothing this colleague says gets any traction.

Similarly, Maria was upset about discriminatory actions and comments she endured from one manager based on her ethnicity. Unfortunately, she became so enraged when this would happen that she consistently misread situations, showed lack of trust in others, and made statements more representative of her emotional state than an intent to win allies or have influence. This, in turn, made it easy for management to point to her missteps in justifying their conclusion that she was a disruptive employee. Thus, despite being rightfully offended by what was happening to her, Maria's angry responses only alienated her allies and gave the offending manager the leverage to further target Maria for reprisals.

But if you manage to respond more skillfully when you're dealing with negative emotions, you can buy yourself a lot of goodwill. Anne was described by a colleague at an advertising agency as a "brilliant employee, a person who is very good at her job, smart, fair, fun, and a lovely person to be around." Despite these strengths, Anne was passed over for a promotion that should have been hers when a new head of her department came in and decided instead to hire a freelancer whom he knew from elsewhere. The move was widely seen as a slap in the face to Anne, who had been an excellent, committed employee through thick and thin. Rather than lashing out in anger, starting to slack off, or becoming bitter and looking for a new job, Anne managed to "rise above the unfairness of it all" and worked to develop a strong relationship with her new supervisor in the hopes that when the next promotion opportunity arose she'd be the obvious choice, rather than someone he viewed as combative and undermining.

Appear to Be on Both Sides, or No Side at All

When you're seeking support from others, you'll fare better if the people involved feel you're acting on behalf of a collective interest *that includes them*. That's hard to achieve if people see your actions as benefiting just a faction or fraction of the organization. External whistleblowing is the ultimate example of this. Once you "take it outside the organization," people are likely to see you as being against them. After that happens, it's hard to recover because people's emotional reaction to those they consider "disloyal" or "traitors" is strong and negative.[10]

A key to being persuasive is to have others believe that you're someone who can be constructively critical while also caring about their needs and interests. This is true even when you're the boss and it's your followers you need to get on board. People are more likely to listen to you if they feel like you're one of them—that you share the same group identity or the same goals.

Take Blake, a functional unit head in his company's Canada operations. When it became clear that internal supply chain problems were causing strained customer relationships, he called out other units at a strategic offsite for their "underwhelming rate of progress" in making necessary investments and improvements to fix the problem. Blake's actions seemed brazen to senior leaders. What they didn't know was that Blake had asked the others in advance if they shared his frustrations (they did), and if they agreed that they would only make more rapid progress if they had an honest conversation at the strategy meeting (they eventually did). His multiple one-on-one meetings with numerous peers helped him shape his message so that it reflected their common view and agreed-to requests of senior management. This led to a reflective meeting in which the group more fully unpacked the issues Blake had raised. Because of the prior steps he'd taken, he found the group was willing to address their weaknesses and come up with a plan to do better.

It's also important to be consistently fair, which means you need to demonstrate, time and again, that your standards are the same for everybody. It doesn't matter whether they are part of the group pushing for change or the group resisting it, whether they're on your team or someone else's. If you want to get nowhere in a hurry, try telling someone else they should "be more objective," "be willing to make cuts," or "push for a higher standard" when you're seen as routinely ignoring these things yourself when it's hard or unflattering for you, your people, or your point of view.

George, a shop manager from a close-knit family in upstate New York, faced this kind of challenge when he hired his nephew. George followed company procedures to the letter, showing no biases in how his nephew was trained or treated. Unfortunately, he soon realized that his nephew was not a hard worker. He frequently took unauthorized breaks to smoke and chat with new friends, left work unfinished, and did other things that disrupted the unit's workflow. When he threatened to fire his nephew, George faced his sister's wrath. She told him in no uncertain terms that terminating her son would have grave effects on their relationship, effectively ending any trust she had in George.

George suffered through sleepless nights because of his sister's ultimatum. He knew he could cover up for his nephew's mistakes, spend extra time training him, and offer him additional chances without being called out by upper management. But George was not a man to compromise on his ethics and the value he placed on efficiency, diligence, and the morale of his team. At the end of his nephew's three-month trial period, George advised that he be fired. George's entire family was and remained critical and unsupportive of his decision, and his sister cut him off for years. But his employees liked and trusted him even more. "I did what I did because rules apply to everyone," George said, "including family." That's what "living your values" actually looks like—doing something even when it really costs you.

If people see you as a person who is fair to everyone—especially when that means putting yourself at risk or costing you something personally—they'll think you'll be fair to them as well.

Optimize Your Autonomy

There are other things you can do that don't necessarily make it more likely you'll be effective in creating change, but that at least allow you to do what you believe is right with less fear of suffering unacceptable economic, social, or psychological consequences. Let's take a look at some of these strategies for "optimizing your autonomy."

Maximize Job Security and Job Mobility

If you've got job security, challenging those with more power can be a lot easier. However, unless you're in the quite rare position of having indefinite tenure—which tends to be the case only for academics, people in legal or consulting partnerships, or extremely strong unions— you're probably not objectively safe if you really rock the boat. Still, there are other ways to make yourself so valuable to your boss or organization that it would be very hard for them to let you go just because you challenged them or pushed hard for change. You could, for example, continually invest in particularly valuable knowledge bases or skill sets, things that would create a huge hole and disrupt business as usual should you be let go. This could be because you can't be easily replaced on the market or because getting someone else up to speed would take too long.

Your unique value doesn't have to reflect something that equates to a high salary or fancy title. You could be the only person who can get finicky machines running again quickly or who really understands the crazy bugs that plague a piece of critical software. This is not the same as being generally competent in your work—there are plenty of employees who are competent *and* still easily replaceable. What I'm suggesting here is that you'll worry less if you provide unique value that makes you hard to let go.

People with high demand or relatively rare abilities also tend to have good job mobility. They know that their skills are highly valued beyond their current organization so they can afford to be less paralyzed by the notion of offending insiders. Software engineers, scientific researchers, and other technical specialists, for instance, often get weekly calls from rival firms and headhunters. This likely contributes in part to the challenging, innovative culture of places like Silicon Valley—it's a lot easier to disagree with policies, practices, or specific individuals if you know you've got lots of alternatives and thus don't feel trapped into silence or submission.[11]

Lilly found herself in exactly this position when she worked for a man who periodically exploded in fits of anger. He'd received all sorts of warnings and coaching over the years, but senior management was never willing to take the final step of removing him. Lilly finally decided this was not acceptable to her after an incident where he questioned her competence and aggressively verbally attacked her. Whereas others felt powerless to do anything, Lilly knew she was considered a high-potential employee, and it was very clear to all involved that she was willing to leave for a healthier environment. Thus, when she went to senior management and explained the impact that her boss's behavior was having on her and her work—and that she would not stay if it wasn't finally addressed—they appeared to listen. When they in fact failed to remove her boss, she had no trouble finding an equally good job where she now has a much better boss.

In contrast, consider Jeremy, a sales assistant in a clothing department at a major New York retailer. One night, an executive, who had a reputation for being rude and verbally abusive, screamed at Jeremy when he had trouble figuring out a small detail on a data analysis task. Hurt and angry, Jeremy decided to quit. The next day, he stepped out for lunch, and then never returned. He didn't even call the office to let anyone know he wasn't coming back. He knew it wasn't the professional thing to do; in the moment, it just felt like the only way to defend his self-respect. But when Jeremy went looking for a new job, he continually hit a wall: HR personnel would call his old employer for a reference and be told how he had left. In retrospect, Jeremy still considered his move courageous, but also called his impulsiveness "stupid." He hadn't laid the groundwork to land on his feet before taking his principled stand, and he hadn't taken his stand in a way that allowed others to vouch for him as he sought a new job.

Avoid Financial Handcuffs

We've all heard about the "golden handcuffs" that companies use to make their highest-paid, most valuable employees feel unable to leave. In my experience studying why people don't speak up, I've indeed found that even very high-status, high-income employees sometimes remain silent and refuse to leave despite knowing that things are very wrong or unsatisfying. Why? Because even if they don't have specific "leave and lose it" financial arrangements, they still feel handcuffed by the belief that they couldn't get an equivalent job that meets their current needs. In short, they say they're trapped.

While there's no denying that adult life brings many responsibilities and obligations, it's also true that sometimes we ourselves have spun the webs that trap us. We all know people who get a raise every year and immediately increase their living expenses by an equal or greater amount. They've got more, but they're no freer from the wage dependency of their job than they were the year before. I've been in that situation plenty of times as I built my own career and family.

It takes real discipline to put yourself in a different position. When Franco Bernabè became CEO of a major Italian company, he purposefully rejected many of the perks that came with the role. He knew that doing so would make it easier to take risks because "if I had lost my job and gone back to something more subdued and less glamorous—well, it wouldn't have changed my life."[12] He not only knew he could quickly secure employment elsewhere, he felt less constrained by the trappings of his current position. "[T]aking risks didn't seem that frightening," he said, because he "didn't have anything to lose."

You don't have to be a wealthy executive for this principle to apply. It's true for people at any level who are willing and able to build themselves a safety net and an acceptable fallback position. This isn't just about keeping other job options open, but also about having enough money in the bank to support yourself and any dependents during an extended transition. It's about having agreed with loved ones that you're willing to make sacrifices should you choose to quit or be pushed out. These are the kinds of things ombudspeople say differentiate those who come forward about unacceptable behavior from those who don't.[13] And they're the kinds of things that make one more willing in general to be a courageous, rather than complicit, follower.[14]

Darren, for example, was a small-town high school science teacher who found himself at a breaking point a few years into his career. He was passionate about his work, spending hours researching how students learn, the psychology of student behavior, and how to make science fun for adolescents. His problems started when school administrators suggested, in not very subtle ways, that he should be more open to presenting "biblical," not just "scientific," views of biology. Darren demurred, arguing that a high school science class was not the place to teach nonscientific views of biology.

Then came his defining moment. A star athlete, who happened to be the daughter of the chairperson of the school board, submitted a paper that was about 90 percent cut-and-pasted from Wikipedia. Darren gave the student a zero for the assignment, which lowered her overall grade for the class. Soon enough, the superintendent and members of the school board strongly suggested he reconsider his decision. Darren stood his ground.

A few months later, his principal told Darren that he would be recommending that Darren's contract not be renewed, and that the school board would almost certainly support this decision. Rather than fight, Darren resigned at the end of the year. "I was free to act as I thought was correct and honest because I did not need the job or the income, explained Darren. "I was teaching because I wanted to teach." He and his wife, who worked in a higher-paying job, were able to live off her salary and allow him time at home with their kids while he contemplated his next step.

Know What's Most Important

Finally, it's worth noting that sometimes what gives you freedom to act isn't an actual level of economic attainment or security but rather the knowledge that there are more important things in your life than your job title, level of income, or other things you get from your current position. For example, if you're clear that time with family members is more important to you than how much money you have to spend on them, or that standing for certain causes is more important to you than "being in the room"—where those causes aren't really being addressed anyway—it can be easier to be more than a "yes man" who focuses on never upsetting powerful others. If you're clear that strong relationships are what matter most to you, you can build them *outside* of work so it doesn't feel as frightening exposing yourself to social losses at work. In short, knowing that the most important parts of your identity or security aren't completely tied to the approval of others at work can be very freeing.

Jeanette, for example, was informed that her division was being dissolved and that she could retain her employment only by moving to a new role in a specific city. In most ways, it was an ideal job for Jeanette—a promotion with a significantly higher salary and the perfect fit for her work skills and interests. The problem was that Jeanette was newly engaged and had already committed to moving to a different state with her fiancé. She asked to be allowed to telecommute, but was told "no" because it was not standard practice in the group. While the choice was difficult, Jeanette "ultimately put [her] personal life and happiness above [her] career aspirations and turned down the offer." For her, it came down to this: jobs come and go, but her first years together with her partner would only come once. It was the biggest decision she'd made to that point in her life, and she was proud that she'd "laid out [her] priority and set that as the line to meet." (Much to her surprise, the company changed its position when she wouldn't accept theirs. In less than twenty-four hours, the hiring manager's boss called and made Jeanette an even better offer. She's since been promoted twice—all while working remotely.)

Exemplar in Action: Catherine Gill

Catherine Gill, the former senior vice president of fundraising and HR at Root Capital, made it her mission to diversify the nonprofit's inner circle. The general sentiment among female employees was that it was harder to succeed at Root as a woman—it seemed that women were less likely to be promoted, that they had to advocate for themselves twice as hard to be considered, and were just not consulted in the same way as their male colleagues. Gill understood that the male executives' similar ages and backgrounds led to a natural fluidity between work and friendship, but she and other female employees at Root nonetheless felt excluded by it. "It's just a man's world" was a common sentiment.

In 2014, Gill and a few colleagues decided to take brave action, making the in-the-moment decision to issue a "call to action" to the male executives at an off-site meeting. As the most senior member of the ad hoc team, Gill was fully aware that the CEO might hold her responsible for what could feel like a revolution or, at minimum, a very public discussion of the array of cultural challenges for which he, as CEO and founder, would be deemed more responsible than others.

And she was right. The CEO was surprised and caught off-guard. But, thankfully, he started his reflections the next day with an honest and brave recognition of the organization's shortcomings. Although he admitted to being somewhat despondent the night before, he came to the next morning's meeting energized and committed to taking the appropriate steps to move forward.

And next steps did come. The team established five leadership principles that sought to bring about actual behavior change. Female employees in Central America now felt able to confront males about gender stereotyping and more explicitly sexual remarks and gestures. These principles, said one female employee, "made it OK to stand up and speak out." Another said employees were now buoyed in difficult moments by having "something to point to on the wall." Men, too, have played active roles in the changes.

Gill was successful because she was warm and competent. She chose her battles carefully, acted with skill during key moments, and followed up. But most remarkable was the way she prepared herself to succeed as a diplomat, not a revolutionary. She worked tirelessly to understand and support those who wanted change *and* to earn deep respect among those who represented the status quo (those who saw no problem with gender-related norms). She made herself the person who "understands the limits of the possible, how to push for change without getting kicked off the island." For as much as people credit her with speaking truth to power, they also respect her for saying "it's not a gender issue" when data did not support the narrative that pay, promotions, or other opportunities were affected by being a woman at Root. Also, her hard work and consistently high performance as a superb fundraiser earned her the trust and attention of those she was challenging. And she inspired her colleagues. Said one:

> Catherine could have easily sat in her position of power and ignored the pain of lower-ranking colleagues around gender, but she didn't. She stood up first, front and center, with a loud and clear message, and has set an example of bravery and tactfulness in truth-telling for all of us. . . . Catherine's example makes these conversations (about gender, but also about so many other things) possible, and even celebrated.

Remember

- Your odds that people will see your courageous act as well-intentioned and worth acting on are higher if you've spent time establishing your warmth and competence beforehand.

- While your intellectual intelligence may bolster the rationale for your actions, your emotional intelligence is likely the more important factor in how your courageous acts play out. Likewise, being seen as fair and able to see both sides is likely more important than being the smartest or most assertive person who is obviously on just one side.

- Because we can never fully control how others react to our courageous acts, it is difficult to eliminate all risks. It is therefore wise to take steps to mitigate the size or impact of those risks by doing things that maximize our internal job security and external job mobility.

- Taking steps to avoid feeling financially or emotionally handcuffed in our current situation allows us to take steps that feel consistent with our values and goals, even if those steps carry risk of upsetting those with power over our current economic situation.

CHAPTER 6

Choosing Your Battles

Allison, a senior manager of marketing and sales, was put off by comments from members of her team about an internal candidate for promotion they were discussing. "I'm surprised no one has mentioned what happened at the party last night, since I know many of you noticed it," said one of Allison's subordinates. "Felicia got up and did that wild group karaoke on stage. I hear she stayed out all night. I just don't think it's appropriate for a manager in our industry—let alone a mother—to behave like that." Another member agreed Felicia's behavior was pretty noticeable but pointed out that there weren't any clients in the room. "Still," said the first, "I just don't know if I can really trust her decision making if that's how she behaves." A few others nodded their heads.

After a few more minutes of discussion, the team leader was ready to end the meeting. But Allison, as the head of the group, was uncomfortable. She didn't like the tone of the conversation about Felicia's behavior, and, in particular, her status as a mother. But, before the meeting, she'd promised herself she'd let her team make the hiring decision. Should she say something?

———————

A llison is in a tough spot. She's always encouraged her team members to speak freely, but in this case, this freedom led to comments about Felica's status as a mother (and, implicitly, her gender) that seem to have influenced the conversation. Would you say something about this? Is it important enough to you, or would you let it go?

Allison's choice is like ones we all face in various forms throughout our work lives. If we take on every issue—no matter the substance or import or the time or place—we'll come to be seen as the critical naysayer whom people try to avoid rather than listen to, and thus we reduce our positive influence. But, conversely, if we always tell ourselves the issue isn't big enough or the time isn't right, we end up standing for nothing and are, said Aristotle, cowards. So how do we decide? What are some good guideposts for helping us discern when to act and when to hold off? That's what this chapter explores.

Is This *Really* Important Enough?

Work life is filled with things that irritate or anger us, frustrate or disappoint us, and fill us with passion about what our organization could be doing more of or doing better. Clearly, though, we can't tackle every one of these issues or we'll get a stress-related illness or get fired. The challenge is to get clarity on when to engage, and when to let go.

This clarity is tough to come by, and deeply personal. What's important enough to *you* to act on, even though there may be negative personal consequences, is likely to be different from what's important for someone else. So we're not looking for objective criteria by which to judge an issue's importance. What I have found, though, are some questions that competently courageous people seem to (implicitly) ask and answer before springing into action.

What Are *My* Key Values and Goals?

"Courage is not the absence of fear, but rather the judgment that something else is more important than fear," said Ambrose Redmoon.[1] Can you articulate what's more important to you than your fear of the economic or social consequences of speaking out or standing up at work? Are you clear about who you are, or want to become, and how you want to be remembered when you're gone? These are heady questions—but if you can't answer them, you'll lack a compass that guides your decisions about which opportunities to pursue and which to let go.

Eulogy Virtues

The admirable people I've studied are better at enacting what David Brooks has called "eulogy virtues"—virtues such as kindness and honesty that people will point to when we die—even at the possible expense of the "résumé virtues" that correlate most directly with getting jobs or promotions.[2] This is no easy feat. While most of us like to think that eulogy virtues are more important than résumé virtues, how many of us really live our lives that way?

Clarifying your key values and goals helps you prioritize what actions you should take. Your felt obligation or duty to act—the understanding that "This is what a person like me does!"—might come from an occupational code (e.g., the Hippocratic Oath in medicine) or from a philosophical or religious base. For example, a study on reporting unacceptable behavior to an ombudsperson found that common reasons for speaking up included variants of "It's my job" (*I'm responsible*; *I'm accountable*; *It's my duty*) and "It's a moral imperative" (*I'm required by my moral code, my religion*).[3] Professors Myron and Penina Glazer found similar motives in industry and government whistleblowers who were explicitly aware of the censure that they would likely suffer as a result of speaking out on issues of client or public safety; and their moral identity was sufficiently central and integral to both their professional identity and core concept of self that they felt compelled to proceed, despite the near certainty of negative outcomes.[4]

This was true for Bryant, one of the people who called attention to misleading accounting at one of the world's largest energy companies. Despite having two young children and knowing there would likely be severe damage to his reputation and employability, his strong sense of right and wrong compelled him to pursue the claim. For ten years, Bryant persevered amid legal battles and financial hardship. His goal throughout was to clear his name, not to seek or accept a large settlement. So when he eventually won a judgment, said the person who told me this story, he was content in knowing that he was right and had been validated.

Family upbringing or current family values can also play a key role in how we respond in defining moments. Byrne Murphy, the highly successful CEO of Kitebrook Partners and chairman and founder of Digiplex, found himself tested time and again as an American entrepreneur working to export the concepts of outlet shopping centers, private residence clubs, and data centers to countries across Europe. He faced extortion attempts, mafia interference, backstabbing by politicians, and all sorts of other social and cultural challenges. Opportunities, and in some cases apparent requirements, to cut corners to get ahead were a regular part of his world for years.

Refusing to compromise his values took a real toll on him and his loved ones. His health suffered from the sacrifices he made to bring his entrepreneurial visions to fruition while sticking to his moral code. When I asked Murphy why he was unwilling to play by the local rules that could have made things easier, he pointed to his childhood. "Growing up seated at the family's dining-room table," he explained, "we learned early on that ethics aren't compromised. Period." Murphy knows that there are different norms around the world, and that the US standard isn't the only one. But he also knows that it can be a slippery slope to use relativist reasoning to justify "doing as the Romans do when in Rome." As to whether his experience proves that his values paid off in the long run, or just means he got lucky, he told me, "Either way, I sleep well."

Make no mistake about it: living your eulogy virtues can involve real costs. Juan, the CEO of a company in Colombia, was informed that his COO had been sexually harassing a young female intern. At the time, the COO had been leading a major technology upgrade and site expansion at a key industrial facility for several years and was thus seen as perhaps the most important employee in the company. The company, said one employee, "had put in his hands most of its future growth." Still, when Juan found out about the harassment, he fired the COO in less than twenty-four hours.

As costly as the decision appeared, Juan thought about the calculus differently: "From a moral perspective, I could not afford to have someone in the organization, with all that power and accountability, behaving that way." But was it costless for Juan personally? Not at all. He had to move to the site, located in a rural area far from his home, and spend two months working tirelessly in the COO's place in order to ensure the successful implementation of the changes already under way.

Being True to Yourself

Clarity about key values and goals also helps a person know when they have to act because "This is who *I* am!" It's about an obligation to ourselves, not just to the requirements of a broader occupational or moral code—a realization that if we don't act to defend our core values, identity, or humanity, no one else can or will do it. It's the clarity that we have to act because it's the only way to feel authentic, to feel proud of ourselves rather than like a fraud in our own skin.

Sheldene Simola notes that the moral exemplars she studied tend to eschew calling themselves courageous despite the high level of personal risk they undertook. For them, the actions were merely a natural extension of *who they are*.[5] Joseph Badaracco likewise describes the critical importance of defining moments in how we shape our life's narrative. Referencing the philosopher Nietzsche, Badaracco urges us to consider whether we want to live distinguished, self-chosen lives or simply join "the herd" who live their lives as interchangeable commodities.[6]

Choosing our own way in these moments requires us to look not backward or outward, but to the future—asking ourselves how an issue at hand, and our response to it, fits the person we want to become, not necessarily the one we've been in the past or even currently are.[7]

Dr. Dara Richardson-Heron, former CEO of the YWCA, has talked about how important it was for her career to find, and truly own, her voice during key moments.[8] Richardson-Heron understands that she can't speak up about every issue, and advises women to therefore be strategic in standing up for what's truly most important to them. Thus, when a male employee commented on how her clothing style (very "buttoned up") made others uncomfortable—something she figured would never happen to a male counterpart—she spoke up. "From this point on, I want you to judge me on my performance, not my appearance," she said. He never crossed that line again.

For Richardson-Heron, this was a defining moment: "You have to be able to look yourself in the mirror and say, 'This aligns with my values. This aligns with my opinion of who I want to be, and my personal legacy.'" Fearing that speaking up will derail them, many people don't take a stand, she realizes. But if you don't, she counters, it's going to derail you personally because you won't be able to say to yourself, "This is who I am."

Putting It on the Line

Enacting your true "who I am" story sometimes requires multiple changes and sacrifices. Wendy studied mechanical engineering in college and began her career in an engineering construction company in the oil and gas industry. It didn't take long for her to realize that she didn't feel connected to or satisfied with this kind of work. She realized, she said, that she couldn't continue on the professional path she was on, that she "wanted to utilize her talents and skills to create a job that was a truthful expression of who I am." Despite significant pushback from family, friends, and coworkers, who wondered why she'd leave a good-paying position for the uncertainty of a loosely defined dream, she quit her job. She immersed herself in all sorts of creative, artistic, and design activities, which revitalized her passion for baking. Wendy then enrolled in a culinary institute and a program in small business creation. Finally, she was ready to open her bakery business, which she did as owner and head cake designer. Beyond the exciting (and stressful) challenges of building and managing a business, said Wendy, she'd created a job that "represents my essence."

To be clear, you may choose to act even if you don't think you'll succeed. Maybe you'll feel compelled to tell the truth, consequences be damned. As Vann Newkirk eloquently put it, it may simply be time to loudly proclaim your humanity.[9] Or maybe you consciously choose to do or say something knowing you're not going to succeed now, but hoping you'll at least draw sufficient attention to inspire others to further action. Those are all completely good reasons to take action, as long as you're choosing them, not doing so unreflectively.

Kenny, a restaurant supervisor, knew his non-negotiables and was willing to defend them. One of the long-time employees was a woman with cerebral palsy. When a new policy came out stating that guests who appeared to be drinking fountain beverages without having paid for them had to be confronted by their server, Kenny was told to fire this employee because her very limited language ability made that impossible. He refused, told his boss to check the Americans with Disabilities Act, and said he'd go both to corporate HR and the employee's parents if they went through with the firing. "That was three years ago," Kenny told me, "and she's still here."

Asked about his inspiration for this stand, Kenny pointed to his sister, who had far more severe special needs. "You don't mess with me on that," he said. *"That is who I am, how I was brought up, and what I believe in."*

As we've already discussed, none of the things discussed here becomes magically easier as you advance. Sure, the specific opportunities for courageous action can differ, but no matter how powerful or high up you are in an organization, the pressures to act in ways that cut against your most important values will still be there, and your responses will be even more closely scrutinized by people coming at you from every angle. If you've spent years compromising your values to get ahead and rationalizing why this was OK, you may have drifted even further from your initial values and ideals than those below you. Fortunately, some senior executives are clear about their core purpose and values and do stand up for them.

Howard Schultz is one of those leaders. Remember his story in chapter 3 where he refused to cut his employees' benefits during a downturn in the face of enormous pressure from investors. Why was Schultz so committed to his employees' health-care needs? In part, it was his own childhood experience. When Schultz was seven, his father broke his leg at work. With no sick pay, disability insurance, or other help, Schultz's family ended up so poor that getting enough to eat became a daily struggle. It was a defining moment for the young Schultz. Having experienced the debilitating effects of lack of health insurance or other employer-provided benefits, he decided that "if I was ever in the position to make a contribution to others in that way, I would."[10] Schultz says his greatest success has been building the kind of company his father never got to work for.

Bill George, the former CEO of medical device giant Medtronic and now professor of practice at Harvard Business School, also understands the difference between an internal compass and external demands as the basis for great leadership. Despite continuous pressure from Wall Street to meet or exceed the preset expectations of external analysts, he refused to manipulate earnings. For telling the truth about results (which were excellent anyway), George faced significant criticism. But he didn't change his behavior. "The test of leadership," he said later, "is ignoring those outside voices and learning to hear the one deep within. . . . The voices clamoring for your attention will be many. Your job is to find your own voice."[11]

Are My Emotions Informing or Controlling Me?

Keeping front and center who you are and what's most important to you provides the energy to act despite risk.[12] That motivational force is more likely to generate actions you're proud of, though, if you're in control of when and how you use this energy. If you're reacting impulsively to every values violation you encounter, you may end up taking stands for everything and achieving nothing because of the way you go about it. Or fooling yourself into thinking you're acting on behalf of others, when in fact it's mostly about yourself.[13]

If you're personally triggered about a minor issue, one way to minimize risk is to avoid acting when your emotions are highest. In my own case, for example, I've become clearer over time that every flash of anger, pain, or disgust I feel is not a sign that something truly important is at stake. A good part of the time, these emotions reflect personal hotspots, based in my own childhood experience and identity; they're not a sign of major problems or issues worth cashing in idiosyncrasy credits to pursue.

Knowing this about myself doesn't make those initial emotions any less strong. So I've learned to use specific tactics to help hold myself back in the moment. For example, at various points I've used the "delay" feature on my email to keep every message I write in my outbox for sixty minutes before sending. Even an hour can be enough time to sort out whether I've said the right things—or whether I should say anything at all. It gives me time to process what happened and how I'm feeling with someone else, testing whether what's "hot" for me has much less emotional valence for others. Second, the time to "get it out of my system" often cools the issue down for me too. Then I can decide more rationally what to do or say before it's too late to take it back.

As you're sorting out the importance of an issue, a good question to ask yourself is, "Do I need to dramatize the situation and demonize others to keep the energy high?" In his excellent book on anger, Dale Olen explains our initial negative reaction to a situation as stemming from a gap between our implicit rules for how things should be done and what we're actually witnessing. For example, you'll experience an immediate flash of anger if and when you've got an internalized rule that says, "All people—irrespective of status, wealth, level, etc.—should be treated with the same respect" and you see someone of higher status or power say something degrading to someone with less status or power. According to Olen, there's not much you can do to prevent that *initial* burst of anger when you experience a "should happen—did happen" gap like this.[14]

You can't avoid those flashes of anger—they're automatic. But you do have a choice. You can fuel the emotional fire by justifying it and sustaining and increasing your outrage. Or you can consciously short-circuit that negative thinking and take steps to douse the flames.

Stop for a minute and recall the last time you had an immediate emotional reaction to something someone said or did. Did you catastrophize, overgeneralize, or engage in black-and-white thinking? Or did you engage in the much, much harder process of looking for reasons why the person's comment or behavior may *not* have come from a place of bad intention or may *not* have been as bad or done as much damage as you initially felt it did?

If you need to keep dramatizing a situation or demonizing others to sustain your emotional reaction, and hence motivation to (re)act, it's probably a sign you're not in a good place to act without potential regret. This isn't to say we should never act when we're angry. Indeed, to the contrary, I think anger may be one of the most important forces for overcoming fear. But if you can only sustain your anger by distorting reality, you might be putting yourself and others at risk. Kenny, for example, was angry when he was told to fire his special needs employee, and he knew that standing up in this situation was central to how he saw himself. But he didn't have to claim his boss was a "*total jerk*" or "*always* does rotten stuff" or was "*eroding the entire notion of moral decency in America*" to know that defending his employee with cerebral palsy was the right thing for him to do.

What Are the Broader Gains and Losses?

When we're negatively emotionally charged, our brains narrow their focus to the present issue.[15] That can make it hard to think rationally about the larger picture, including what might be gained and lost long term as a result of anything we do now. To be clear, the suggestion "Think first!" isn't an invitation to *never* do anything. Rather, it's a reminder that challenging everything tends to lead to accomplishing nothing much, or even causing more net harm than any good you do create. If you care about the consequences, which I imagine you do, you want to be what Stanford professor Debra Meyerson calls a *tempered* radical, not just a radical.[16] That requires you to think through the relative risks and rewards of both what you do and don't do now, and how that will affect your ability to act effectively going forward.

Sometimes the better part of valor is to do nothing. This is not always an easy call because there might be some harm if you don't act and, if you did act, some good might result. Still, the choice of inaction is not necessarily a sign of cowardice. It may instead reflect what William Miller, a law professor at the University of Michigan, has called the "practical wisdom" of knowing when it's not the time, place, or issue for a stand.[17] Inaction might reflect the judgment that doing something will only make a problem worse, or the reasonable estimate that the bad that might come from your action could outweigh any benefits.

Those who exhibit competent courage seem to be particularly skillful at ascertaining what's only a battle and what's the overall war, and at avoiding spending capital on battles that, even if won, might actually undermine their broader mission.[18] For example, you might be tempted to dump a current customer to take an immediate stand for more respectful treatment or better terms, or to refuse to sell a product with a few warts even though it's entirely safe and functional. Those might be courageous acts in their own right, but they might also undermine your ability to achieve your longer-term objectives of having a different customer base or a more refined product because you'll have reduced the profits needed to pursue those objectives.

Remember Allison's choice at the start of this chapter: Should she let a comment made by someone on her team go or point out her concern that the female applicant's status as a mother was irrelevant and inappropriate to the decision about who to promote? Allison *did* politely confront her team, suggesting that they needed to be conscious of the biases they might be bringing to the discussion. She suggested that their concerns about Felicia's "fit" might be less about her abilities as a manager and more about their views of right and wrong behavior for females or mothers. As a female minority, Allison commonly heard people make comments involving someone's race, gender, or ethnicity in ways that suggested implicit bias. For example, she doubted that anyone in the meeting would have described dancing at the company event as inappropriate "for a father" had it been done by a male candidate.

Allison knew she had to choose her spots. If she spoke up too often, her team would start tuning her out and would hesitate to speak freely and provide honest feedback. They might also start to label her and like her less, common outcomes women face for speaking up about this kind of issue.[19] In this case, though, Allison was willing to broach a sensitive topic and risk alienating her direct reports because she felt that hiring and promotion decisions were the most important times to avoid the long-term, ill effects of implicit bias. After all, as she reasons, what difference will it ultimately make to the advancement of women and minorities to speak up about every bias-driven microaggression if advancement itself is not ultimately forthcoming based on merit?[20] To Allison, acting to make sure deserving women and minorities get promoted is a eulogy virtue worth practicing.

Is This the *Right Time*?

Competently courageous people pay attention to timing. They recognize that even the most reasonable comment or idea, presented in the most constructive way possible, may still fall flat or lead to trouble if delivered at the wrong time. Though some crisis situations or difficult conversations must be dealt with immediately, many issues can be addressed after you consider the best timing. It's usually worth asking yourself when in the day or week might be best for a certain conversation or when on an even longer timescale might be the optimal time to make your move.

Don't take my suggestion as equivalent to saying, "Wait until there's no risk, and it's totally easy." That could easily become a *permanent* rationalization for inaction. As Mary Gentile, creator of Giving Voice to Values and professor of practice at the University of Virginia's Darden School of Business, correctly notes, it may *never* feel like the right time to take on value conflicts or other tough issues. There will always be reasons to tell yourself it's not the right time. So if you have to admit to yourself that you've said it's not the right time a whole lot of times, it might be worth flipping things around and asking yourself if for some issues or things you really care about, it can never really be the wrong time either.[21]

If there's one thing my data has consistently shown, it's this: it never gets easy. No matter how much time passes, or how high you rise, you'll likely still have a boss, you'll still care to some degree about being socially ostracized, and you'll still be hesitant at times to challenge norms. So be careful about letting yourself off the hook with any version of the "When I get promoted, I'll do it" story.

Even in academia, where getting promoted as a professor means you have lifetime tenure, I've seen a pretty strong pattern: people can always find reasons to avoid risks. Assistant professors hold back, saying they'd like to speak up but worry that offending someone will be held against them when their tenure decision gets made. After promotion to associate professor with tenure—that is, promotion to a role with lifetime job security—the reasons for silence and compliance become fear of harming one's chance to be promoted to full professor and of being shunned by the peers you're going to be around for decades. Even for a full professor, there's always the risk of not earning an "endowed chair" (granted to only a portion of full professors) if you anger people, so many are still careful. Finally, should you decide that you'd like to take a leadership role within your department, college, or university, you don't want to have upset too many people or you might not get selected. These rationalizations are similar in consulting, law, and lots of other environments.

Returning to our discussion from chapter 5, sometimes "the wrong time" reflects that you don't yet have the credibility or data that would help you succeed if you acted now on a particular issue. That's the situation Mandy found herself in when she joined the production and product development department of an accessories and apparel company as a product manager. Soon after starting, she began experiencing problems with one of the company's manufacturing partners. Its employees were dishonest and manipulative, they communicated in a demeaning manner, and the organization was delivering subpar products. They'd swap cheaper, lower-grade materials for the ones specified in the contract, only to be found out when her company's customers returned defective products; and they refused to be transparent about their costs or suppliers. But this partner had been working with her company since its inception, serving as its sole supplier of key product lines for years. This made her company's management reluctant to change, lest customers notice the difference. Plus, a friendship between the key managers at the two companies seemed to lie behind her company's tolerance of unjustified price increases, poor quality, and product delays.

Recognizing all this, Mandy chose not to speak up immediately. Instead, she spent months researching alternatives, including working with other manufacturers to prove they could match or beat the current manufacturer's quality and price on the key lines. She carefully developed a proposal, detailing how they could make the transition without affecting any shipping schedules. Only then did she make her pitch directly to the VP of her department, risking her reputation with the managers she bypassed in doing so. Seeing her arguments as data-driven and her solution viable, Mandy's VP ended the relationship with the longtime partner.

Other times, you may be in the opposite situation—you've got credibility and data on your side, but you're still better off not rocking the boat right now because you've recently cashed in a lot of idiosyncrasy credits.[22] Perhaps you've just secured new resources for a project, or just gotten people above you to acknowledge something involving them was off track. In that case, pushing on the same or new issues too soon risks getting you branded as the broken record or someone not really on the team, and hence tuned out or worse. Leaders might start to avoid you because they don't have the energy for whatever you'll throw at them next, or because they see you as someone more interested in talking about new ideas than doing the harder work involved to implement ones already approved.[23]

Sometimes, it's not really about you at all. It's about something in the broader external or internal environment that makes it a better or worse time to pursue something. As Sue Ashford (a professor at the University of Michigan's Ross School of Business) and I reported in 2015, successful "issue sellers" were far more likely to have considered whether the larger context made the timing right than those who failed to garner support for their issue.[24] For example, the managing director of an Ecuadoran holding company's luxury division waited two years to pitch his idea about pursuing an untapped market in Peru. When he first got the idea in 2007, Peru was just coming out of a period of significant civil unrest and his division still had room for growth in its home market. So he held off on trying to sell his idea internally. But by 2009, "Peru had the best-performing stock market in the world," the director told us. He thus began to explore his idea more systematically, and eventually concluded that Peru was now ready for the investment. That, along with the home market now being more saturated, made it the right time. The director thus sought and got internal approvals and opened two new stores in 2010. Over the next three years, one of those stores alone accounted for 40 percent of the division's profits.

Macroeconomic or political conditions can be two obvious indicators of whether the time is right for pushing your idea. It's also important to consider if there is any current momentum related to your specific issue, or whether internal or external events suggest that now is your best chance to get positive attention and action. Billy, for example, had watched a couple of leaders above him bully and harass others for some time. While he wasn't proud of his silence, he suspected that no one at the top would be willing to listen as long as financial results stayed strong. When the organization faced a crisis, though, he sensed it was his chance to draw attention to what he considered a pattern of unethical and inappropriate behavior. At the risk of losing his job, he and some colleagues seized the moment and publicly confronted those who had abused their power.

Staying attuned to "attention cycles"—a term first used to describe the process by which issues emerge and stay active on the public policy scene—is a good way to assess the timing for making your move.[25] For most issues, the attention cycle unfolds as follows.[26] First is a "pre-problem" stage, where key decision makers are not even aware of or paying attention to the issue. Some triggering event then catapults the issue into broader awareness, and a period of energy and enthusiasm for doing something about the problem ensues. Eventually, of course, the "dramatic elements" needed to sustain energy pass, and attention shifts to something new. If sufficient changes have been made and institutionalized by then, real progress is likely. If not, the moment has been lost.

Successful actors, therefore, tend to choose their timing carefully. They try not to act before anyone is ready to take them seriously, but also not wait until the moment is lost.

According to historian Doris Kearns Goodwin, Abraham Lincoln's outstanding sense of timing played a major role in his becoming perhaps our country's greatest president. Observers noted that Lincoln neither wasted time fighting battles prematurely nor waited for external events to drag him into action. For example, Lincoln had drafted the Emancipation Proclamation well before he delivered it. "It is my conviction," he later explained, "that, had the proclamation been issued even six months earlier than it was, public sentiment would not have sustained it."[27] We know the value it ultimately had.

Exemplar in Action: Tachi Yamada

Tachi Yamada was born a sickly, three-pound baby in June 1945, in war-torn Tokyo. Kept swaddled in a closed dresser drawer, his parents were worried he wouldn't survive. But survive he did, making him a "child of destiny" in his father's eyes.

Throughout his remarkable career, which includes stints as chairman of R&D at GlaxoSmithKline (GSK) and president of the Global Health Program at the Gates Foundation, Yamada has used his talents and positions of influence to make the biggest positive impact he can on the world. As a physician and leader, that's meant never forgetting that he has accountability for others' health and lives and using that as a reminder that any risks to himself for acting courageously were trivial in comparison.

While the head of R&D at GSK, he challenged the company's board of directors to support the establishment of a lab for the treatment of diseases in the developing world—a decision that had little to no likelihood of paying off financially but was nonetheless the right thing to do.

At the time, many within GSK were upset about the company's lawsuit against Nelson Mandela and the South African government for allowing domestic companies to circumvent international patent law to manufacture cheap HIV drugs at a time when one in nine South Africans had HIV and most could not afford treatments from companies like GSK. "For those who are in it because they want to make a difference in people's lives, including me, this was devastating," said Yamada. "We're going to sue people who can't afford our medicines?"

So what did he do? He looked for a win-win—a way to address the disaffection many inside the company now felt while also showing those on the board that he understood the need to make sound financial decisions. He needed to get the board to more fully appreciate that for the researchers he represented, motivation and commitment to the company came from their efforts to save and extend lives. That, in short, was the essence of their scientists' answer to the question, "What does a person like me do?"

Yamada found his solution in a Spanish lab that was a candidate for closure because of the recent merger. Here was a facility that Yamada couldn't justify keeping open from an R&D perspective, but that served useful commercial purposes and that could do something to show people within GSK and the broader public that big pharma did care about medicines for the poor. He convinced the board to support his message to that facility: you can stay open if you focus on treating diseases of the developing world and if you seek more funding through alliances with those, such as the Gates Foundation, who are focused on this mission. "I succeeded in conveying my belief [to the board]," he said, "that this would show our people that we could do more and do better."

The move paid off. Far beyond saving the jobs of those in the Spanish lab, it showed those in R&D that the company did care. According to Yamada, there were many requests from employees around the world to transfer to Spain to work on those medicines. In the years since, the lab has done important work toward the development of new therapies for malaria. More importantly, says Yamada, the lab has served "as a symbol of the pharmaceutical industry's commitment to doing something for people in the developing world."

Yamada's success with the incident above depended in part on his keen understanding of how to connect issues and compel others *at the right time*. He knew the GSK board felt a sense of urgency because of external criticism and internal dissatisfaction. And he used his understanding of a burning platform to successfully push for change in other instances as well. For example, the merger between Glaxo and Smith Kline Beecham—both of which had thin pipelines at the time—presented an opportunity for him to restructure the entire R&D function around disease areas rather than the typical vertical silos (e.g., drug development, preclinical, regulatory affairs) despite strong initial resistance from people on both sides.

Well into his seventies, Yamada is still driven by his father's belief that he was a child of destiny. The man who once wondered why he went to medical school and why science even mattered remembers when it all became clear: "I realized when I saw patients that if I didn't know the science, I'd be putting people's lives at risk. It was a moment of great awakening and shame. I was slacking off, fooling around, thinking I was taking shortcuts when what was needed was deep concentration and focus." That clarity of purpose—what he was meant to do with his life—has propelled Yamada for more than four decades and continues to do so today. It's an always-present passion to alleviate human suffering that has led Yamada to repeatedly take calculated risks for worthy causes. To be courageous at the right times.

Remember

- If you want to have high impact, you can't act on every opportunity. Guide yourself by clarifying your key values and objectives and choosing opportunities most consistent with who you are and want to be.

- Be informed, not controlled, by your emotional reactions. Where possible, use strategies to step back from and lessen the intensity of your emotions before choosing consciously whether or not to act.

- Clarify whether an opportunity to act represents a battle or the war itself. When it's a battle, ask yourself before acting whether whatever you might gain is likely to help or detract from the broader objective(s) (the war).

- Pay attention to timing. Sometimes building more credibility or an evidence base is worth waiting for; other times, the momentum or opportunity for success created by internal or external events requires immediate action or you'll miss the peak of the attention cycle.

CHAPTER 7

Managing the Message

Melinda, a senior product manager at a major consumer goods company, was in a tough spot. Based on new science, the R&D team had recently reclassified a key ingredient in a major product to its lowest rating, which essentially meant "don't use." Following this, R&D had spent millions of dollars over the past six months searching—to no avail—for an alternative ingredient that would be safer but equally as effective. Melinda was pressed for time. Since the company's annual product safety report was due in a month and would be shared with the public, she had to recommend a plan to the senior team.

As Melinda saw it, she had three options: (1) recommend sticking with the existing product for now, even though it still contained an undesirable (but legal) chemical, (2) recommend switching to the new product, knowing that it was inferior but unquestionably safer, or (3) recommend removing the old product from the market until R&D came up with a safer alternative that also worked well.

None of these options was ideal. Sticking with the old product seemed to violate the company's commitment to safe products. Using the new but inferior product could anger customers and lead some to stop using the company's products. Taking the product completely off the market until a better alternative was found meant forgoing about 5 percent of total company revenue during that period.

After days of agonizing about the choice, Melinda and her team settled on recommending the second option—replacing the existing product with the safer but less effective alternative. She knew that it was risky: evidence from *prior moves to safer alternatives was mixed. In some cases, sales had stayed the same or gone up; in others, sales had definitely gone down initially. Given this history, Melinda had to figure out how to frame her recommendation to the CEO and top management team. How could she convince the array of people on that team that this was the best (or least bad) way to live the company's values and also minimize financial downside?*

M elinda has decided what to recommend, but she's still got a lot of choices about *how* to make her recommendation. Whom, if anyone, should she invite to join her in making the recommendation? What data will she use, and in what kind of presentation format? What kind of message framing will make her recommendation most compelling to the executives assembled? Should she lead with the cultural values that support her recommendations or focus on the short- and long-term financial implications? Should she describe her recommendation as an opportunity to be pursued or a threat to be dealt with? Can she help the executives see this as somehow advancing their agenda rather than just being a major problem?

Like Melinda, you have a host of options when you need to persuade others. You can consider inviting others to help you make your case, use the right data the right way, and utilize various framing strategies that my colleagues who study "issue selling," "voice," and "persuasion" have found to increase effectiveness.[1] Of course, if your goal is just to "get something off your chest," you might not care about effectiveness. But assuming that's not your only objective most of the time, it's worth thinking a bit more strategically about the who, where, and how of what we say in big moments.

Getting Ready

Let me start with an obvious statement that is often ignored in practice: the reason to take a problem or idea to one or more "target(s)" is precisely because you need someone else's help or approval. If you accept that, then a related assertion should also seem reasonable: understanding how *they* see the world is critical. I'm not saying that your values, beliefs, preferences, and priorities don't matter. What I am saying is that understanding your targets' values, beliefs, preferences, and priorities is equally, if not more, important. Melinda, for example, has her opinion on what the company should do, but if she can't convince senior managers to accept her recommendation, her perspective is irrelevant.

Time and again, though, we automatically frame situations the way *we* find most compelling. Then we get frustrated, angry, or hurt when things don't go as well as we hoped. "It was so compelling," we tell ourselves (and anyone who will listen). Yes, to *you* it sure was.

If you've ever given a presentation using solid data and reasoning but didn't think through how your new ideas could stoke fears or create new work and challenges for others, the aftermath probably looked something like this. People pushed back, shot down your ideas, and asked questions that you hadn't anticipated. You, in turn, grew defensive and tried to make the (good) questions sound unreasonable or stupid. Your ideas (whatever their merits) went nowhere.

To avoid these types of situations, try to see your targets' interests as "currencies" with which you can bargain.[2]

Consider Getting Others to Help

Sadly, sometimes other people just won't take you as seriously as they will someone else, even if you say the same thing in the same way. This can be particularly true when you're standing up for yourself or for fellow members of a group with which you identify.[3]

For example, in his doctoral dissertation at the University of Washington, Benjamin Drury found that when targets of prejudice (women and Black people, in his studies) confronted the perpetrator (men or White people) they were taken less seriously than when other men or White people did the confronting.[4] Whether that's because it's easier to say the offended person or group is "just overreacting" or "too

personally connected and emotional," the fact seems to be that issues often get more traction when those who can't be labeled as over-
identifying also get involved. Thus, no matter how important an issue
is to you personally, it's worth considering whether a broader coalition
of people who can't be easily labeled and dismissed would also be willing to act with—or even for—you.

Getting others to act along with you can be especially helpful when
the potential consequences are the largest. For example, people who
report unethical or illegal behavior note that it's easier to act when
it's clear that multiple people see the situation the same way and will
stand with them. This isn't just about the relative safety of knowing
your organization probably can't or won't fire you all (something you
might be very afraid of if acting alone)—the increased confidence in
one's position and motivation to act also comes from knowing that
others share your view.[5] This "social proof" also increases the likelihood that something actually gets done.[6]

Even if others are unwilling to join you publicly, your attempts
to involve them can still be beneficial. You'll know more about how
broadly shared your concern is, what underlies others' fear or futility
concerns, what data they have that is relevant to the issue, and what
they know about the best ways to approach your target. This can be
particularly important when you're newer to an organization or know
less about the people you want to influence. As professor Mary Gentile
has noted, others can fill you in on what's led to change in the past
and what's led to highly negative reactions.[7] For example, someone
else may know if you should appeal to your target using emotional
stories or, instead, data and analyses.

While people may agree with you in private, don't forget that they
may act differently under pressure. Cheryl was put off by the lack of
raises at her company, and her colleagues told her they were upset as
well. But when Cheryl spoke up in an all-employee meeting, and the
president asked if everyone else felt that way, no one said a word. The
president then said times were tough and that he'd look into it. Nothing changed, except that Cheryl got a poor performance review that
year. Though Cheryl's coworkers supported her in private, she hadn't

secured a commitment to shared action in any meaningful way. She hadn't asked them to commit to specific speaking parts or to other forms of public support, or to sign a letter she'd share to document their position. So when her assumption proved wrong, she alone suffered the consequences. Disappointed in both management and her colleagues, Cheryl left the company.

Choose the Best Context

Generally, people don't like to feel ambushed or ganged up on. So if you have a chance to speak to someone in private—at least for the first time—you're likely to get a better reception. Jake, for example, told me that diving right into a public discussion with his narcissistic and strong-willed chairman only led to crazed reactions that derailed meetings. But if a single employee laid out the truth, with sufficient facts and tact, in private, the chairman reacted more calmly. He was able to save face by knowing the points of disagreement or new proposals before things were discussed in the open.

Kelly similarly chose her place and time to good effect. As part of a team that included her CFO and operations leaders, Kelly was in a negotiation to sell the company. At one point in the conversation, which required her particular expertise, Kelly took the lead and politely held firm when the potential buyers again stated an untenable position. In the middle of a sentence, the CFO tapped Kelly's legs several times to get her to stop talking, which everyone could see, and then took over the conversation.

Kelly was stunned. She sat silently, feeling her body heat rise. Her instinct was to begin speaking again, or at least use instant messaging to tell the CFO how angry she was. But she held herself back and let him finish the conversation with the folks across the table.

The next morning, Kelly went to the CFO's office. She told him she considered him a friend, and that she held him in high esteem. But what had happened the day before made her feel unappreciated. It also sent the wrong message to the potential acquirer because it made her look angry when she was just doing her part in the negotiation.

"If you believe I was sounding aggressive," she told him, "please find other ways to tell me because I would welcome that feedback." No longer caught up in the stress of the negotiation, the CFO readily admitted he had done wrong, apologized to Kelly, and thanked her for the honest feedback.

There are, of course, times when raising an issue in front of others makes sense. For example, some decisions are discussed only once, in public, and if you don't use that opportunity to say something there won't be another chance. Other times you might consciously choose to use a public venue to try to create a commitment to action that can't be easily rescinded without embarrassment for the target.

Bring Data and Solutions

Most of the time, the problems we want to alert others to are not actual emergencies, and those with the power to fix them won't consider them as urgent as we do anyway. So you'll need to convince them. According to my research, presenting data and offering solutions can make a meaningful difference.[8]

To give an illustration: A senior manager in a *Fortune* 50 company believed that there was strong potential in a currently untapped market segment. For years, though, the division's president had disagreed and prevented the organization from pursuing this opportunity. Knowing he would continue to lose a battle based on opinion, especially since others on the leadership team were unwilling to challenge the president, the senior manager decided he would compile an extensive new set of analyses to back up his recommendation. With these in hand, he was finally able to convince the president to allow a small pilot. When the pilot yielded overwhelming empirical support for the idea, the president finally acquiesced. The market segment became a global priority and produced some of the highest profit margins in the company. The senior manager? He was one of the youngest in the company's history to be promoted to the next level.

Bringing data and solutions can be particularly beneficial when you're addressing the most serious kinds of wrongdoing, like those involving illegal, unethical, or highly inappropriate behavior. They can help others really understand why it's important to stop or change something, or simply make them aware that ignoring or retaliating against you is likely to get them in (more) trouble.[9]

Additionally, people often put their head in the sand because they're afraid and don't see a way out, so offering them solutions can make a real difference.

Choose the Data

Don't forget that the data and solutions that matter most are those that your target, not you, finds compelling. Remember, too, that your data and solutions are not *the only* data and solutions out there. You might have data that people in your unit are dissatisfied with something. Senior leaders, though, may have other data that indicates there's an even larger problem elsewhere in the organization that needs their attention or resources right now.

Otis, a team leader in a small pharma company, showed a keen understanding of how to select and use data skillfully. He knew that his only chance to successfully challenge his company's chief medical officer about the optimal development path for a product was to present a proposal aligned with the organization's larger objectives. Otis also knew that his CMO would readily dismiss his team's point of view as just "your expertise versus mine," so he included multiple forms of scientific support such as the clinical precedence for their proposal and the results from simulated models. Faced with the kind of evidence the CMO himself frequently cited as compelling, the CMO had little choice but to accept Otis's proposal.

While it's important to use the kind of data that will be compelling to the specific target(s) of your action, it's also worth paying attention to the kinds of data that carry the most weight in your organization overall. In some places, "not invented here" logic prevails: if you can't point to internal data, or solutions that come from within, you're wasting your breath. You'll present a beautiful example of how your idea works somewhere else, and the response will be, "That's fine, but that's not us" or "That's not how we do things." Perversely, your attempt to make the place better at your own risk—something that seems like true loyalty to me—may only end up having people question whether you understand the organization or are a loyal member of it.

On the other hand, in "the best ideas come from somewhere else" organizations, you'd better find something related from elsewhere to share, even if the idea really originated in your head or at one of your facilities. At a different pharma company I studied, for example, scientists told me, "We hire the best people in the world, but then it seems like we're all considered inferior to scientists elsewhere within a couple of years." As a result, when researchers there wanted to garner support from higher-ups to continue exploring potential breakthroughs in their own labs, they presented related evidence or theories from competitor firms and academics because that's what it took to compel senior R&D leaders to take them seriously.

Finally, don't forget that good data or viable solutions are not themselves a compelling story or case. As leadership professors Noel Tichy and Warren Bennis have articulated, data and potential solutions usually become compelling only when you connect them to an existing narrative or a new story line you also share.[10] If you doubt this, think about politics for a second. Whatever your leaning, it's likely that you routinely hear data and ideas that don't resonate with your overall point of view and that, as a result, you downplay or dismiss altogether. What resonates are the data and proposed paths forward that fit the overall story line you're already committed to and are probably overconfident about. The trick, in the language of social science, is to help people overcome their strong "confirmation bias" by presenting disconfirming evidence in a way that doesn't get ignored or rejected out of hand.[11] That takes some clever framing, for sure.

Making the Strongest Case

Successful framing involves persuading others that there is common ground between what you're doing or saying and how they see the world, what they value, and what they want or expect to happen. As Jay Conger, a leadership professor at Claremont McKenna College, explains in *The Necessary Art of Persuasion*, it's about helping others see that there are advantages *to them* for accepting what you're saying.[12] Here are some specific ways to approach this task.

Advocate for Growth, Not Destruction

In most cases, the reason you're proposing a change—a growth strategy, a new direction, a different behavior—is because something currently happening isn't ideal. You think someone's behavior could be better, resources could be more profitably deployed, or a process could be more efficient. No matter how you say it, there's an implicit criticism of the status quo. The key, therefore, is to say things that don't make others think that you're criticizing their prior or current choices or behaviors. One way to do this is to frame what you're proposing as "taking the next step." That's the language of growth and improvement, rather than of rejection or destruction.

Mary Gentile provides related advice: help others see prior decisions as having already paid off, as having already produced something useful.[13] If you can do that, even if the benefit was largely just the valuable learning that has occurred, you may make it easier for people to accept your proposed next steps without feeling (unconsciously, perhaps) that they need to admit and own prior mistakes. Remember, your goal is to get support for moving forward, not to get people to admit they were wrong or stupid or be willing to "abandon" what they built or believe in.

Show Intent to Win *Together*

To state something else that sounds obvious, but often gets ignored in practice: people will respond much better if accepting your point of view or suggestion doesn't also imply they're wrong, a loser, or out in the cold.

Bill, a technology project manager at IBM, used his influence to make major improvements to a client relationship that his predecessors had failed to accomplish. When Bill inherited the program, there was already a long history of budget and scheduling disagreements and widespread dissatisfaction about the way people were performing and interacting. He gathered all parties and spoke clearly about how they needed to operate moving forward to get results. Together they established new targets, rules of accountability, and consequences for both parties of not meeting these new commitments. It worked, said Bill, because he approached the situation as a true collaboration, setting up collective goals that meant the only two options were for both his organization and the client to win, or for both to lose.

One way to prevent others from feeling defensive is to adopt an "and stance," a method described by Douglas Stone and colleagues in their excellent book, *Difficult Conversations*.[14] First, acknowledge how the other person sees a situation, and then help them see how you think things could move forward. I and my colleagues David Webster and Bobby Parmar call this "empathize, then solve." Until someone feels you really care about how they're feeling, and that they can therefore be vulnerable enough to work together with you on a path forward, there is little real chance of moving forward in a way both parties feel good about.

Raul demonstrated this type of empathizing when he had to give feedback to his subordinate Pete. He needed to tell Pete that several higher-ups believed that he wasn't engaged and didn't really care. Worried that Pete would feel shamed or angered by this news and thus leave, Raul "approached it from a place of collaboration," telling Pete that he "had received similar feedback early in my career and it was some of the best feedback I'd ever received as 'impressions are everything.'" Rather than becoming defensive or tuning out, Pete embraced the feedback and subsequently improved significantly.

In contrast, you'll undermine yourself if you use "but" statements. "I appreciate what you do, but . . . ." When people hear these kinds of statements, they automatically view everything you said before "but" to be irrelevant. If Melinda, in making her recommendation about the dilemma described at the start of this chapter, tells the senior team that "profits are important, *but* customer safety is clearly paramount here," folks like the CFO and CMO may well walk away remembering, "Melinda doesn't care about profitability." She's more likely to convince them, and keep her reputation in good standing, if she uses "and stance" framing such as, "It makes me proud to be at a company where we recognize that profits are necessary and important *and* that customer safety is paramount in certain situations."

Connect to *Their* Priorities

Imagine you've got a few really good people on your team who you're worried about losing unless you can give them something new and exciting to work on. The problem is that your area isn't growing—and isn't even seen as particularly aligned with the organization's current priorities. What do you do?

You find areas of the organization that senior management *is* most excited about right now. For example, you might suggest your talented people be given special projects in hot areas. Your bosses might not have time or energy to care about your subordinates' development, but they do care about getting help with their top priorities.

When Tachi Yamada managed to save a GlaxoSmithKline research lab in Spain, he couldn't justify it on traditional research and financial bases, so he proposed converting it into a lab that would focus on the treatment of diseases in the developing world. This was exactly the kind of tangible proof that big pharma cared about more than making wealthy shareholders richer that senior GSK leaders needed to counteract the highly negative reaction they'd generated by suing Nelson Mandela and the South African government for producing cheaper versions of copyright-protected HIV drugs. In short, it connected something Yamada found compelling with something that those above him were focused on accomplishing at the time.

Sometimes we don't speak up because we're worried that our issue won't be seen as important enough. In that case, it can be useful to "bundle" your issue with other related instances or programs that collectively show that this is a bigger deal.[15] If, for example, you're worried about losing some women on your team, and your organization is trying to rectify longstanding problems retaining and promoting talented women, you'd be smart to connect your concern to the broader problem.

Consider *Opportunity* versus *Threat* Framing

Should you frame your problem as an opportunity or a threat? Sometimes it's obvious. If you're laying people off, no one wants to hear that the cuts are an opportunity for the company to be more profitable. You're better off pointing to legitimate competitive or macroeconomic threats, framing the decision as something unfortunate that has to be done to avoid putting many more jobs at stake.

Many times, though, your approach should depend less on the issue than the person you're trying to persuade. Some people are promotion-oriented, meaning they're inclined to take risks and do something new if they see sufficient upside. Others are prevention-oriented, and thus more likely to change when they become aware of what could go wrong or be lost.[16] You can raise your chance of success simply by knowing whether your target tends to respond better to opportunities or threats and aligning how you frame your issue or idea.

Remember that what you're ultimately trying to do is *motivate* someone, to create enough attention and interest that someone feels compelled to do something. Often, that someone is very busy, so hoping they'll act just because they care enough about you is wishful thinking. So make sure the opportunity or threat you link to your issue is one your target simply feels he can't let pass.

Ted, for example, watched one of his coworkers at a children's camp be disrespectful toward the kids they supervised. The coworker was mean to and neglectful of the kids and talked negatively about them behind their back. The coworker was also a jerk to Ted, at one point threatening violence because of Ted's sexual identity. Because of all of this, Ted quit and wrote a detailed letter to the director explaining why. Still hurting, Ted focused almost exclusively on how he'd been treated. Unfortunately, the camp director wasn't sufficiently motivated to do anything on behalf of a now-former employee, so no follow-up occurred with the coworker. Had Ted focused on the threat this person posed *to the kids* and, hence, the legal risks of inaction, he may have jolted the director into action.

Choose *Instrumental* or *Cultural* Framing

Sometimes, you may think something should be started or stopped because it has business implications *and* because it's the right or wrong thing according to some important principle(s). The question is which framing is likely to get you further with those you must influence.

Though far from a universal rule, "instrumental" framing often trumps "cultural" framing in its effectiveness, though cultural framing can also be incredibly powerful (especially in highly purpose-driven organizations).[17] For example, Karla, who worked at a construction company, was concerned that employees were working too long in the heat without breaks. Although the company's practice was unethical and inconsistent with its stance on employee safety, Karla avoided mentioning this. She thought management would think she was calling them callous and negligent (and maybe even hypocritical). Karla therefore avoided cultural framing altogether, instead using instrumental framing to describe the business costs and benefits of the breaks she was recommending. She shared that workers were becoming so exhausted from the heat that they were purposefully slowing down to cope and were making more mistakes. The company would have *better* business outcomes, she argued, if they would add a few more breaks during the hottest days. This made it very easy for her supervisors to agree to her proposal.

A useful rule of thumb might be to lead with instrumental reasons, following with cultural reasons as additional rationale where doing so won't come off as an attack on people's ethics. Ethan, for instance, wanted his company to be more evidence-based in its work for clients. But he framed his argument by saying the current approach was "unethical," which triggered defensiveness in his boss and led to no change. Had he started instrumentally by suggesting that a more scientific approach would attract new clients and help retain existing ones, he might have defused this response and then have been able to add that the proposed changes were a perfect fit with the company's culture of "going the extra mile for clients."

Exemplar in Action: Mel Exon

Yeo Valley—a family-owned organic dairy brand in the UK—was an unlikely candidate for a hip, breakthrough advertising campaign early in the social media era, but Mel Exon thought differently when she led the account as an executive at Bartle Bogle Hegarty (BBH). Since the brand faced stiff competition from the global food giants who were increasingly touting their own "100% natural" product lines, as well as the public perception that organic foods were over-priced and elitist, Exon was convinced that a forward-thinking campaign was needed. Yeo Valley's marketing director agreed. So, rather than play it safe, as many in the industry would have, Exon and her team decided to go for broke.

The segment they produced was highly unusual: a music video set on the Yeo Valley farm, in which farmers *rapped* about their pride in their products, sustainable farming, and the land. Upping the ante, they invested almost the entire media budget on a single TV ad that ran for two minutes during the first episode of that season's *X Factor* in the United Kingdom.

If the huge TV audience didn't resonate with the commercial and no one visited the online platforms they built, BBH likely would have been fired by Yeo Valley, creating significant blowback for Exon's team. (Yeo Valley's internal marketing lead may also have lost her job.) And BBH's reputation would surely have taken a hit in the industry. In the relatively insular marketing community, everyone knows the agency behind a campaign, and the trade press is quick to note failures. As BBH colleague Rosie Arnold recollects, Exon could easily have been named "Turkey of the Week" in one UK trade magazine.

The agency's executive creative director (ECD) wanted Exon to "unsell" the project. "He absolutely loathed it," is how she and Arnold remember it. The ECD and others (including the agency's country director) thought the rap was cheesy and corny, and they were deeply concerned about moving the project forward. This wasn't primarily about getting fired (they doubted that would happen), it was about professional identity. Explained Arnold, "You spend your career being judged by your latest work. Usually you feel buoyed up despite that because insiders understand that." With so many skeptics inside BBH, the identity risk felt all the more salient. Amidst all the fear they already felt in the months leading up to the launch, it was even harder knowing that the top creative leaders—whom they considered mentors—didn't respect this campaign. There were many sleepless nights for Exon, her emotional state vacillating between excitement and fear. "It was only advertising," Exon knew, but BBH's, Yeo Valley's, and her own reputation were nonetheless on the line.

Exon and her team pushed forward. How did she get the powers that be to accept this (before it ultimately became a smashing success)? She "never came across as doing anything for herself," said colleague Saneel Radia. She'd shown that she was "in it for BBH for a long time," so that "her meaning and intentions [we]re hard to doubt." Exon recalled a comment from BBH's founder and CEO, Nigel Bogle, that exemplifies how her behavior is perceived. "You understand the fundamental DNA of BBH," he told her, "and try to build on and improve it rather than change it."

Exon also skillfully framed her position in ways that made them attractive, or at least palatable, to those whose support she needed. Exon is, said Radia, a master at speaking "in your terms," no matter what her target's particular area of expertise or starting point may be. Her perspective taking helped her shape messages so colleagues could hear them as being on the same side even when she was pushing them beyond their comfort zone. She helped insiders see that this type of innovation was highly consistent with BBH's culture, and that whatever learning the campaign produced would benefit them all. During the Yeo Valley experience, and in other instances throughout her career, Exon's success, to sum it up, has been aided by being a master of managing the message.

Remember

- Beyond the *what* of your message, *who* delivers it and *where* it gets delivered can make a big difference in the reception. Consider inviting others to help and think through the best place and time to make your case.

- Offering data and solutions is usually superior to just pointing out problems or ideas with no evidence. Remember that the best data and solutions are those that the target(s), not you, finds most compelling. Also remember that data alone is seldom compelling; it's the accompanying story line that compels.

- The same message can be framed in ways that are less likely to offend and more likely to resonate with the target(s). People are more likely to accept your message when they believe you want to build on their prior efforts, include them in the future, and help them achieve their current priorities.

- Some people are more inspired by opportunities; others are more reactive to threats. Some people are driven to protect and promote personal or organizational values; others are more responsive to instrumental objectives in work settings. Studying prior responses of your target(s) helps you frame your messages in ways most likely to compel action.

CHAPTER 8

Channeling Emotions

After working with Steve for two months, Reyna, a project engineer at a consumer products company, was frustrated with his working style. Unlike Reyna and others on the team, who preferred to manage their workloads and stress levels by being ahead of the curve, Steve operated on more of a just-in-time basis. Steve would agree on a schedule for his responsibilities, and he generally managed to get things done at the last minute. However, this often didn't include time for others on the team to carefully look over what he'd done and suggest or make changes.

Though she wasn't direct about her feelings, beliefs, or the basis for her dissatisfaction, Reyna had tried talking with Steve about his working style and how it wasn't comfortable for her or others on the team.

Because Steve had a strong desire to keep everyone happy, he tended to avoid difficult conversations and seek to end them by quickly becoming very apologetic and promising to try to do better.

But nothing really changed.

In their last conversation, after a particularly stressful race to a deadline, Reyna spoke to Steve in an increasingly angry tone, telling Steve she was tired of his "screwing things up with your procrastination" and "hiding your lack of professionalism and commitment to this team behind some nonsense about 'your style.'" Steve finally became visibly angry in response, nearly screaming at Reyna, "You're so frickin' rigid. It's gotta be your way or the highway. I'm sick and tired of your dictatorial attitude. The only problem with this team is you." They both glared at each other and then walked away.

How could Reyna have handled this situation better? What would *you* be inclined to do if you found yourself in Reyna's shoes—feeling frustrated about a colleague's ongoing behavior and with just subtle hints or nudges producing no change? Would you be willing and able to say something earlier, so you didn't get to the point Reyna did, where her anger got the best of her? Would you be able to speak in ways that created an openness in Steve to possible change rather than leading to his own anger and defensiveness?

What about Steve? If you were in his shoes—caught off-guard by a colleague's harsh verbal attack—how would *you* be likely to react? Would you be able to stay calm rather than attacking her back? Do you have the right strategies and skills to turn this into a productive dialogue rather than a shouting match?

Most of us, if we're honest, struggle mightily to handle these kinds of situations. We're not sure what to say or how to say it, and we're scared of all the ways it could go wrong. Whether our tendency under stress is to fight (to angrily confront others), to freeze (to become so paralyzed we can't say anything in the moment), or to flee (to avoid difficult conversations like this altogether), we often undermine ourselves when dealing with intense, emotion-laden situations.

Managing your own emotions doesn't guarantee that others will react well but, as with the other competencies we've covered, it increases your odds of getting your message across in a way that keeps you safe and produces something positive for others. Let's take a look at some strategies for doing this.

Managing Emotions

Emotions play a huge role in how courageous acts turn out. In my own study, actors' management of emotions—their own emotions and those of their target(s)—strongly differentiated the successful and unsuccessful examples.

When you're cool and collected, you can carefully consider your target's preferred way of seeing the world and how to frame your issue most effectively. Likewise, with enough time and a calm state of mind, you can think about what allies might help you when you raise your issue, and about the right time and right place to do so. But we all know that controlling or concealing our fear and anger, and managing the emotions of others, can be difficult and complicated.

Fear can stymie our best-laid plans for acting. While it's obvious that freezing or freaking out in a physical emergency can lead to disaster, I've heard countless stories about fear derailing people's ability to act, or act skillfully, during all kinds of situations not involving physical risk. In many settings, fear is the dominant reason people don't speak up at all, or the reason they retreat the second they sense a negative reaction from those they're speaking with.

And then there's anger. Anger can be a really positive motivational force, an emotion "enlisted to do battle against fear" that often holds us back during opportunities for courage.[1] If fear inclines us to freeze or flee, anger often triggers a fight response. At work, this anger and inclination to "fight back" can come from seeing others we care about mistreated or harmed or from seeing the organization itself, or its key values, undermined by harmful behavior.[2] This strong desire to right a wrong that anger evokes in the face of unethical, inappropriate, and hurtful behavior is why psychologist Jon Haidt has called anger the "most underappreciated emotion."[3]

The problem is that anger can cloud our ability to think clearly and to behave effectively. Research has shown that angry individuals feel more optimistic and in control than they actually are, which can lead them to take risks that they wouldn't otherwise.[4] When we're angry, we tend to speak more loudly, more aggressively, and in more black-and-white terms, all of which elicit defensiveness in others. Look at Reyna and Steve's interaction; her anger led to his anger, and she ended up further from a solution than she was before she spoke. It can be a vicious cycle.

Manage *Your Own* Emotions . . . before the Act

"Anger and nervousness," a manager told me, "can contaminate a discussion before it starts." The manager had an employee with a reasonable request—to buy equity in the company. But since the employee came in so hot, it derailed the conversation and the request—which otherwise would likely have been approved—went nowhere.

Contrast that with this episode. Rita became irate when she heard about a new policy that would significantly reduce her and her coworkers' take-home pay. Her initial instinct was to march right into the district manager's office to demand a reversal of the decision. But she caught herself and talked with coworkers to calm herself down. With a clearer head, she realized that the district manager wasn't the one who had made the decision anyway. She carefully crafted a letter, detailing her concerns without negative words or emotions, and sent it on to HQ for consideration. As professors Robin Ely, Deborah Meyerson, and Martin Davidson would describe it, Rita learned to view her anger as a "signal, not as a springboard for action."[5] We can all learn from this. Over time, we can adopt strategies to temper our reactions and avoid undermining ourselves.

Though preparing ourselves emotionally for a tough situation warrants a book of its own, let me share here one idea I find highly compelling: if you want to learn to control, rather than be controlled by, your emotions, you need to recognize and own the distinction between your immediate, instinctive reaction and what you do next. Then you need to accept that what comes next is up to *you*, not the person you think is causing your reaction.

Your instinctive reactions—those immediate flashes of fear or anger—are pretty much hardwired and automatic based on what NYU neuroscientist Joseph Ledoux calls our brain's "defense circuitry."[6] If you stay on autopilot, you'll likely fuel the initial emotional heat. Unfortunately, many of us do just that, engaging in thinking patterns that throw logs on the fire, not recognizing that *we* (not the initial trigger) are now the cause of our pain and inability to respond optimally. However, you *can* take steps to defuel the fire that's been ignited in your body by working to consciously interpret what's going on in a way that calms you down.

Here's an illustration. Imagine you've spent significant time and energy preparing a proposal to your boss. When you get a chance to share your idea, he simply says, "Thanks, but I don't think this is the right time for this," and then moves to the next topic with no further discussion. Immediately, you feel the signs of anger: Your muscles tighten, your face gets red, your heart races, and you sit there and stew for the rest of the meeting.

You go back to your office and immediately schedule a one-on-one to revisit the issue that afternoon. At this point, you've got a choice. You can do something to reduce the anger you're feeling, and thus increase the chance you'll approach your boss in a better frame of mind later, or you can keep stoking that anger and end up approaching him just as angry as you were when he dismissed your idea earlier. Too often, we take the wrong path here. We mindlessly add fuel to our initial reaction, sustaining our anger with thoughts like, "He *always* does this," "We're *totally screwed* because of him," "He's such a *total jerk*," or "He'll *kill me* if I keep pushing." By using these kinds of cognitive distortions (e.g., overgeneralization, catastrophizing, black-and-white thinking), we stay angry (and perhaps now become afraid too) and thus minimize our chance of taking the conversation forward in a positive way.[7]

If, on the other hand, we learn to catch ourselves fueling the fire, we can also choose to tell ourselves an alternative story that calms us down and allows us to proceed in a less emotion-driven way.[8] This, in essence, is the goal of cognitive behavior therapy. For example, instead of accepting those negative thoughts listed above, you could instead tell yourself, "This is his natural reaction, but he becomes more open once you make it clear you're not piling more work on him," "This would be unfortunate if he's not ready for this, but we've got lots of other good things going," or "He'll be upset with me for a while if I keep pushing, but he'll still respect me as long as I stay calm."

The point of choosing these latter alternatives isn't just that they're likely to be more accurate (because most of the time we're not actually in the realm of "always," "total jerk," "kill me," or "totally screwed"); it's that you're much more likely to calm down if you can see the situation this way, and thus much more likely to continue the interaction with your boss in a way that gives you some chance of success. You'll be less likely to say things that make it sound like you're attacking or insulting your boss.

If you think I'm wrong about the basic contention that *you*, not the person you're reacting to, are the source of your ongoing emotional state, ask yourself this question: "Why am I sometimes in situations where I'm scared or irate, but other people experiencing the same situation seem to be just fine?" They all heard the boss make that insulting comment or announce that seemingly unfair or ill-advised decision, but they're responding calmly—while you're freaking out. If *the boss* is causing your reaction, how come everyone experiencing his behavior isn't feeling exactly the same? Clearly, there's something about how each of us processes external stimuli (e.g., a boss's behavior) in our head that differentiates us. We have some control over, and total responsibility, for that. If we can't accept that, we'll likely spend our whole lives blaming others for our inability to successfully navigate emotion-laden situations.[9]

Manage *Your Own* Emotions . . . during the Act

OK, you've got yourself into the right emotional state. It's a good start, but clearly not enough. If you panic or blow a gasket as soon as the interaction gets rolling, you might only make it worse for the very people you're trying to help. That's what Robby did when he "tried to be a gentleman" by standing up for a female coworker who was the target of derogatory comments by another peer. He made such a scene when confronting the offender that the firm's partners got involved. He was trying to help, but only made it worse when everyone in the office now knew what had been said about his coworker.

The same goes for anyone you're dealing with. You can just as easily undermine your own objectives and status with subordinates if you lose your cool. Sure, yelling and other behaviors that create fear in employees may work in the short run. But as a consequence, you also get "work to rule" behavior, hard-to-detect counterproductive behavior, and a staff looking to avoid you as much as possible. Dave admitted that this happened to him when he blew up at a direct report who was consistently frustrating him with his bad attitude. As a result of what Dave realized was his "unprofessionalism" in the shouting match that ensued, the two never got back on track. Dave was still the boss, but he'd lost his ability to influence his subordinate through mutual trust and respect. The same thing happened to William, a senior manager at an engineering company, when he badly mismanaged a meeting with his engineers. The team was engaged in a technical debate, and when William grew frustrated that a consensus wasn't emerging, he loudly declared, "You need to just do what I'm saying because I'm the director in this room." What did William get in response? Stunned silence—and a bad reputation among the many "disappointed and dissatisfied" engineers who shared this story around the watercooler.

What's clear is that you have to stay calm, or at least present yourself that way even if you're terrified or raging inside. It's hard to overstate how impressive it can be, and how much more likely we are to create positive outcomes, when we take a principled stand without losing our cool. Terrence, a young Black man, did just that when he confronted his significantly older, White boss about using racial slurs at work. It was a bold move for Terrence to call out this behavior in public given the hierarchical nature of the place and the knowledge that there were "a lot of racist people working there in higher positions." Despite the strong emotions he felt in the situation, Terrence didn't show any anger. He was firm, but level-headed and polite when he spoke, showing compassion and a desire to help correct rather than shame or scold his boss. This allowed his boss to see the ignorance and hurtfulness of his statements and, according to Terrence's colleague, led to the boss no longer talking like this at work.

The same principle holds even when the issue itself isn't as potentially explosive as a conversation about racism or other unethical or illegal behavior. For example, Erik was a manager whose objective was to grow the solar business at one of the world's largest companies. He had to repeatedly share unpopular truths with executives in the company's traditional business units and faced criticism and pushback when presenting his analyses: "We don't do that" and "That will never work here" were the knee-jerk reactions of defensive leaders. Despite feeling quite frustrated, Erik continued to engage "by *not* participating in emotional discussion" but instead by diving deeper into how money could be made in this space. He forced himself to see the emotion-laden critiques of those above him as evidence of their fear of the unknown, not personal attacks, and thus was able to calmly continue what he told himself was as an internal education campaign. He eventually got buy-in and saw a strong pivot toward his recommended strategy.

The point of these examples isn't to claim that staying in emotional control guarantees positive outcomes. Terrence's boss, for example, could certainly have gotten defensive and ugly toward him despite his calm demeanor. Still, it's worth remembering two things. First, you'll feel a lot better about yourself, knowing you did the very best you could, no matter how the other party reacts. You'll have less regret about the "how" of your action. Second, there might be some positives that only come about later. Erin, for example, got into an unpleasant exchange with her VP during the debrief at the end of a day of training. After Erin said she wanted to lead people, not boss them, her boss condescendingly responded, "We hired you to be boss." Erin calmly replied that they must just hold different views of leadership. Although he "continued to be a jerk" to her then, she stuck politely to her point of view. In the days following the meeting, others complimented Erin for the skillful way she held her ground. And perhaps the VP learned something about Erin, because from then on, he was much more respectful toward her.

In contrast, if you let your emotions get the best of you, you're likely to struggle in the moment *and* potentially create longer-term negative fallout. Jenna, for instance, worked at a startup under a supervisor who was rude, played favorites, gave contradictory guidance, and had unrealistic expectations for her people. Jenna carefully compiled instances of the problematic behavior and then scheduled a meeting with her supervisor and their skip-level boss. As Jenna shared the examples, her supervisor became angry and attacked back, pointing to trivial instances of Jenna's tardiness or missed deadlines. Jenna took the bait and became so enraged that she lost her cool. Deviating from the facts she'd written down, she started personally attacking her supervisor. Understandably, the senior leader's attention was diverted to calming down both Jenna and the supervisor, and nothing productive came of the meeting. Jenna was so discouraged that she soon quit. Not long after, three more employees quit on or got fired by the same supervisor. Despite Jenna's evidence and best intentions, the supervisor kept her job.

One final clarification: "good emotional control" does *not* equal "show no emotions." Time and again in discussing emotional intelligence with managers, I've heard the mistaken notion that good leaders don't get emotional. I think that's a belief born from witnessing too many people display their emotions very poorly, which imprints the notion that emotions are dangerous and lead to poor outcomes. But as an overall conclusion, it couldn't be further from the truth (or more impossible) to say emotions should (or could) be kept out of the workplace. Think about it. Has someone who behaved like a robot ever influenced or inspired you? Of course not. You are not emotionally skilled if you appear emotion*less* in situations where emotional reactions are normal and expected. The key is to find, as professor Jay Conger has written, the delicate balance between appearing too emotional and seeming too emotionally distant.[10]

Manage Your *Targets'* Emotions

So—you've got your emotions under control. Now, let's deal with other people's emotions.

For starters, you need to understand why others feel the way they do and, at minimum, acknowledge that you have heard how the situation looks from their perspective. For example, Rhonda was being harassed by a coworker and scheduled an appointment with her new VP to report it. Though she was understandably angry and wanted immediate, severe action, she also forced herself to consider her VP's perspective. He was new, and male, both factors that she expected would condition how he responded. Sure enough, he became visibly uncomfortable when she raised the issue. He tried to minimize his need to do anything and to quickly move on to a new topic. But Rhonda was prepared for this and calmly asked him to explain the situation from his perspective. When he pointed to the difficulty of doing something about an employee he didn't know that well and of starting his tenure negatively by focusing a lot of attention on this issue, Rhonda acknowledged those concerns. She then reminded him of the legal risks of not responding and of the ways in which HR could take the brunt of the action. She then offered him time to work out a plan. Her respect for his perspective helped the VP move forward productively.

You should also be clear that you are merely offering *a* perspective—not *the only* perspective or relevant facts. Avoid common phrases like "*the* explanation . . . ," or "*the obvious* problem . . . ," or "it's *totally clear* that . . . ." When we speak this way, we're not just implying that there's only one point of view; we're implying the valid view is *the one we hold*, and that others who don't see it that way are stupid or self-interested. This is what psychologists call *naive realism* because it's not an accurate view of the world.[11] Falling prey to naive realism can be particularly damaging in the realm of ethically charged situations, where coming off as holier-than-thou is among the surest ways to invoke anger (and other negative emotions) in others.[12]

Even small changes to counteract this tendency can be powerful. Rather than saying something is "*the* . . . ," say "*a* . . . ." "It seems too simple to make a difference. But it does. Speaking in less definitive terms is acknowledging that you, too, have only a partial view of reality.[13] It's acknowledging that you are sharing your perspective, not the only acceptable or true way to see or feel about a situation. It shows humility and openness and makes it much less likely you'll offend someone or see them shut down.

Another tip: keep it behavior-focused, and keep it specific. That is, mention only the behavior or policy you find problematic, while avoiding assumptions about the reasons for someone's actions or behaviors. For example, telling someone "I felt hurt when you said X" is simply naming the behavior and owning your feeling about it. Conversely, saying "You didn't even care that you offended me when you said X" states not only the behavior and your feeling but also an assumption you're making about the speaker—namely, that he's not a good or sensitive enough person to care that he's hurt you. That might not be what you mean, but that's how the recipient is likely to hear it. They'll probably try to defend their character rather than addressing the issue at hand. So, unless you actually want to debate how good or bad, or smart or stupid, or caring or insensitive a person is, stick to the behavior or issue you want to see improved.

It's also useful to give specific examples right away. Say you're angry or upset that your boss doesn't seem to listen to you or give you credit for your contributions. You could say, "When I said, 'I think we should do X' in our meeting earlier, you dismissed the idea, but then ten minutes later, when John said the same thing, you said it was a good idea worth exploring further. That leaves me feeling you don't value me." Being specific not only decreases the likelihood your boss will feel you're attacking his overall character, it also avoids a whole back-and-forth in which he is likely to deny that your general statement is true, or just ask you for examples (which if you wait too long, she can't remember well anyway).

This is something my wife and I have learned over many years. We have always wanted to be respectful and accountable to each other for our behavior. But often we would lob these generic statements at each other—"You don't listen to me," "You're being critical," or "You're blaming me for your feelings"—and then derail into an argument about the truth of the generalization. Only as we got better at pointing out in real time the specific behavior triggering the generalization were we more able to really hear the other and either immediately apologize or talk the issue through without defensiveness. In sum: people can much more readily accept that a specific behavior of theirs needs work than they can accept feedback that translates in their mind to "He's saying I'm a bad *person*."

So. Focus on the behavior only. Keep it specific. And, one last suggestion: do it in person. It seems by now that this should go without saying, but people continue to use email or other online forums to address challenging situations. Sometimes this seems to stem from a conscious desire to publicly embarrass or shame the person we're confronting, a choice that probably reflects that our emotions are taking over and leading us to do something likely to accomplish little except get ourselves into trouble. Other times, we do this because of a story we've told ourselves about how this actually improves our effectiveness—for example, "I get so nervous in real time that writing it down in an email allows me to get it all out more rationally." While it may well be true that writing it down is very helpful—it allows you to organize your thoughts and assess what's better or worse to actually say—there's no reason you have to *send* what you wrote down via what is referred to, in media richness theory, as a lean communication medium like email or text messaging.[14]

Lean communication mediums simply don't convey *intent* well. They don't allow the recipient of your message to see that you care, to hear in your voice that you're hurt but not attacking, or to immediately engage in clarifying questions or statements that you can use to calm that person's emotional reaction. So, whatever your rationale, avoid sending a missive instead of having a conversation. You could use your notes as preparation for a face-to-face conversation, and even take them with you if you need to. Documentation and follow-up notes can be important (especially if you're concerned about retaliation or later denial or distortion), but they're seldom a good way to start a conversation off on the right foot.

One last reminder about managing others' emotions: pay attention to nonverbal signals. Often what people say, or even how they say it, is significantly less indicative of how they're really feeling than what their body language says. For example, you may be pitching an idea or reporting something problematic and think it's going well because your boss is saying "I understand," "That's interesting," or "Keep going." But if she's leaning way back or has angled her body away from you, she may not actually be that interested. If her lips are pursed, her eyebrows furrowed, or jaw muscles tensed, there's a good chance she's feeling something beyond those encouraging words she's just used. And if she's got her arms folded across her chest or her fists clenched, you've got reason to suspect she's feeling at least a little defensive. As Carol Goman, an authority on the impact of body language in the workplace, has described, this is the "silent language" of leaders—the myriad nonverbal ways in which people unintentionally convey what they're actually feeling.[15] Whereas many of us have learned to consciously manage our verbal reactions—knowing, for example, that it's normative in most environments to suppress *spoken* signs of anger or boredom—few of us are skilled at masking other bodily reactions that accompany these emotions.

Think about how this knowledge might help you. If you pay attention only to your boss's words when he says he understands and wants you to keep going, you might plow ahead, thinking you've got the situation under control. You might start to reveal even more about the problem or idea, bringing more of your own emotions into the conversation, and then be surprised when he appears to "suddenly" become quite defensive. If you'd been paying attention to his body language, though, you might have noticed much earlier that he'd been uncomfortable. If so, you might have attended to those cues in ways that helped keep him calmer and kept yourself from a situation that now feels unsafe.

Exemplar in Action: Anthony Wedo

On the morning before the most important product launch of his career, Anthony Wedo, the thirty-year-old VP of one of KFC's five US divisions, greeted 250 store managers for a final kick-off meeting. It had been a fast and demanding process—preparing to launch rotisserie chicken in a big, urban test market—and Wedo wanted to get things started on a positive and energetic note.

What happened next startled him. As he addressed the group of store managers and employees, he could tell they were distracted, and the enthusiasm he had been used to seeing from these people was absent. And, as he looked out at the crowd, he noticed that some of store-level leaders that he had counted on since he took over the division were equally distracted or physically absent.

Wedo kept going, thinking perhaps the local managers, like him, were also just anxious. But nothing changed. The crowd, on whom this career-defining launch depended, continued to stare back at him with blank faces. Now Wedo was moving from "nervous but confident" to "downright terrified."

Something was up. Wedo could feel it. So rather than plowing forward and potentially making matters worse, he cut his remarks short and called an unplanned break.

Wedo found his troubled-looking local HR lead in the hallway and the two ducked into a private room. What he was told was shocking and tragic: at midnight, just hours ago, a group of three local restaurant employees, plus the teenage son of a beloved store manager, had died in a head-on collision with a drunk driver.

The GM whose son had died was related to at least twenty-five employees in the test market and had trained most of the region's managers in her restaurant. The employees assembled in the ballroom were devastated at the loss suffered by someone most considered the matriarch of an extended family. Wedo himself was distraught. He had developed a special relationship with the GM as they worked together over the past three months preparing for the launch. He had come to count on her, her team, and her knowledge of the managers and of the consumers in the market. He believed that without this GM's support, the product launch would be doomed from the start in this region.

Wedo collected himself as best he could, breathing deeply to keep himself from panicking. He knew that he needed to control, not be controlled by, his emotions; everyone was looking to him for direction. He needed to decide what to do, and he'd have to do it on his own: his own boss wasn't arriving until tomorrow.

Wedo directed his HR lead to go postpone the restart for thirty minutes, and then immediately prioritized the calls he needed to make before reappearing on stage. This did not include calling the grieving GM right away, as he knew this would only make him more emotional and not help him decide what to do anyway. In short order, Wedo concluded that there was no way to proceed with the launch the following day.

When he returned to the ballroom, he expressed his deepest sympathy and let the group see how personally sad the news made him. He then told everyone present that the launch would be postponed for one week and canceled the rest of the daylong meeting. He next spent that afternoon talking to people at corporate and working to stem the various losses associated with the delay (e.g., PR and advertising contracts). All told, the direct costs of the delay were estimated at over $1 million—including the costs of closing affected restaurants on the afternoon of the GM's son's funeral.

Wedo's conclusion was poorly received by most at headquarters. His decision only validated the perception that Wedo, who was a decade younger than any of his counterparts and the only one without an Ivy League degree, didn't fit the mold. He was told that his choice to delay was a "terminable offense."

So why did he anger nearly everyone above him, and put millions of dollars at risk? Because, says Wedo, it was the emotionally intelligent thing to do. Sure, he could have forced the launch to go as scheduled the next morning. He knew, though, that customer-facing employees' emotional state is critical to customers' experience. He also knew that employees who were sad or angry were more likely to make mistakes, thereby risking customers' first experience with the new product being an unsatisfactory one. And, he knew that in the tight-knit ethnic community he was dealing with, the enduring damage he would sustain in employee morale and commitment by appearing to be a corporate blue-suiter who didn't really care about their loss would cost him far more in the long run. In sum, he knew that respecting employees' current emotional needs wasn't a case of compassion *versus* profitability; it was a case where business success depended on understanding and respecting their current emotional state. "We simply could not have pulled off the launch given the state these people were in," Wedo believes to this day.

The launch the following week was met with an overwhelming response. KFC, and Wedo personally, received local acclaim for "doing the right thing" in the aftermath of the tragedy. Sales rose 22 percent and transactions more than 25 percent in the test market, compared to the norm of 3 percent to 5 percent for a new product launch. Overall, it was considered the most successful product launch in the history of the brand.

Remember

- Learning to recognize the earliest signs of our own strong emotions and to separate those automatic feelings from what we consciously choose to do next can prevent both action and inaction that we regret.

- Emotional intelligence is *not* the lack of emotions. Emotions are key to human connection and successful persuasion, so the goal is not to eliminate them. The goal is to have your emotions be the motivation for action, but not the driver of *how* you behave.

- Perspective taking isn't just a nice thing to do. It conveys respect, increases understanding, and helps us to *give* our own perspective in ways that increase the chance of acceptance.

- Keep it behavior-focused, specific, and do it in person. Generalities that imply character faults tend to land poorly, especially when conveyed well after-the-fact. Stick to the specific behavior, without attributions around intent, and do it in person as soon as possible so your meaning and intent are easier to understand.

CHAPTER 9

Taking Action after the Act

Sarah was frustrated with Pat. Since being promoted to partner, Sarah spent additional time mentoring junior associates, leading internal initiatives, and working on firm-level strategic planning, while Pat, also a newly minted partner, often left work early, had stopped coming to many meetings, and hadn't developed much new business. On top of that, Pat's assigned mentees felt neglected and now regularly came to Sarah. While Sarah understood that Pat had young kids and a partner who worked crazy hours, she felt unwilling to continue shouldering the burden of Pat's attempt to have it all.

Hoping to improve the situation, Sarah decided to use a quarterly meeting of partners and senior partners to raise the issue. Her goal wasn't to call out Pat; it was to draw attention to the toll that the work culture had on working parents in general. She knew that some of her peers shared her perspective. She also knew what other organizations were trying to do to balance the needs of the business and their employees. When she spoke up, she articulated the ways in which the company culture was causing stress, which, in turn, was putting the firm at risk of losing top people and ultimately jeopardizing both talent development and business performance. The senior partners listened intently, asking several questions.

During the discussion, a senior leader asked Sarah whether her stress and frustration was a broader problem. "Yes," she replied, "but this isn't about me personally. It's a larger issue." She then quickly shifted back to the need for systemic adjustments and never named names in anything she said. Nonetheless, she noticed out of the corner of her eye that Pat was visibly angry. The conversation continued a few more minutes, until the leader of the meeting said, "OK, we need to move on. This is an important issue, Sarah, thanks for bringing it up."

As the meeting shifted to another topic, Sarah glanced down and saw her colleague had scribbled a note on her notepad. "Good job," it read, "but you realize Pat now hates your guts, right?"

Sarah has just raised an issue that is important to her and, she believes, the whole organization. And she took the approaches discussed in the prior chapters—she used data, she tried to frame the issue in a way that would appeal to senior leaders, and she didn't let her anger control what she said or how she said it. That's all good, but now what? If you were Sarah, what would you do in the hours or days after this meeting? Would you approach Pat?

If Sarah is like most of us, after enduring the stress of speaking up, she's probably inclined to retreat and lay low. While understandable, that's often the worst thing to do if you want your action to produce positive results. In fact, the net result could be negative. Since senior management didn't commit to next steps, they're unlikely to make changes. And, now, Pat knows how Sarah feels. He probably felt that Sarah had called him out in front of the other partners. If Sarah moves on without talking to Pat, her relationship with him is sure to suffer.

As we'll discuss in this chapter, what we do *after* a courageous act is often more important than the big moment itself. To put it simply: following up is critical, as is being realistic about the likely amount of time and further effort it will take to see through whatever positive change you're hoping to make. Competent courage involves addressing head on any negative emotions or relationship damage you may have unintentionally created, thanking and sharing credit with those who've helped so far, and confirming next steps with key stakeholders. It also involves persistence. That is, rather than giving up when the outcomes of your courageous act aren't optimal, you'll need to treat the aftermath as an opportunity to learn more and to glean helpful information about how to keep pushing forward.

Following Up

No matter how well or poorly you think your first attempt has gone, you can usually make things better by choosing to take further action. Sometimes those acts are courageous too.

Solidify Next Steps

In my study comparing the outcomes of courageous acts, people who experienced positive outcomes were significantly more likely to have touched base with their targets to discuss next steps and to thank those who helped out with the act itself.

As Harvard Law School's Douglas Stone and Sheila Heen have noted, if we've ended a conversation without explicit action plans, metrics, and benchmarks, there's a good chance we'll be disappointed by what comes next.[1] Busy people will forget what was discussed; people who weren't that dissatisfied with the way things are will revert to the status quo.

That's true enough. But if you don't get specific agreements the first time you raise an issue, you can follow up. You can schedule another meeting for as soon as possible and go in this time with the explicit purpose of establishing next steps. If your bosses seemed to like your idea but didn't commit to action the first time you brought it up—as happened to Sarah—you can follow up with distinct asks. If your peer finally seemed to hear what you were asking him to do differently, but you didn't lock in agreement on what progress would look like and when you'd next touch base, you can ask to talk again with that as your agenda.

When you seek specific commitments, it can help to distinguish between outcome goals and metrics—the ultimate state of performance you want to achieve—and process goals and metrics—steps you believe are critical to achieving those outcomes. For example, imagine you gave a presentation on increasing representation throughout your company. Your outcome goals, such as "equal representation of men and women at all managerial levels," are of ultimate importance. But if your follow-up involves trying to pin down senior managers to commit to getting to "50 percent within three years" when you're at just 10 percent today, there's a good chance you'll walk away empty-handed. If, conversely, you ask them to commit to specific process goals and metrics, such as "at least five targeted recruiting events per year," "a specific leadership development program for a hundred high-potential females," and "a promotion process that utilizes technology to help with de-biasing," you may have better luck locking in their commitment.

Address Negative Reactions

No matter how skillfully you frame the change you're suggesting or making, there's a reasonable likelihood someone will be hurt, angry, or confused. After all, change implicitly says that something currently happening is a problem. You can ignore others' feelings, hoping they'll just get over them, but letting this negative energy fester can be bad for the changes you want.[2] And it's almost certainly a bad idea to ignore others' feelings if you care about those relationships. In short, it's usually worth it to address what you sense or know are lingering negative feelings, even if doing so feels like yet another courageous act.

When Catherine Gill made an in-the-moment decision to launch a "call to action" for cultural change at Root Capital during a leadership retreat (detailed in chapter 5), she knew she had caught the CEO off guard and that he might have felt that the conversation was an indictment of him. So Gill purposefully checked in with him privately that evening. Yes, she wanted change. She also cared about the CEO and knew how critical his support was going forward. Gill assured him that no one was trying to single him out for blame or doubting his intentions. Nor, she said, was anyone trying to start a revolution;

they were trying to be part of the firm's further evolution into its ideal form. The CEO admitted that he was still processing what had happened but looking forward to continuing the conversation.

In other cases, even if your motives were pure or you really had no reasonable alternative, it will be obvious that you've hurt or angered someone. As uncomfortable as it may be, you really only have one good option: face their feelings and try to make things at least somewhat better.

That was Marin's choice. Marin had played a vital supporting role in a merger that was producing a lot of disruption and uncertainty. Some of her team members were at risk of losing their jobs. The situation was uncomfortable. But Marin didn't hide. She faced those employees and offered to help them find better opportunities—either at the newly merged company or another. Much to the chagrin of HR and other senior leaders, Marin met weekly with her team members. She helped them work on the skill sets needed in the new environment and also encouraged and supported those who wanted to pursue other options. "I adhered to management's requests and read their scripts," Marin said, "but I also spoke from my heart as an individual. I made it clear that I was not representing the company when I worked to hold them up as human beings and to help them work through their emotions." Some did leave, but many stayed with the company due to Marin's willingness to address rather than ignore their pain.

Sometimes, you'll upset someone but you won't know why—as when Jack announced the launch of a task force to explore reorganizing some departments to better serve clients. Though he assured his employees that nothing had been predetermined, and that he expected whatever the task force brought forward would be grounded in careful analysis of data from many sources (including input from the people in the room), a member of his team made several snarky remarks.

Jack decided not to ignore this negative reaction and therefore visited that employee's office within thirty minutes of the end of the meeting. He didn't want to do it, but he thought the discomfort might be worth it if he could learn about the employee's resistance or resentment and lessen or eliminate it up front. Jack was direct: "You seemed very upset when I announced the task force. Can you help me understand what you were reacting to?" It turned out that the employee shared Jack's belief that things could be done much better and was quite supportive of the task force's mission. But when Jack had listed "potential savings" as one of four reasons for the task force's work, he had been triggered and didn't process anything else Jack said. All it took was for Jack to clarify that "getting it right" was the main objective, whether it saved money or not in the end, for the employee to feel better. The follow-up took less than five minutes, but it converted a key team member from being in "blocker" mode to fully supportive.

Give Thanks and Share Credit

If you've enlisted the help of others, you need to thank them—even if you failed to persuade your boss or tame the bully. At minimum, they kept you from standing alone, and that's worth your thanks. And a simple gesture of gratitude may be enough for them to try again on other occasions.

When things have gone well, don't get so caught up in your success that you forget to share or give credit to others. Sharing credit isn't just the right thing to do. It's also, according to Harvard Business School professor Rosabeth Moss Kanter, an important part of motivating people to undertake similar efforts in the future.[3] When Teddy Roosevelt successfully resolved the largest early crisis of his presidency—a major coal strike in 1902—he immediately shared credit publicly for the outcome. He penned thank-you letters to each member of his own team, and to other key stakeholders like J. P. Morgan.[4] If the president of the United States could make time for gratitude, it's probably fair to assume we can and would be wise to do so too.

Remember It's a Journey

The outcomes of some courageous actions are determined immediately—like when you intervene to prevent physical harm to a fellow employee who is doing something unsafe. Often, though, it takes a long time to determine what's possible, and the best outcomes accrue only to those willing to keep trying and learning over an extended period of effort.

Be Persistent

Here's a frank, but hard to disprove, statement: if you're only willing to try one time, you're either (1) naive about how change actually comes about or (2) not that committed to what you're trying to accomplish. As noted by Bertie Forbes (the founder of *Forbes* magazine) and documented by John White in his book *Rejection*, history shows that the most notable achievers usually experienced repeated setbacks before finally succeeding. Winners won, said Forbes, because they "refused to become discouraged by their defeats."[5]

You're sure to face pushbacks and setbacks—especially in a business setting. When Cindy, a manager in a commercial real estate company, tried to convince senior leaders to make a formal commitment to sustainability, she met with resistance. But she kept pushing and renewed her focus.

Rather than making a general case for sustainability, she needed to show that money could be made, not just spent, on sustainability efforts. So she joined a program in which some of their properties would receive regular payments for agreeing to be on standby in the event of a power grid emergency. She then got several other properties to pilot an energy efficiency program that showed tangible cost savings. Now she had internal data to use to make her case. But she took one more step. Since her senior leaders always paid careful attention to an annual industrywide survey that outlined emerging trends, she spent significant time getting the association in charge of the survey to make sustainability-related questions a major focus. Eventually, her tireless efforts paid off: her firm now has an established sustainability committee and support from the board for organization-wide efforts.

Persistence also increases the admiration and appreciation you get from colleagues. Trying once is often appreciated, for sure. But, if you keep trying in the face of setbacks and rejections, you'll truly earn the respect of those around you.

Chuck, for example, worked for a manager who was routinely abusive to members of Chuck's team. Because the manager "kissed up and kicked down," everyone felt it was risky to speak up about his behavior. At the potential risk of his job, Chuck nonetheless reported the manager to both HR and to his skip-level boss. The manager was given a slap on the wrist, after which he improved for a short while.

Then the manager went back to his abusive ways. Again, no one would speak up. The inconsequential response to Chuck's report only cemented in others' mind that it was neither safe nor worthwhile to try to do anything. Only Chuck, who watched another team member suffer from ulcers from working with their boss, refused to let it go. This time, he went all the way to the top, telling the VP of HR about the consequences of the manager's behavior. The manager was fired, and the morale and health of Chuck's team recovered quickly. How do I know this? Because Chuck's coworkers told me.

Adopt a Learning Orientation

You have two choices when you face setbacks: you can view them as conclusive results or chances to get data you can learn from.

If you view situations through what Stanford psychologist Carol Dweck calls a *fixed mindset*, you'll see the first sign of failure as evidence that you're just not capable of accomplishing your goal.[6] "Things are what they are," you'll tell yourself, "so there's no point expending more energy and putting myself at further risk." If, conversely, you view the same initial setback through a *growth mindset*—and choose a learning orientation—you'll take what happened as evidence about what doesn't work, adapt your strategy, and use what's happened as motivation to keep working to achieve your goal.

That's how Duke University's Mike Krzyzewski ("Coach K"), the winningest coach in the history of college basketball, treated his team's loss in the semifinal game of the NCAA tournament in 1989.

Most would have packed up and headed home, utterly disappointed. But Coach K told his team they were going to stay through the national title game two days later. It was important, he told them, to see what the success they were seeking looked like. Years later, he reflected on that decision: "Sometimes in a defeat, you can set the stage for future victory." To be clear, he didn't want his team to like losing; he wanted them to understand they could learn more from it than the pain they felt. This required forgoing a *performance orientation* for a *learning orientation*.[7] In the former mode, all the team would have done is harshly judge every mistake; in the latter, they analyzed them as opportunities to grow. In the next two years, Duke won its first and second national championships.

Part of developing a growth mindset and a learning orientation is to let go of the myth that the people who succeed are just innately better than the rest of us. They can create change or achieve greatness in their domain because they were born different, we tell ourselves. It's a convenient way to let ourselves off the hook, but it's largely untrue. As Dweck reminds us, Michael Jordan—perhaps the greatest player in the history of professional basketball—was cut from his high school varsity team and didn't get recruited to his top college choice (North Carolina State). He became what he did because he used every setback as motivation to do something different and better. He practiced longer and harder than anyone around him, focusing on ways to hone his strengths and shore up his weaknesses.

Scientists and entrepreneurs can't possibly succeed without a learning orientation. Scientists have to be willing to design experiment after experiment in which they continually learn what *doesn't* work if they hope to eventually find what *does*. That's why the process of drug discovery, for example, takes many years and billions of dollars. By the time some form of a drug has proven safe and effective in humans, many alternatives have failed at some point along the way. The same is true for would-be entrepreneurs: if you're not willing to view initial failures as a chance to learn rather than *the* indicator of your ability to build something new, you probably shouldn't head down that route in the first place.

But it's not enough to simply view what went wrong as a learning opportunity. There's an additional—and pivotal—step: you need a good process to make sure that you've actually learned all you can from the event. What you need is some form of after-event review (AER).[8] You may have heard of AERs being used after hospital mistakes, airplane mishaps, oil spills, and major explosions or fires. A personal, scaled-down version of an AER may seem unnatural, especially since our instincts are to quickly blame others for what happened and engage other defense mechanisms to distance ourselves from our negative emotions around the event. But it's an essential part of the learning process.

AERs can take different forms. If I were advising Sarah—the partner who was angered by her coworker Pat—I'd suggest she begin her after-action review with a quiet period of introspection. At first, her mind may drift to self-serving attributions ("It's not my fault that Pat's freaking impossible to deal with") or self-defeating criticisms ("I screw it up every time I try to speak up"), but she should push past that phase and move toward multiple and more plausible explanations and perspectives. Sarah might jot down things like, "Pat might be less angry if I'd let him know in advance I was going to talk about this" or "It might have been better if I'd brought this up in a smaller, less public context."

Next, Sarah needs to gather information from other sources—maybe an audio or video recording that could be played back. Often, though, the best data available is perceptual in nature—feedback from others about how they experienced the situation and what they'd suggest we could have done differently. While Sarah may think there was no reason for Pat to feel implicated personally by what she said, how did other colleagues perceive it? How did she come off to observers—as someone talking calmly about an organization-wide problem, or as someone choosing an indirect way to attack Pat? In what ways do they see Sarah's behavior as having contributed to the problem? If she's really interested in learning, she'll go talk with Pat, and ask similar questions. The point here is to acknowledge that our learning will be quite limited if we stick with only our own recollections. We have to be

willing to consider other sources of data that add to, and even contra-
dict, our inevitably limited and biased interpretation. Remember, the
point of a personal after-event review is to increase the odds we'll do
better next time. If you only use it to confirm your starting position,
it's a waste of time.

Exemplar in Action: Fred Keller

While walking the plant floor at Cascade Engineering, a manufacturing company headquartered in Grand Rapids, Michigan, founder
Fred Keller and employee Ron Jimmerson hatched a plan to give people on welfare a chance. "It seemed like the right thing to do," recalls
Keller. "Going back to the '60s, I believed 'the system' wasn't working,
and I'd cared about intergenerational poverty since I was a young
man." His values-driven rationale: "I've got a business that might be
able to help. Why not try to do something about it?"

Their first effort to establish a welfare-to-career (W2C) program,
which included Jimmerson renting a van and looking for potential
workers in a low-income area of Grand Rapids, was a bust. Cascade
wasn't sufficiently prepared to help the new hires succeed. "We didn't
know what we didn't know," recalls one of the supervisors, so they
resorted to a "tough love" approach that just didn't work.

To Keller, the initial outcome was simply data: the first attempt
hadn't worked, he reasoned, so clearly there were things to learn before taking another step.

Unfortunately, their second attempt—which included potential
Cascade employees first working at a local Burger King for six
months—didn't work either. Part of what Keller and others misun-
derstood, because they still didn't really understand intergenerational
poverty and the challenges of getting out of it, was that the barriers to
consistent attendance and performance remained too high.

After several years, Keller's team managed to hire several dozen
welfare recipients. But the company was struggling to truly integrate
them. Turnover remained significantly higher for the W2C group,

and those who worked with or supervised them were frustrated or angry. The few W2C employees were often late, distracted, needed to leave early, or just didn't show up because they had problems with transportation, their children's schooling or health or childcare, or a myriad of other life challenges. In this context, it was hard to sort out legitimate frustrations from stereotypes about people in poverty. When supervisors tried to cut these new employees a little slack, long-term employees voiced concerns about fairness. On-the-ground managers were thus feeling it from all sides: they were expected to stick with the program because senior management wanted it, and they were expected to hit existing quality and quantity production goals despite the challenges posed by the new employees' attendance and performance. "This is not gonna be good," a plant supervisor at the time recalls thinking. Even the local Goodwill president wondered if this was a "good idea that just wasn't going to fly."

Keller persevered, requiring first himself and then everyone in a managerial position to undergo focused training on intergenerational poverty. Equipped with better understanding of the "hidden rules" of poverty and how standard middle- or upper-class strategies and responses simply don't work, Keller and his team renewed their commitment to finding solutions. He also continued to be a cheerleader, encouraging everyone to see the broader purpose of the endeavor. But while beliefs and attitudes were beginning to change, challenges persisted. With more than a few W2C workers on a shift in any plant, problems with attendance, output, and factory culture were still prevalent. Clearly more was needed if the program was going to succeed.

To address this, Keller and Andy Zylstra (a Michigan County director at the Family Independence Agency) formed a novel company-state partnership after reaching a bold conclusion: they needed to put a state social worker *on-site* at Cascade. In this way, social workers could get real-time input and help solve problems before they escalated. In theory, it was a win-win-win: if more employees got off welfare, it would ultimately save the state money; W2C workers would get more effective help for their nonwork challenges and become permanent members of the workforce; and Cascade would reduce turnover, meet its production goals, and thus show that it was possible to do social good while still making money.

With Cascade agreeing to pay half the social worker's salary for several years (until evidence about the program's ultimate costs and benefits could be collected and assessed), the state accepted this creative proposal. While it certainly wasn't smooth sailing from then on, people at Cascade today consider the intergenerational poverty training and on-site placement of a social worker to be the key turning points. With those supports in place and a never-give-up, continuous learning culture infused from the top down, the W2C program slowly but surely found solid footing. Managers—who now believed in the project—pushed through the hard times, iterating toward new processes that facilitated effective employee-social worker interaction, overcoming perceptions that there were two sets of standards, refusing to bow to employees' threats to leave, and eventually letting go some employees whose attitude got in the way of their performance.

Cascade's W2C program persists to this day, with turnover rates now as low for W2C employees (whom most within Cascade can't even identify) as overall turnover at Cascade (and statewide turnover in the manufacturing sector). Cascade's program is widely studied and celebrated. It has been publicly lauded by Michigan's governor as a model for state efforts to help get people into the workforce and off welfare. And it served as a template for iteratively developing other bold programs at Cascade, like their "Returning Citizens" program for former felons and their anti-racism program. Internally, these are now taken-for-granted parts of how Cascade operates and why people want to work there.

None of this would have taken place had Keller thrown in the towel after the first, second, or even third attempts at building these new models proved extremely challenging. Nor would Cascade be where it is today had Keller not routinely shared credit and followed up in myriad ways that helped others collectively own the company's truly unique culture. It took courage for Keller to take these steps, well beyond the significant financial resources he risked: by being willing to make himself vulnerable by admitting shortcomings along the way, by standing firm when people said he was crazy or out-of-his-lane as a businessman, and by standing up for populations who themselves initially thought his position of privilege meant he would never truly understand or help them.

Remember

- What you do *after* your initial action is also a critical part of being competently courageous. Following up to garner specific commitments, set specific timelines, and agree on specific goals and metrics is critical to turning your courageous act into meaningful outcomes.

- Addressing negative or uncertain emotional states is also critical follow-up work. Sometimes our initial courageous act requires another one in the form of approaching those who are hurt or angry about what we said or did.

- Persistence is needed to see through almost any systemic or deep-seated behavior change. If you're only willing to give it one try, you might be better off not acting at all in many cases.

- Adopt a learning orientation, where you view initial outcomes from your action as data to be learned from, not the final evidence of whether your objective can or will be achieved.

PART THREE

CLIMBING YOUR COURAGE LADDER

CHAPTER 10

Cultivating Courage

*You gain strength, courage, and confidence by every
experience in which you really stop to look fear in the face.
You must do the thing which you think you cannot do.*

—Anna Eleanor Roosevelt

W hether speaking truth to power, confronting peers or subordinates, or engaging in other challenging actions, the people
I've studied all shared an awareness that what they were doing
was risky, and most felt at least some degree of fear. That's right: like
the thousands of military personnel Stanley Rachman studied, even
the people who appeared so calm and cool in the stories I've shared
often acknowledged they were afraid.[1] They, too, had sleepless nights
worrying about the consequences of their actions. But they acted
nonetheless. So let's be clear. Fear isn't a sign that you shouldn't move
forward; rather, it means the stage is set.

It's time to decide: Will you start climbing your own courage ladder, one rung at a time?

The Path to Competent Courage

There are three routes to competent courage. First, we can change how we *think*. That's the logic behind cognitive behavioral techniques—understanding and modifying the unhelpful thoughts that get in the way of desired behavior. Second, we can add useful tools to our *behavioral toolkit*, such as specific techniques for conducting difficult conversations. This is the realm of communication strategies, such as learning how to "sell issues," negotiate conflicts, and skillfully challenge without offending in emotionally charged situations. Third, we can change or better control our *physiological responses*. Here we're talking about managing our body's automatic defense circuitry, whether that means learning how to dampen those responses or to behave skillfully despite them.

Let's take a closer look at the kinds of changes you can make.

Thinking More Productively

To think productively about the challenges you'll tackle, start by accepting that your interpretation of life's events isn't just about, or even primarily about, what is objectively happening; it's about what you *perceive* is happening and the story you immediately start telling yourself.

Sporting events provide the perfect illustration of this point. Imagine you're watching an (American) football game with your friend. It's a tense game. Your favorite team is driving for a winning score late in the game, and the quarterback throws a perfect pass to a wide receiver streaking down the sideline. But just before the ball can fall softly into the receiver's hands, a defender bumps him and knocks the ball away. You're livid, screaming at the TV for a pass interference penalty. To you, it was a blatant foul. But your friend, who's a fan of the opposing team, vehemently disagrees. He thinks it was a great, legal, game-saving play.

You both watched the same play; you both accuse the other of being biased. What objectively happened on the play is irrelevant because, like so many things in life, it's what we see and tell ourselves that determine how we feel and behave.

That's why cognitive behavioral therapists focus on helping people identify, question, and replace limited and limiting thought patterns with more helpful or accurate ones.[2] To stick with the football example, that might mean learning to check yourself when you start *overgeneralizing* ("My team always gets screwed by the referees" [surely bad calls happen to all teams]), *catastrophizing* ("We'll never win a championship" [one call surely doesn't predict eternity]), or *labeling* and *name calling* ("Their fans are a bunch of ..." [their fans are likely no more or less biased or bad than your team's fans]).

It's probably not worth developing a self-improvement plan to deal with our responses to a game. But if we're talking about how we handle difficult situations at work, that's different. There, our ability to respond skillfully in the moment and our willingness to keep approaching rather than avoiding similar situations in the future is quite important to us and others. Learning to see things differently and tell ourselves more productive stories in real time is really valuable.

As I've discussed, learning to recognize and change unproductive thinking under stress is pretty hard if you haven't even practiced in less stressful circumstances. That's why psychologists recommend learning new ways of seeing a situation and rehearsing them over and over.[3] This is what John Lewis and his peers did to prepare to nonviolently resist and is the essence of Mary Gentile's approach for learning to competently "give voice to values" at work.[4] For example, you have to *script out* the reminder you're going to silently give yourself at the first sign you're starting to distort what's happening; you have to *think through* what you'll tell yourself when someone starts shutting you down; and you have to *mentally rehearse* what you're going to say or do at the first sign your action is derailing.

Trust me, I'm not lecturing you from a place of presumed perfection. I continuously push for change at work, and thinking productively under stress is something I struggle to master to this day. When I share an idea and it's not immediately met with open arms, I often feel a flash of anger and my mind races to generalizations (e.g., "He *never* supports innovation") and catastrophizing (e.g., "This is why higher education is *doomed*"). Since these thoughts are both inaccurate and sure to create negative reactions if verbalized, I remind myself ahead of time to counteract these automatic reactions with more helpful thoughts. For example, I might prepare to defuel my initial reactions by writing down alternative narratives, such as "His initial reactions often soften as more compelling data is shared."

What about you? As you think about taking small steps up your courage ladder, what unhelpful thoughts do you want to practice recognizing and changing? On the left side of a sheet of paper or spreadsheet, jot down one or two common thought patterns you have under stress that you realize are unhelpful. Then, on the right side, write down one or two alternative things for each you'd like to tell yourself when you next have that thought. Also record somewhere how, specifically, you're going to remind yourself of these goals before your next stressful interaction.

Mastering New Communication Tools

We've already talked about the importance of framing your actions in ways that are less offensive and more compelling to others. Let's look here at some other powerful tools for succeeding in difficult conversations, including some additional types of inflammatory language to avoid in already hot situations.

Imagine you were recently promoted and one of your direct reports is someone significantly older than you. Now let's add a twist. That same older colleague was your boss and mentor before your promotion. For months, you've tried to discuss his feelings and how you could still work together well. But he's been unwilling to talk and has largely carried on as if nothing has changed. This is undermining your authority and causing confusion with other stakeholders such as clients.

The problem is this. You're thinking, "You owe it to me to change your behavior immediately," but he sees it another way: "You screwed me. The least you can do now is leave me alone." If neither of you skillfully moves the conversation beyond these conclusive statements—or what the late Harvard professor Chris Argyris described as the top rung of each person's cognitive ladder of inference—all that's likely to happen next is that you'll escalate the volume and harshness with which you each lob your convictions back and forth.[5] If you're the higher-power person (which you would be in this situation), you might appear to "win" because your subordinate is likely to give up sooner out of fear. But what exactly have you won? You have no better understanding of his feelings or reasoning, and he understands yours no better. And while you may be able to coerce some short-term, visible change from him, you've certainly only further alienated him and increased the likelihood that he's giving less effort and going to continue subtly undermining you.

Getting past this kind of "top of the ladder" impasse requires skillful use of both "advocacy" and "inquiry."[6] Advocacy is *not* about simply stating your *conclusion* (your top rung) more loudly or articulately; it's about revealing what's below your conclusion on your cognitive ladder. At the lowest level is the *data* you're drawing from as the basis for your conclusion. In the example here, you might point to facts such as, "I've tried to discuss this with you, and have given you time to process your feelings and adjust" and "I've not corrected your inappropriate behavior in staff meetings."

Your next step is to reveal your *reasoning* (which is driven by the data and experiences you're paying attention to). You might, for example, say, "I have been patient and empathic and given you time to adjust to the new reality." Having shared your data and reasoning, the bases for your conclusion ("That's why I'm saying that I need you to change your behavior") are clearer. He still might not like this conclusion, but at least you've started to create a common pool of understanding from which the conversation might proceed.

But even if you skillfully advocate by revealing your own ladder of inference, you're at most halfway to a conversation that might produce a mutually satisfactory outcome. You've also got to engage in skillful inquiry, which involves getting your new subordinate to reveal what's below *his* conclusion ("I owe you nothing. You should leave me alone."). Remember, there are a lot of relevant of facts or data points out there, and many plausible interpretations of most data. Your job is therefore to learn about your subordinate's data and reasoning.

In this case, your inquiry might involve questions such as, "Can you help me understand why you think I screwed you? What data or experiences support that conclusion?" or "What's leading you to think that just leaving you alone and leaving things how they are is healthy and productive for the team?" Your goal at this point is not to further debate his conclusion; it's to truly try to understand *why* he's concluded that. Most of us espouse the value of perspective-taking, but doing it well requires a skill most of us haven't practiced nearly enough: helping others share more than their conclusions with us.

Let's say you do skillfully inquire and he reveals facts like: "I spent years mentoring and developing you," "I trusted you on a million occasions," and "Some of our clients are not comfortable with you yet." He then shares his reasoning from these data: "You aren't the friend I thought you were" and "You still need me."

These would be painful things to hear, for sure. And are you now guaranteed to reach a better place for both of you because you've revealed your cognitive ladder fully through skilled advocacy and gotten him to reveal his through skilled inquiry? Of course not. But your odds are better because you've finally gotten insight into his recent behavior and what it's going to take to repair this relationship or at least make it functional at work.

Don't underestimate how hard it is to skillfully advocate and inquire in the manner described above. Nearly all of our training (think of high school or college debate, standard communication training, or even how you argued at home growing up) leads us to assertively push our conclusion, with or without skillful revelation of our reasoning and data. We're taught that overwhelming someone with our point of view is the way to "win." Conversely, it's quite rare to have learned to skillfully inquire during difficult conversations. Sadly, this is a mistaken notion of winning that leads to a lot of pyrrhic victories at best—we might get others to give up and pretend to accept our point of view, but this certainly doesn't mean we've come to the best solution for both parties or for our group or organization. If the latter is your goal, then you should welcome the idea that once you hear someone else's data and reasoning, you might conclude that they've got the better idea for moving forward productively.

Walking down ladders of inference through advocacy and inquiry is a powerful communication tool. But that doesn't mean it's easy or comes naturally. Phrases like "The answer here is . . ." and "We should do this because . . ." roll off our tongues readily; conversely, it takes conscious effort to say things like, "Can you help me understand what you're feeling or thinking about this?" and "Can you share the experiences or data you're drawing from here?" Like most of what we've discussed in the realm of developing competent courage, you have to *practice* employing advocacy and inquiry until you can use it in ways that feel and sound authentic to you and others.

Deborah Kolb, an emeritus professor at the Simmons School of Management in Boston, developed another method—"reframe-problematize-anchor on purpose"—to help people unfreeze their current positions and work together toward solutions. You start with *reframing*, which involves providing an alternative construction or interpretation of the situation. You then *problematize* the situation, which requires you to not only state the problem, but also to clearly articulate your request that the other be an active partner in working toward a mutually acceptable solution. Finally, you try to *anchor on a shared purpose* that can be advanced by working productively together.[7]

To see how this works, imagine a discussion between two managers at odds about their response to a competitor trying to steal business leads. Britt decides to use this tool to counter Jerry, who is advocating a "fight fire with fire" approach—namely, "going after those unethical jerks" using methods that are themselves ethically dubious. Britt starts by reframing the situation away from the competitor's behavior, saying, "Our core problem, as I see it, remains lack of site approval from any local government so far, not what our competitor is doing."

He then tries to problematize Jerry's position, saying something like: "You seem to be focused on retaliation. Help me understand why this is your focus rather than finding ways to bring a deal to completion ASAP without adding further risk to our plate." Notice that this problematizing involves inquiry—his request that his peer reveal what's below his conclusion on his ladder of inference. Finally, Brett tries to remind Jerry that they have a shared purpose, saying, "We both want to make money bringing our concept to consumers. Let's figure this out so we can get back to making that happen."

Beyond practicing specific techniques like the ones above, it's also worth the effort to eliminate certain words or phrases that, whatever your intent, tend to just create anger, defensiveness, and denial. Table 10-1 contains some of these trap words and phrases to avoid, along with the reason they tend to make a bad situation worse. For example, it's common when we're upset or passionate about something to use words indicating extreme (in)frequency, such as "You *always* . . ." or "You *never* . . ." This tends to go poorly for two reasons. First, your claim is likely not true, as very few things actually happen always or never, and exaggerating like this just undermines your overall credibility. Second, when you tell someone they always or never do something, it's quite likely you're going to get derailed from the issue at hand as the person starts a debate about frequency. "That's not true," they're likely to retort, "I did it on this date, and on that occasion, and that other time." If your intent is to get someone to start or stop doing something, keep the focus on that. Not on exactly how often they do or don't do it.

Breaking bad habits of language that get in the way is hard work, as is successfully using new communication tools. But both can be done, and when you start changing your work conversations, you're likely to see benefits in other spheres of your life, too. Albert, for example, learned and practiced new tools in the realm of business situations during his time in our leadership lab. When he reflected a few months later on the experience, he noted that he was regularly using the same tools in his personal life. Rather than aggressively fight back, which has been his default strategy for as long as he remembers, he'd

TABLE 10-1

Words or phrases to practice eliminating

Avoid:	Why?
Hot-button words like "inappropriate," "unethical," "unprofessional," "ugly," "bad"	They feel like character attacks. Words that threaten human needs to feel morally decent, competent, and likable quickly put people on the defensive.
Words negating room for doubt, such as "obviously," "clearly," "unambiguously," "beyond doubt"	They imply others are too stupid to see or understand or agree with what you're claiming or not open to other interpretations.
"Should"-ing others	Telling others what they should do feels like an order, and it suggests that there is some value violation they will be committing if they don't do what you say they should.
Telling people to "not take it personally"	If it feels necessary to say "It's not personal," then part of you knows it *is* personal. It's better to avoid this phrase altogether and acknowledge the pain or other emotions associated with things that *are* personal.
The words "You are . . ." to describe a specific behavior or fact	This sounds like you are labeling the entire person (e.g., their character) rather than just a specific behavior or situation. Saying "That's wrong" focuses attention only on whatever "that" is; saying "You're wrong" focuses the person hearing this on defending him- or herself more generally.
Saying, "You make me . . ." to describe feelings you are having	Feelings originate from within our mind and body and are controlled by us, not others. When you try to make someone feel bad for making you feel something, they will likely become defensive. If you own your feelings— saying, "I feel . . ."—others are more likely able to hear you and be willing to do something to help rather than be focused on defending themselves.
Exaggerations, especially those involving claims about frequency ("always," "never")	Your goal is to be credible, which is undermined by hyperbolic statements. Also, getting into an argument about how often something happens just sidetracks you from the issue itself.

recently used these tools to navigate a difficult conversation with his brother about the best way to plan their mother's birthday and to handle a difficult situation with several friends.

What will you work on? As you think about next steps, how might you practice revealing what's going on below your conclusions, and learning about others' reasoning and data through inquiry? What's a specific conversation you could try during in the days ahead?

Or for what conversation might you script out and then try the reframing-problematizing-anchoring on purpose technique? What trap words or phrases that you use are you willing to work on eliminating? If you're not sure, share the list with someone you trust and ask their opinion. Then ask them to alert you when they hear you saying one or two of the things you'd like to stop using.

Changing or Controlling Physiological Responses

Having healthy internal dialogue or a full communication toolkit won't be enough if you're so emotionally aroused that the more primitive parts of your brain have taken control. As discussed in chapter 8, competent courage also requires an ability to keep your physiological reactions under control, whether that means by doing things that keep you from getting overly emotional in real time, or learning to behave skillfully despite physiological arousal.

Mindfulness and meditation are increasingly looking like powerful tools for helping us cope with acute and chronic stress. Mark Bertolini, the former CEO of Aetna Insurance, began meditating when the pain from a skiing accident that broke his neck in five places was so unbearable that he was feeling suicidal. Finding that it changed his life, he became an evangelist for mindfulness practices at work, creating in-house programs for both yoga and meditation.[8] A double-blind study conducted on Aetna employees, who were randomly assigned into a workplace yoga program, a mindfulness-based program, or a control group (who did nothing new), found that those in both mind-body intervention groups showed significantly greater improvements on perceived stress, sleep quality, and a heart rate variability measure.[9] These benefits came from a program that totaled only twelve to fourteen hours of formal training over twelve weeks. So, while you won't be a Zen master overnight, you also don't have to move to Nepal and join a monastery for years to reap the benefits of mindfulness practice.

If you're not ready to make time for a mindfulness or meditation practice (even though you could start by devoting only a few minutes a day using all sorts of apps now readily available on mobile devices), you could instead just force yourself to focus on your breathing right before and during moments of intense interaction. Folk wisdom about "taking a deep breath" or "silently counting to ten while breathing deeply" actually aligns with the science on how our stress response works. When we're stressed, our sympathetic nervous system is dominating, as indicated by increased heart rate and blood pressure, shallow breathing, and other telltale signs. Slow, deep breathing, in contrast, activates the vagus nerve—the control switch for our parasympathetic nervous system—and thus actually does calm us down as the two components of our central nervous system return to a more balanced state.[10] So, while you can't usually stand and do some tai chi when you're in a stressful meeting at the office, you certainly can train yourself to take a few slow breaths before speaking or continuing to speak. And, if you can do that yoga pose, stretching, short walk, or something that makes you laugh before a big moment, do it.

To be sure, mastery of our automatic emotional reactions takes lots of practice. You don't quickly retrain brain circuitry that has evolved for thousands of years to keep us alive, but you can make real strides if you're willing to work at it. *What will you try?*

Rehearsing Mentally Is Good, but Not Good Enough

Let's revisit the notion of mental practice or rehearsal. The concept is simple: you play the situation out in your head, imagining the sequence of what you hope to say or do. Athletes do this all the time: gymnasts "walk through their routine" mentally, baseball players "see the pitch," and golfers "imagine the shot" they want to hit.

We can all do the same thing, imagining what we're going to say or how we're going to respond to all kinds of work situations. For example, Ken got flustered and nervous and had trouble "finding his place" whenever he interacted with someone more powerful than him. It had gotten to the point where he went into full-on fight-or-flight mode before important meetings and therefore "gave others full control of the conversation before even entering the room." Working with a coach, Ken learned that engaging in a specific "mental preparation ritual" helped him not just organize what he wanted to say, but also calm his nerves and bolster his confidence so that he can be questioned and challenged without losing his footing. Ken now uses this mental rehearsal strategy regularly and finds that he's actually enjoying the kinds of business interactions that he used to find terrifying.

As valuable as mental rehearsal can be (it's been linked to actual performance in lots of domains[11]), don't forget that two things will still be true: (1) no matter how much you practice in your head, others won't know you'd like them to start, stop, or change something until you actually speak or act; and, (2) no matter how much you practice in your head, where it's psychologically safe and you can therefore stay calm and think rationally, you can't really master "hot" situations unless you practice under circumstances that mirror that emotional intensity. Dress rehearsals can be helpful, but you've ultimately got to control your emotions and actions when there's an actual crowd out there judging you.

That's why colleagues Bobby Parmar and Connie Dunlop and I created an experiential leadership development lab (ELDL) at the University of Virginia's Darden School of Business. Our ELDL seeks to provide the kind of "graded realistic training" that Rachman studied in military contexts,[12] but to do so with a focus on helping people become more skillful in the kinds of workplace situations where the risks are primarily economic, social, and psychological.

Our actors are trained to do everything they can to mimic the emotional intensity of real difficult conversations and situations where people feel exposed, vulnerable, and on the edge of control. We are purposefully exposing participants to stress (in an otherwise psychologically safe context[13]) so they can learn to recognize and then change their reactions. Said one young leader, "it wasn't until I was actually confronted by an abrasive, abusive person [in the lab] that I realized how tongue tied and helpless I was in resolving situations like this." Said another: "The repetition and feedback have been invaluable. Instead of just talking about how I would handle firing someone, managing a hostile meeting, or pitching a board, now I know how I would react. Now I can walk into most hostile business situations like these with the confidence that I have seen it before and that I have the tools to be successful."

This book, unfortunately, can only describe the benefits of this kind of controlled exposure. To improve how you react under stress, you've got to actually step into situations that trigger a danger response and practice taming it with those alarm bells ringing. You've got to commit to action, not just contemplation.

Commit to Action

If you're serious about the challenge of cultivating courage, it's time to start converting your intentions into real action. Let's look at two specific steps to take next.

Set Good Goals with Implementation Intentions

Start by getting your courage ladder back out (or building it for the first time if you didn't in chapter 4) and setting some *challenging, specific* goals. Intuitively, we all know what hundreds of studies have shown—that lack of specificity means lack of real commitment and little likelihood of success.[14]

We say, for example, we're "going to lose fifteen pounds by fifteen weeks from tomorrow" when we're truly ready to commit; in contrast, we say we're "going to lose some weight this year" when we're not truly ready to get started and stick to a plan. The same is true for any behaviors you've put on your courage ladder. If your goal is no more specific than "Speak up to my boss more," how will you know when you've accomplished it? Is once enough? Twice? About what issue(s)? And how will it be motivating enough to get you past your fears since you can always tell yourself you'll do it some other time?

Make your goal S-M-A-R-T. First, your goal should be *Specific*. You might, for example, say "I will speak up to my boss *next week* about *inequities in our travel policies.*" That's a goal with specific "what" and "when." This goal is also clearly *M*easurable—you will know if it happens. If your goal included to speak up to your boss *while avoiding sounding angry and using inquiry to understand why she thinks the travel policy is fair,* then you likely need others to help you assess how you did. You might not have felt angry and think you inquired, but is that how it sounded to someone else?

Talking constructively to your boss about travel policies is also *A*ctionable—it's something you have control over and can do right away. Talking to your boss about the travel policy is also *R*ealistic, assuming you have access to her and that this is an action toward the bottom of your ladder. Finally, this goal is *T*ime-bound—you've given yourself until the end of next week to have the conversation.[15]

Let's say you're not ready to commit to speaking up to your boss because you aren't sure you've laid the groundwork described in prior chapters or have the tools yet to do so effectively. In that case, you can set goals related to those steps. For example, if the issue is that you get tongue-tied every time you try to speak when you're nervous, what specific commitment can you make to work on that? Don't just think about how valuable improv training might be; sign up, pay for it in advance, and get to your first class this month.

Here's one more thing you should do to increase the odds of follow through on your goal—add what Peter Gollwitzer, a psychology professor at NYU, calls *implementation intentions.*[16] The core idea is to use stimulus cues (things that happen in the situation around your desired goal behavior) to make that desired behavior happen automatically rather than allowing yourself the chance to make excuses for not taking action.

For example, say your goal is to exercise more regularly. The problem is that there are always reasons cropping up to avoid exercising. If you planned to do it first thing in the morning, it's not irrational to tell yourself, "I slept poorly; this would go better later in the day when I'm less groggy." When your day has extended too long, it's also not irrational to think, "I'm supposed to go the gym now, but need to get home to spend time with my kids before they go to bed." But now it's evening and you "can't exercise right before bed or I won't sleep," so you've managed to talk yourself out of exercise all day without any untrue or irrational thinking.

Gollwitzer's method to address this problem is to build "if-then" statements to help yourself eliminate this type of rationalized avoidance. For example, you might link your exercise goal with the following cues from your body: *"When I have to use the bathroom*, I will walk up at least two floors to do so" and *"When I am so tired that I yawn at my desk*, I will get up and walk for ten minutes." You might even sleep in workout clothes and put your tennis shoes next to your bed, telling yourself, *"When my foot hits my tennis shoes stepping out of bed*, I will put them on." If you trained yourself to *automatically* use the bathroom two floors up, to *automatically* get up and walk when you yawned, and to *automatically* put those shoes on, you'd start exercising more without having to consciously battle your brain's amazing ability to rationalize it away one choice at a time.

This might seem too simple to make much of a real difference, but it's actually quite powerful. Recently I shared this concept and the example above with managers at a major construction company. A week later, I got a note about Tom, whose goal had been to review more architectural drawings because failure to catch errors leads to major rework expenses. The problem was that Tom just didn't think he had time, and so hadn't really committed to any new strategies for doing more reviews. After our session, he decided that he'd set a pile of drawings in a visible place on his desk and spend ten minutes reviewing them every time he got up to visit the bathroom. That created twenty to thirty minutes a day that he started automatically reviewing drawings (because he didn't decide to do [or not do] it each time, he just did it). Within one week, he'd identified three mistakes and avoided $50,000 or more in rework.

Implementation intentions have also been shown to help people reduce and take action despite their anxiety.[17] You can do the same with your courage goals. Think in simple if-then terms—for example, "If *my boss says X*, I will . . . ," "If I *feel my face flush*, I will . . . ," or "If I *notice Y happen in the meeting*, I will . . ."

Your brain will always try to avoid things that are hard. So if you're serious about moving forward, take some time now to write down some implementation intentions that will help you avoid copping out. What "if" and "when" statements will be your triggers to action? And what, specifically, will you automatically do when those triggers occur?

Commit Publicly

All right—let's do one last thing to lock in some action: tell someone or commit publicly in another way. This makes failure to act costly, in part because it makes it about our integrity. If we don't do what we say we will, it's clear to ourselves and others that we've failed to live up to a commitment.[18]

In *The Mystery of Courage*, Michigan law professor William Miller talks about the strategies used by seventeenth-century Italian soldier Raimondo Montecuccoli to eliminate possibilities for chickening out in warfare.[19] Montecuccoli purposefully let the enemy cut off lines of retreat, he burned his own ships and the bridges his troops had already crossed, and he assigned people to shoot retreating soldiers. While these extreme measures aren't exactly fitting for the average modern workplace, the point is that we can increase our commitment to action beyond merely telling others about our goals.

The company stickK, for example, helps people follow through on goals by having them sign a "commitment contract" and then providing various forms of support.[20] This includes having users agree to donate a defined amount of money to a cause they despise (an "anti-charity") if they fail to follow through. This clever approach is based on the principle of loss aversion—people do not want to lose what's at stake, especially when it's for something they would feel terrible about supporting.[21] Imagine the motivational boost if you're for major limitations to gun ownership and you've agreed to donate to the National Rifle Association if you don't meet your goal. Or you're a staunch Republican and you've agreed to donate to and canvas for the Democratic candidate in the next local election if you don't follow through on your goal.

Beyond the motivational benefits, sharing your goals can also create opportunities to learn and be supported. When others know you are trying to do something new or better, they can provide insights, resources, and contacts. And they can be on the lookout for ways to help you. For example, if your goal involves some kind of speaking up, they can pay attention to how you do it and offer feedback. If they see you didn't act when an opportunity existed, they can point that out too. Even if things don't go as well as you hoped when you stretch yourself, you've now got one or more people who know how hard you're trying and who will be ready to help you process the experience and get ready for the next time.

Climbing a courage ladder is hard work, with some falls likely. There's no good reason I can think of to go it entirely alone. So, who will you tell about your goal?

Remember

- Like any skill, competent courage comes from significant practice. We develop mastery over difficult, fear-laden situations by carefully exposing ourselves to, not avoiding, these situations.

- Increased competence in courageous situations can come through three types of changes: improvements in how we *think* before and during stressful moments, improvements in our *behavior* due to mastery of new communication tools, and improvements in how we handle the *physiological reactions* that can undermine our desired behavior.

- Everyone's courage ladder is different. The route to improvement involves building one that is specific to you and designing a plan to climb it one step at a time from the bottom rung.

- Setting SMART goals with implementation intentions can help make your desired changes a reality. Making your goals public can increase your motivation and your ability to learn from and with others.

CHAPTER 11

It's Up to You

*Hoping or thinking that we will be courageous when a
critical moment arrives is a cowardly approach. We cannot
become someone in 30 seconds that we haven't been for the
past 10 years. The critical truth of courageous leadership lies
in how we live every day, not just flashes of the extreme.*

—Colonel Eric Kail

love the above quote by the late Colonel Eric Kail. To me, it summarizes the core message of this book: things can change—for you and for others—but you've got to be willing to put in the work. You've got to let go of the idea that there's some magical personality type that makes all courageous acts easy, or a genetic endowment that equips some at birth with the skills needed to stand up, speak out, or step outside the box successfully. Similarly, you've got to let go of the false hope that you'll be ready and able when the big moment comes if you haven't been preparing for it by doing something time and again in many smaller moments. You've got to accept that real change requires a fair bit of your own perspiration, not just the inspiration provided by others. Doctors, nurses, firefighters, and others who risk their lives for us are capable and willing to act in stressful situations precisely because they've spent years training to effectively own this kind of responsibility.[1]

That's why I've focused in this book on competent courage as a set of skills to be developed through regular practice and a set of actionable steps you can take before, during, and after moments of courage that increase your chance of success and decrease the likelihood of personal trouble. We've learned about many ways to reduce the perceived and actual risk you face, and how to slowly but surely increase your "*can* do it" attitude through prudent exposure to challenging situations.

In the end, though, there's no way around the reality that courage ultimately comes down to your willingness to act despite, and in spite of, risk and fear. It's great if you can eliminate 100 percent of the perceived risk from a situation, but once you do so, it's no longer an opportunity for courage. That's why, in the end, courage also requires a "*must* do it" attitude. Your courage at work (and elsewhere in life) requires a willingness to endure potential personal pain on behalf of something more important than that pain and other negative consequences you might face. As management consultant and writer Patrick Lencioni has articulated, it's about deciding which values are truly core to you, and therefore worth enduring pain to stand for, versus those that are merely aspirational.[2] I'd add that it's about following your heart, not just your head. Indeed, the word *courage* comes from the Latin word *cor*, meaning heart.[3]

What leads us to conclude we *must* act despite the potential for personal pain? For some, it's a deeply internalized sense of responsibility—an inability or unwillingness to assume that someone else should do it, a refusal to be a bystander. Whether they're trying to understand who sheltered Jews during the Holocaust, who refused to administer electric shocks in the famous Milgram experiments, or a number of other risky or nonconformist behaviors, psychologists have had a hard time identifying concrete personality traits or other individual characteristics that reliably differentiate those who act from those who don't. What's been common, though, is a description shared by those who acted that they felt *personally responsible* for helping, that they *had to* do it, and that doing so was a matter of *personal integrity* or *authenticity*.[4]

Sometimes the drive to act comes from an intense focus on others.[5] Psychologist Stanley Rachman, for example, found in his military studies of courage that both airborne and ground combatants reported that their desire to avoid letting down their comrades played an important role in pushing past their fears.[6] That's also what Clemson psychology professor Cynthia Pury and colleagues found in their study of ways to increase courageous action. Mental rehearsal and other cognitive techniques were reported as helpful, but most common were strategies focused on the outcomes to be achieved through action. Specifically, those who acted courageously were likely to bring to mind those whom their action would help or, more generally, to remind themselves about the value of the goal they were pursuing.[7]

The sense of purpose and obligation that drives courageous action is independent from the sense that you're fully competent or ready. For Tachi Yamada, it was about contributing as much as possible to the alleviation of patients' suffering even when he was in new situations and navigating unchartered territory. For the schoolteacher who got fired for refusing to brush off a cheating incident involving a star athlete who was also the school board's daughter, it was about defending the principles of learning and fair play. For Fred Keller, it was about using his business to do social good when that involved trying things no one else had yet done successfully. For the many others whose stories I've shared in this book, it was about some driving force that made the risks worth taking.

Whether you respect his choice or not, it's also what drove Colin Kaepernick—then the starting quarterback for the San Francisco 49ers—to sit and then kneel during the playing of the national anthem before football games. What Kaepernick just couldn't do any longer was ignore the inner voice telling him to use his platform to raise awareness of ongoing racism and social injustice in America. Asked at the time if he feared being cut for this silent form of protest, Kaepernick said if it happened, he'd "know [he] did what was right" and that he could "live with that at the end of the day." Asked if he feared for his safety, he replied, "If something happens, that's only proving my point."[8] That's what *must do* looks like.

In the end, Kaepernick did find himself out of a job and still hasn't been hired by any other NFL team despite having better statistics than nearly every backup quarterback in the league and some teams' starters. It's a consequence, as he said, that he was willing to live with.

The same is true for Sallie Krawcheck, who says she "knew I would get fired" from Citigroup but still went ahead and did what she felt she must. Krawcheck was the CFO at the beginning of the financial meltdown in 2008. She argued that Smith Barney, which was part of Citigroup, had sold some investments that were much higher risk than people had thought. "We were dumb," said Krawcheck, so she advocated to the board of directors that they return some of their clients' money. It was a sound decision that would ultimately strengthen relationships, she thought, because it would "demonstrate to clients that we would do the right thing by them." Eventually the board sided with her on this issue, but Krawcheck was fired not long afterward.[9]

As I've shown throughout this book: you don't always get fired for doing what you feel you must. I'd never have written this book if I thought that was the case. Take Dara Khosrowshahi, the CEO of Uber. Following the disappearance in 2018 of journalist Jamal Khashoggi (who was eventually confirmed to have been killed by agents from Saudi Arabia), Khosrowshahi was among the first to cancel his attendance at the high-profile Future Investment Initiative hosted by the Saudis. This was no easy decision, given that Uber had received a $3.5 billion investment from the Saudi sovereign wealth fund less than two years earlier and one member of Uber's own board headed that fund (which was sponsoring the conference). Said Khosrowshahi, "I chose to end my participation because, quite simply, it was the right thing to do."[10] Not everyone loved his decision, but he remained CEO.

Outside the spotlight, there are many more unsung heroes who act courageously without getting in trouble. Martha, for example, stood up against the sexual harassment she and others experienced from their boss, the company president. She decided that either things were going to change or she was going to leave. Martha confronted the boss and gave him specific examples of what he had done, and how they made her feel anxious, depressed, and unable to trust him or herself. She told him she assumed that this was unintentional—that he thought he was just creating a fun environment and didn't know he was causing her to feel this way. Nonetheless, she said, it had led her to believe she was never going to be seen as an equal or promoted on merit alone.

Having gotten that out, she sat silently, waiting for him to either explode and fire her, or to invalidate her by saying she was being too sensitive and should just toughen up. He did neither. He apologized. He praised her for having the courage to come and say to him what no else had, even though now he was horrified to realize other women probably felt the same way.

Over the subsequent months, Martha's boss sought a lot of input from Martha and others. He then issued a formal apology to all staff, pledging to make the workplace a safe and equal opportunity business. He also promoted Martha to a VP position. In making the announcement, he praised her willingness to speak up and stand against actions that are wrong and asked her to lead the charge in continuing to improve the culture of the organization. It was an incredible place to be for someone who had believed there was no way the president would ever promote a woman in his company to this level of power and authority.

Is this the perfect ending we all hope for? Not exactly. A couple years after her promotion, Martha told me with disappointment that her boss had slid back into his old ways. But this time she didn't doubt herself, and she knew what the next right step for her was: finding a new place to deploy her talents. She'll move on with no regrets—she had stood up, demanded respect and change, and was willing to walk away.

A Note to Leaders

If you're in a position of formal leadership, where you manage people and also have an influence on your organization's culture and systems, I hope you've read this book from two perspectives. First, I hope you've considered how you, personally, can be more competently courageous. That's important for yourself, and it makes you a model for others.

Don't underestimate the symbolic impact that your behavior has: people pay attention to power. They see those above them as "embodiments of the organization," the living illustrations of what the organization really values and is like.[11] If you're not taking courageous action yourself—speaking up to your boss, taking prudent risks to defend and promote others, putting your foot down when you know something is wrong—the message is all too clear: "courage may be given lip service, but it isn't actually expected or rewarded around here." It won't matter that you *say* you want others to be courageous because, as Ralph Waldo Emerson once wrote, what you *do* will speak so loudly that no one will hear you.[12]

Second, as a leader, I hope you've also been thinking, "What am I going to do more broadly about this? How am I going to get the important behaviors described in this book to happen more frequently?" You might do what numerous organizations are doing these days, which is to claim courage as a core value and even use phrases like "encourage courage" as a mantra.[13] Sure, I've clearly been encouraging courage in this book. I think that makes sense when the focus is on ourselves—what each of us wants to do to be our best selves and make our greatest contribution to the world during our one short life. But if you're a leader of others, especially one with significant control over the organization's policies, practices, and cultural norms, are you really running a healthy organization if you've got to encourage people to routinely accept significant risk just to do important parts of their job? Put starkly by author and ethicist Rushworth Kidder in his book *Moral Courage*, "Something is clearly wrong with a culture that requires routine courage by employees."[14]

Said another way, encouraging courage without addressing the underlying reasons for your people's fear is essentially telling them, "You're right, it's not safe, and it isn't going to be. Please act courageously anyway." From my perspective, that's a serious case of displacing responsibility onto those with less power: you're telling the people below you to be more courageous without also doing everything *you* can to change the conditions that make key behaviors feel so risky.

So if you're a leader who finds yourself lamenting that "no one around here has enough courage," I implore you to investigate why everybody needs so much courage to work in your unit or organization and then to get serious about doing things to change that. Indeed, when leaders tell me they're interested in encouraging courage, I ask them why they wouldn't instead want to focus their efforts on decreasing the perceived need for courage. That involves doing things to create what Harvard Business School professor Amy Edmondson has called "psychological safety"—the belief that one won't be punished or humiliated for engaging in behaviors that help the organization learn, even if things don't turn out perfectly or feelings get hurt along the way.[15] For example, maybe rather than focusing training primarily on how employees can speak up more effectively it's also worth investing resources training people to receive and respond to feedback more constructively. Or, rather than pressuring employees to step out of their comfort zone, it'd be better to redesign evaluation and reward systems that convince people it's easier to get ahead by trying new things than by playing it safe.

These approaches—encouraging courage and decreasing the perceived need for it—aren't mutually exclusive. A senior marketing executive told me a story that illustrates how an organization can purposefully design a system to help change an important behavior from one that employees find nerve-racking and hard to do well to one that they have mastered and look forward to doing. When Pat Lafferty—now a marketing and advertising executive with senior leadership experiences in the world's top agencies—first started at Chicago-based ad agency Leo Burnett Worldwide, he was terrified at the meetings where creative work was reviewed. The entire chains of command on both the business and the creative sides were there, and the junior account person (which Lafferty was) was required to give feedback first. In the early days, Lafferty had the same physiological reactions he remembered feeling in his high school Latin II class. He was short of breath, sweating, and trying not to make eye contact. He tried to say as little as he could get away with in the meetings.

When Lafferty or other junior account associates did speak, they tended to "get their asses handed to them." From the perspective of Lafferty and his peers, the natural place to start one's feedback was as the "voice of the client." For example, the client may have said something like, "Our consumers really like it when we show people enjoying the food, including smiling while they are chewing." In turn, the junior account would relay this fairly directly, offering something in the review meeting like, "We should be showing more food enjoyment." This kind of feedback, however, was routinely shut down. Not surprisingly, Lafferty's and his peers' first response was to hold back in future meetings, even though they were closest to legitimate client input, so as to not get shot down again.

At first blush, this seems like a lousy, callous approach to training people. It appears to be creating embarrassment and fear and stoking avoidance tendencies. Actually, though, it was intentionally designed that way to help junior people learn. It was encouraging—in fact, requiring—courage from the junior folks. Yes, it was painful the first couple of times you gave feedback. But you were in the room (rather than excluded as a junior person) for a reason: to learn how to do it skillfully. You watched others do it better and worse, and you took notes about what worked well. You learned what you should be doing ahead of the meetings to be more prepared and how to deliver the right messages, the right way during the meetings. Over time, this decreased the sense that honest participation was a courageous act. Success made it feel much less risky.

The key, says Lafferty, was learning how to give the feedback in a way that built on others' ideas rather than appearing to tear them down. He explains:

> It really is as simple and as difficult as, "How can I help this work live and grow? How can I help it reach the potential?" At the risk of sounding overly dramatic, you should look at

the idea as you would one of your children. You wouldn't (or shouldn't) look at your kids and start with all that is wrong with them. You look at what is wonderful and special, and you help build on that.

This didn't mean that people at Leo Burnett learned to avoid talking about legitimate concerns. It meant that they learned to become masters of the "and stance" strategy discussed in chapter 7. They learned how to first affirm what was good or working with a project and only then move to how more value could be added. They learned to remember that any project was "someone's baby," so success in those meetings required beginning with validation and making clear you wanted to help that baby thrive. When the project's "parents" sensed this intention, they became able to hear the rest and accept help. Conversely, when someone just jumped in with what was wrong, the project's parents got defensive and wouldn't listen.

In relatively short order, Lafferty became skilled at framing his feedback and the other things he could do before, during, and after the meetings to add value without engendering negative reactions. Rather than looking down, he confidently made eye contact and contributed with confidence. He felt great being included in a key process undertaken by a team focused on doing great things. Sure, he still had plenty to learn, but the review meetings became enjoyable, and the self-confidence he gained in them positively impacted all aspects of his work.

It's Up to You

More than a half century ago, professors Philip Slater and Warren Bennis predicted in *Harvard Business Review* that "democracy was inevitable" in organizations.[16] Without "full and free communication, regardless of rank and power," and related behaviors that foster learning and creativity, an organization simply wouldn't survive, much less thrive amidst intense competition, they said.

Sadly, we're still a long way from most organizations being fearless democracies in the eyes of most employees. Among US federal government workers, for example, at least one-third of respondents to the annual employee survey in recent years have disagreed that they can disclose a suspected violation of any law, rule, or regulation without fear of reprisal.[17] As we've discussed, this same fear of speaking up or standing out pervades many other for-profit and nonprofit contexts. In a 2020 poll of 14,500 employees across industries conducted by the Yale Center for Emotional Intelligence, 80 percent said they felt constrained in speaking truth in their organization, including when they are under pressure to act unethically.[18] People worry generally about getting fired or punished materially for being honest or bold, and they worry about the social and psychological consequences that can also come from these actions. They assume that the way to get ahead is to be a "yes man," not an innovator or truth-teller.

So where does that leave us? One answer might be "in a state of despair." I certainly can't deny that courageous acts can lead to all sorts of negative consequences. It would be an irresponsible lie for me to claim otherwise. Still, for me—and I hope, for you—another place to land is "highly motivated to do something." Work environments are often dysfunctional, far from being great places for humans to spend the majority of their waking hours and far short of fostering opportunities to maximize potential to make the world a better place. In such environments, we desperately need more courageous acts from everyone. Not just from those for whom it seems to be easy (it's not), or for those we think were somehow genetically endowed with skills that we don't have (they weren't). From everyone.

The choice is yours! Are you willing to do the hard work of preparing yourself for moments of courageous action, to take steps to maximize your ability to act competently and confidently, and to do so with the best possible chances of success? And are you willing to act despite the risks that will always remain, choosing to stand for things that are more important to you and others than your personal success or popularity?

The irony in this all is that while courageous action should be done in the services of others, for principles more noble than self-interest, in the end it really is about yourself. It's about your choice to do what it takes to respect *yourself* even if not everyone else does. It's about the regrets *you* will or won't have. It's about knowing that in twenty years, *you* will be "more disappointed by the things you didn't do than by the ones you did."[19]

Both research and anecdotal evidence suggest that lasting regret is indeed far more likely to come from things we know we should do but don't than from things we do even if they go poorly. Recently I read business writer Amy Gallo's blog post about how to speak up about ethical issues. Among reader comments that followed, one man noted he'd done the things she outlined as best practices. Nonetheless, what transpired was a nightmare for him and his family. Yet he also said he'd do it all again. "Integrity cannot be sold, that firm is better off for it now and voiceless employees were represented," he explained, and further noted that his children "learned an important lesson of integrity which they carry with them as adults." And, he concluded, he would never want "silence in the face of injustice" to be the legacy he leaves.[20]

That writer will, I suspect, die feeling "good tired." As described by author and businessman John Izzo, good tired comes from focusing on the things that really matter to you, and being worn out but content.[21] Bad tired, in contrast, results from efforts to win in the eyes of the outside world while knowing you aren't being true to yourself. One way we fail to be our true selves is to allow fear and calculated short-term self-interest to prevent us from taking enough prudent risks. When Izzo asked the older participants in his study if they'd risked enough, almost every one of them said no. For many, that led to regret.

If Eric Kail pushes us to practice courage regularly by reminding us that we can't become someone in thirty seconds that we haven't been in the past ten years, Izzo's findings also warn us against waiting thirty years before becoming courageous in our last ten seconds.

We'll have a lot of regrets, and likely be "bad tired" if that's been our strategy for living.

I leave you with my favorite quote. It's from playright and political activist George Bernard Shaw. "The reasonable man," he wrote, "adapts himself to the world: the unreasonable one persists in trying to adapt the world to himself. Therefore, all progress depends on the unreasonable man." In the world of work that most of us inhabit, daring to speak up or stand out is still often seen as unreasonable. I hope you'll do it anyway, because all progress depends on it.

NOTES

Preface

1. M. Richtel, "Frightened Doctors Face Off with Hospitals over Rules on Protective Gear," *New York Times*, March 31, 2020, https://www.nytimes.com/2020/03/31/health/hospitals-coronavirus-face-masks.html; N. Kristof, "'I Do Fear for My Staff,' a Doctor Said. He Lost His Job," Opinion, *New York Times*, April 1, 2020, https://www.nytimes.com/2020/04/01/opinion/coronavirus-doctors-protective-equipment.html?action=click&module=Opinion&pgtype=Homepage; as told to Eli Saslow, "'No mask, no entry. Is that clear enough? That seems pretty clear, right?'," *Washington Post*, July 18, 2020, https://www.washingtonpost.com/nation/2020/07/18/Covid-pandemic-store-clerk-north-carolina/?arc404=true; R. Gates, "Kansas State Football Team Announces Program of Protest," *247sports.com*, June 27, 2020, https://247sports.com/college/kansas-state/Article/Kansas-State-football-team-announces-protest-of-program-K-State-offensive-tweet-Josh-Youngblood-Chris-Klieman-148609553/.

2. Like Amy Edmondson, author of *The Fearless Organization* (Wiley, 2018), I have been committed to trying to reduce fear in organizations for two decades. This book acknowledges that however important that task is, most people work in organizations where fear is still present and must therefore decide if and how to act in spite of it.

3. R. Lacayo and A. Ripley, "Persons of the Year 2002: The Whistleblowers," *Time*, December 30, 2002, http://content.time.com/time/specials/packages/article/0,28804,2019712_2019710_2019677,00.html.

4. M. Egan, "I Called the Wells Fargo Ethics Line and Was Fired," *CNN Business*, September 21, 2016, http://money.cnn.com/2016/09/21/investing/wells-fargo-fired-workers-retaliation-fake-accounts/index.html; Jack Ewing. "Volkswagen Says 11 Million Cars Worldwide Are Affected in Diesel Deception, *New York Times*, September 22, 2017, http://www.nytimes.come/2015/09/23/business/international/volkswagen-diesel-car-scandal.html?emc=eta1&.

5. https://www.gallup.com/workplace/266822/engaged-employees-differently.aspx.

Chapter 1

1. All quotes from https://www.theringer.com/2020/1/15/21066392/stuart-scott-espn-sportscenter-career-death-broadcaster.

2. Keith Olberman tribute to Stuart Scott, ESPN, January 5, 2015, 6:19 p.m., http://espn.go.com/video/clip?id=12125173.

3. All stories told in this book are true. However, to protect identities, I often use only a first name in sharing someone's story and change that name and any other nonsubstantive details to preserve anonymity. For example, "Chris's" story

is real, but this is not his actual name. In contrast, when a story is already in the public domain or I have received explicit permission, the person's full name and other details are revealed. For example, Stuart Scott and others named in his story are actual names.

4. Since the earliest recorded tracts of Aristotle, Plato, and the Chinese poet Mengzi—all before the common era (BCE)—courage has been written about in nearly every domain of intra- and interpersonal social life. Most dominantly, though, discussions of courage have centered on the physical bravery needed in battle. Plato, for instance, focused mostly on courage in military settings; likewise, the "good soldier" was the measure of courage for Aristotle. While social scientists and philosophers have focused more attention in recent decades on other types of courage, rigorous attention to the concept of *workplace* courage is still nascent.

5. This definition of workplace courage put forth by Evan Bruno and myself includes the two components widely agreed upon in the broad literature on courage: (1) action taken despite *perceivable risk* and (2) action that is in service of a *worthy cause*. Note that this definition does not require the cause to be "moral" or "morally good." Here is a simple example that illustrates why I believe some workplace acts are worthy enough to be called courageous without having to meet some formal ethical threshold. In one study I ran, each participant read about an employee, "Maya," speaking back to a defensive boss about one of four different issues: (1) a product line not well aligned with market trends, (2) unrealistic sales goals, (3) hiring trends not aligned with the organization's needs, or (4) unethical comments about people's looks, race, ethnicity, or sexual orientation. While all have potential value to the company, only the last issue involves a clear violation of ethical standards or standard conceptions of morality. Yet all of these behaviors were seen as reflecting significant, and a similar amount of, courage by Maya.

Whereas there's widespread agreement about action taken despite perceivable risk or for a worthy cause as core components of courage, there are other components less consensually argued to be central to the definition of courage that are not included in our definition. For example, philosophers have often consensually agreed that an act is not courageous if it was not carefully deliberated. In this view, no spontaneous acts can be accorded the attribution of courage. If this is true, those of us who think that running into the burning World Trade Center's towers on 9/11 was courageous are wrong. It likewise makes many people in one of my experiments wrong for thinking there is no significant difference in the courage level of a spontaneous challenge to an unfair criticism versus the same challenge voiced after a minute, a few hours, or a few days. The "deliberation required" view also seems inconsistent with neuroscience research showing that people can "automatically" or "unthinkingly" do all sorts of highly worthy, laudable acts.

Similarly, despite arguments by some, it's not clear that a behavior has to (1) be fully volitional or (2) involve recognized fear to be considered courageous. For example, we've run some experiments in which participants evaluated the courage of someone who engaged in a risky, worthy act because they felt coerced by a boss (who threatened to fire them if they failed to act) or by coworkers exerting implicit or explicit social pressure. In both cases, participants didn't rate these "forced" acts as significantly less courageous than when the same acts were described as freely chosen. Likewise, given that fear is increasingly recognized as the cognitive label we place on a set of physiological reactions and actual stimuli (that is, what's happening around us), there is no reason why people have to label their reaction "fear" or "being afraid" just because they recognize there is potential risk in an action.

6. P. J. Palmer, *Let Your Life Speak: Listening for the Voice of Vocation* (San Francisco: Jossey-Bass, 2000), 34–35.

7. The notion that courage is like a muscle that grows stronger with use was popularized by Ira Chaleff; see Ira Chaleff, *The Courageous Follower: Standing Up to and for Our Leaders* (San Francisco: Berrett-Koehler, 2009).

8. As reviewed by Catherine Sanderson, the primary difference between those who were complicit and those who defied authority in the Milgram obedience experiments, and between bystanders and those who intervened in actual dangerous situations, was prior training in the relevant kinds of skills and strategies (*Why We Act: Turning Bystanders into Moral Rebels* [Cambridge, MA: Belknap Press, 2020], 16 and 72).

9. Winston S. Churchill, "Unlucky Alfonso," *Collier's* magazine, June 27, 1931.

10. C. S. Lewis, *The Screwtape Letters* (London: Fontana Books, 1955), 148–149.

11. In surveys I've done, students ranging from their twenties to their sixties, and holding all types and levels of professional and leadership roles, rate a leader's courage even higher than technical expertise, intelligence, and work ethic in importance to long-term leadership success. They also rate courage as more lacking than those other qualities in ratings of leaders whose careers derail. Interestingly, though, it's clear that people have an intuitive sense that courage doesn't always go well in the short run: for differentiating short-term leadership success, my students rated intelligence and work ethic as more important than courage.

12. Some "going along" makes perfect sense, as it's hard to imagine a functional or healthy workplace where people didn't agree to abide by certain rules or be good followers most of the time. Whatever we may feel about hierarchy and rules, we don't like utter chaos or isolation very much either. So it's logical that we've created and largely accept systems (and associated cultural norms and social pressures) that require at least some degree of deference to authority and interpersonal agreeableness. But sometimes this tendency to favor stability and avoid conflict presents a direct challenge to our sense of integrity or authenticity, or to our aspirations to make things better.

13. Our desire to be liked is what makes Michael Bloomberg's conscious willingness to be unpopular so unusual and inspiring. Toward the end of his time in office, Bloomberg told *The Atlantic*, "Leadership is about doing what you think is right and then building a constituency behind it. It is not doing a poll and following from the back. . . . If I finish my term in office . . . and have high approval ratings, then I wasted my last years in office. That high approval rating means you don't upset anybody. High approval rating means you're skiing down the slope and you never fall. Well, you're skiing the baby slope, for goodness' sakes. Go for a steeper slope." From James Bennet, "The Bloomberg Way," *The Atlantic*, November 15, 2012.

14. In my own research, I've been surprised by how many types of jobs present at least periodic opportunities for physical courage. Restaurant employees, for example, sometimes need to step in front of combative or violent guests, as do store managers or bartenders whose fellow employees are being put at risk by irrational or intoxicated customers. Store employees show up despite the risks of being robbed, and keep coming back after it happens. For example, I interviewed a restaurant manager who'd been held at gunpoint early one morning and forced

to empty the contents of the safe into the ski-masked robber's bag. He was then left tied up and gagged until other employees arrived and found him. After calling his wife, he then helped open the store and stayed until mid-afternoon. Why? "Because we had a store to run," he told me. Sometimes it's employees themselves who bring violence—and weapons—into the workplace. When an employee pulls a knife on another or starts to physically assault someone, others on the scene face imminent physical risk.

15. In every organization I've personally studied, I've found people all the way to the top who are aware of the career risks of speaking up. They, too, worry about losing status, future opportunities, income, and more. Like the rest of us, they have their ambitions, mortgages, and kids' futures on their minds when considering pushing the envelope at work.

16. Charles Perrow, "A Society of Organizations," *Theory and Society* 20, no. 6 (1991): 725–762.

17. These career risks are highly visible in the realm of external whistleblowing. Though it's hard to get truly accurate statistics on whistleblower retaliation, and the figures vary quite a lot, we know that the percentage of people who suffer significant negative career consequences for speaking out about illegal, immoral, or illegitimate organizational practices is well above zero. From nurses to financial employees to federal workers, whistleblowers face real risks. Whether it's 5 percent, or 25 percent—or even some higher number—people do get harassed, demoted, reprimanded, denied promotion, physically accosted, or fired and incur other consequences for this extreme form of courageous action. See S. McDonald and K. Ahern, "The Professional Consequences of Whistleblowing by Nurses," *Journal of Professional Nursing* 16, no. 6 (2000): 313–321; M. T. Rehg et al., "Antecedents and Outcomes of Retaliation Against Whistleblowers: Gender Differences and Power Relationships," *Organization Science* 19, no. 2 (2008): 221–240; J. Mont, "The Whistleblower Retaliation Epidemic," *Compliance Week* 9, no. 106 (2012): 36–63; and R. Moberly, "Sarbanes-Oxley's Whistleblower Provisions: Ten Years Later," *South Carolina Law Review* 64, no. 1 (Autumn 2012): 1–54.

18. W. Deresiewicz, *Excellent Sheep: The Miseducation of the American Elite and the Way to a Meaningful Life* (New York: Simon & Schuster, 2015).

19. M. Egan, "I Called the Wells Fargo Ethics Line and Was Fired," *CNN Business*, September 21, 2016, http://money.cnn.com/2016/09/21/investing/wells-fargo-fired-workers-retaliation-fake-accounts/index.html.

20. L. Wong and S. J. Gerras, *Lying to Ourselves: Dishonesty in the Army Profession* (Carlisle, PA: Strategic Studies Institute and US Army War College Press, 2015), 28; https://www.politico.com/news/2020/06/19/navy-fires-brett-crozier-aircraft-carrier-coronavirus-329716#.

21. K. D. Williams, "Ostracism," *Annual Review of Psychology* 58 (2007): 425–452.

22. For more on the risks of social rejection, see R. F. Baumeister et al., "Social Rejection Can Reduce Pain and Increase Spending: Further Evidence That Money, Pain, and Belongingness Are Interrelated," *Psychological Inquiry* 19, no. 3–4 (2008): 145–147.

In light of these deep-seated fears of isolation, it's not surprising that research on reasons for employee silence include "relational" concerns. People don't want to upset coworkers, create tensions, or hurt others' feelings (see C. T. Brinsfield, "Employee Silence Motives: Investigation of Dimensionality and Development of

Measures," *Journal of Organizational Behavior* 34, no. 5 [2013]: 671–697; see also F. J. Milliken, E. W. Morrison, and P. F. Hewlin, "An Exploratory Study of Employee Silence: Issues That Employees Don't Communicate Upward and Why," *Journal of Management Studies* 40, no. 6 [2003]: 1453–1476). Is this because we're all so nice? That's part of it. But there's also a more self-interested reason: we realize, often subconsciously, that upsetting others also poses a social risk for ourselves. When probing for the reasons that people don't speak up or push for change, I commonly hear sentiments like the following (from a research scientist in a *Fortune* 100 company): "You might look like a show-off, not a team player, and then your peers would isolate you."

23. According to his friends, Raymond is willing to be unpopular and to not be liked as a result of doing what he sees as unquestionably right. But the fact that his case got so much attention suggests that his courage is the exception, not the norm. Indeed, a sergeant above Raymond chose not to submit a promised recommendation letter to higher-ups on Raymond's behalf, citing his need to "protect myself and my job and my family" (S. Knafo, "A Black Police Officer's Fight against the N.Y.P.D.," *New York Times Magazine*, February 21, 2016, https://www.nytimes.com/2016/02/21/magazine/a-black-police-officers-fight-against-the-nypd.html).

24. S. Polk, "How Wall Street Bro Talk Keeps Women Down," opinion, *New York Times*, July 7, 2016, https://www.nytimes.com/2016/07/10/opinion/sunday/how-wall-street-bro-talk-keeps-women-down.html.

25. E. Bruno and J. Detert, "The Workplace Courage Acts Index (WCAI): Observations and Impact," presented at the Academy of Management Annual Meeting, Boston, MA, August 13, 2019.

26. S. Lohr and L. Thomas Jr., "The Case Some Executives Made for Sticking with Trump," DealBook, *New York Times*, August 17, 2017, https://nyti.ms/2vl9fMe.

27. E. A. Cohen, "America's Crisis of Courage," *The Atlantic*, November 8, 2017, https://www.theatlantic.com/politics/archive/2017/11/americas-crisis-of-courage/545063/.

28. For instance, a 2016 Russell Reynolds survey of large public company board of directors from twelve countries consistently rated courageous behavior in directors as most important to creating strong board cultures and high performance. Specially, "possessing the courage to do the right things for the right reasons" was rated the most important director behavior, with "willing to constructively challenge management" and other similar behaviors rounding out the top five (with a significant gap between these five and the next dozen or so). See Russell Reynolds, "Global Board Culture Survey. Understanding the Behaviors That Drive Board Effectiveness," (2016).

29. J. Ewing. "Volkswagen Says 11 Million Cars Worldwide Are Affected in Diesel Deception," *New York Times*, September 22, 2017, http://www.nytimes.come/2015/09/23/business/international/volkswagen-diesel-car-scandal.html?emc=eta1&.

30. See https://www.c-span.org/video/?c4472965/user-clip-robert-gates-leadership.

31. R. Pieters and M. Zeelenberg, "A Theory of Regret Regulation 1.1," *Journal of Consumer Psychology* 17, no. 1 (2007): 29–35.

32. J. B. Izzo, *The Five Secrets You Must Discover before You Die* (San Francisco: Berrett-Kohler), 47.

33. S. Steiner, "Top Five Regrets of the Dying," *The Guardian*, February 1, 2012, http://www.guardian.co.uk/lifeandstyle/2012/feb/01/top-five-regrets-of-the-dying.

34. https://www.everytable.com/mission/.

35. J. F. Bonnefon and J. Zhang, "The Intensity of Recent and Distant Life Regrets: An Integrated Model and a Large-Scale Survey," *Applied Cognitive Psychology: The Official Journal of the Society for Applied Research in Memory and Cognition* 22, no. 5 (2008): 653–662.

36. A. MacIntyre, *After Virtue: A Study in Moral Theory* (Notre Dame, IN: University of Notre Dame Press, 1981).

37. Brendan Spiegel, "From Safety of New York, Reporting on Distant Home," *New York Times*, November 19, 2011, https://www.nytimes.com/2011/11/20/nyregion/from-safety-of-new-york-reporting-on-a-distant-homeland.html?searchResultPosition=1.

38. Yoko Wakatsuki and Jethro Mullen, "Japanese Parliament Report: Fukushima Nuclear Crisis Was 'Man-Made,'" cnn.com, July 5, 2012, http://www.cnn.com/2012/07/05/world/asia/japan-fukushima-report/index.html?hpt=hp_t1.

Chapter 2

1. E. R. Burris, J. R. Detert, and D. S. Chiaburu, "Quitting before Leaving: The Mediating Effects of Psychological Attachment and Detachment on Voice," *Journal of Applied Psychology* 93, no. 4 (2008): 912–922.

2. C. Anderson and S. Brion, "Perspectives on Power in Organizations," *Annual Review of Organizational Psychology and Organizational Behavior* 1, no. 1 (2014): 67–97; M. Stanley, *Obedience to Authority* (New York: Harper, 1974); S. T. Fiske and S. E. Taylor, *Social Cognition: From Brains to Culture* (Thousand Oaks, CA: Sage, 2013).

3. H. C. Kelman and V. L. Hamilton, *Crimes of Obedience: Toward a Social Psychology of Authority and Responsibility* (New Haven, CT: Yale University Press, 1989), 53.

4. K. Flannery, *The Creation of Inequality: How Our Prehistoric Ancestors Set the Stage for Monarchy, Slavery, and Empire* (Cambridge, MA: Harvard University Press, 2012).

5. M. L. Fein, *Human Hierarchies: A General Theory* (New Brunswick, NJ: Transaction Publishers, 2012); C. Boehm, *Hierarchy in the Forest: The Evolution of Egalitarian Behavior* (Cambridge, MA: Harvard University Press, 2009).

6. As noted by Omoyele Sowore, a web news provider about all things Nigeria: "It is not so much a problem of freedom of speech, but freedom after speech. You can say a lot of things in Nigeria, but the question is: Will you still be a free person? Will you still be alive after you freely express yourself?" (quoted in B. Spiegel, "From the Safety of NY, Reporting on Distant Home," *New York Times*, November 20, 2011). Unfortunately, there are still many places in the world where speaking out against authority figures might indeed put one at serious physical risk.

7. Kelman and Hamilton, *Crimes of Obedience*, chapter 6.

8. N. H. Frijda, *The Emotions* (Cambridge, UK: Cambridge University Press, 1986); A. Ohman, "Fear and Anxiety: Evolutionary, Cognitive, and Clinical Perspectives," in *Handbook of Emotions*, ed. M. Lewis and J. Haviland-Jones (New York: Guilford Press, 2000), 573–593.

9. R. F. Baumeister et al., "Bad Is Stronger Than Good," *Review of General Psychology* 5 (2001): 323–370; J. S. Lerner and D. Keltner, "Fear, Anger, and Risk," *Journal of Personality and Social Psychology* 81 (2001): 146–159.

10. Ohman, "Fear and Anxiety."

11. S. J. Ashford et al., "Out on a Limb: The Role of Context and Impression Management in Selling Gender-Equity Issues," *Administrative Science Quarterly* 43 (1998): 23–57.

12. For example, Milliken and colleagues found that 85 percent of their MBA respondents had felt unable to raise an issue with a boss (F. J. Milliken, E. W. Morrison, and P. F. Hewlin, "An Exploratory Study of Employee Silence: Issues That Employees Don't Communicate Upward and Why," *Journal of Management Studies* 40, no. 6 [2003]:1453–1476); Ryan and Oestrich found that 70 percent of their diverse interview pool had hesitated to speak for fear of repercussions (K. D. Ryan and D. K. Oestrich, *Driving Fear out of the Workplace: How to Overcome the Invisible Barriers to Quality, Productivity, and Innovation* [San Francisco: Jossey-Bass, 1991]), and I found that only about half of thousands of employees in a *Fortune* 100 multinational said it was safe to speak up (J. R. Detert, "To Speak or Not to Speak: The Multi-Level Leadership Influences on Voice and Silence in Organizations " [doctoral dissertation, Harvard University, 2003]).

13. I. Chaleff, *The Courageous Follower: Standing Up to and for Our Leaders* (San Francisco: Berrett-Koehler, 2009).

14. D. E. Meyerson, *Rocking the Boat: How Tempered Radicals Effect Change without Making Trouble* (Boston: Harvard Business Review Press, 2008); Ryan and Oestreich, *Driving Fear out of the Workplace.*

15. Rothschild and Miethe, for example, reported that half or more of observers of illegal or unethical behavior remain silent (J. Rothschild and T. D. Miethe, "Whistle-Blower Disclosures and Management Retaliation: The Battle to Control Information about Organization Corruption," *Work and Occupations* 26, no. 1 [1999]: 107–128).

16. Both Worline (M. C. Worline, "Dancing the Cliff Edge: The Place of Courage in Social Life" [doctoral dissertation, University of Michigan, 2004]) and Koerner (M. Koerner, "Courage as Identity Work: Accounts of Workplace Courage," *Academy of Management Journal* 57, no. 1 [2014]: 63–93) have noted the frequency of this type of courage in their coding of qualitative accounts of courageous acts.

17. J. J. Dahling et al., "Breaking Rules for the Right Reasons? An Investigation of Pro-Social Rule Breaking," *Journal of Organizational Behavior* 33, no. 1 (2012): 21–42; P. Schilpzand, D. R. Hekman, and T. R. Mitchell, "An Inductively Generated Typology and Process Model of Workplace Courage," *Organization Science* 26, no. 1 (2014): 52–77; Rothschild and Miethe, "Whistle-Blower Disclosures and Management Retaliation."

18. For example, Okuyama, Wagner, and Bijnen summarized research showing relationships between nurses' level of speaking up for patient safety and care quality and team performance in medical settings; see A. Okuyama, C. Wagner, and B. Bijnen, "Speaking Up for Patient Safety by Hospital-Based Health Care Professionals: A Literature Review," *BMC Health Services Research* 14, no. 1 (2014): 61.

19. Whiting and colleagues also examined voice behavior through challenging the status quo for organizational improvement and found that when individuals spoke up about issues on a new product, they were rated higher in performance

evaluations (S. W. Whiting et al., "Effects of Message, Source, and Context on Evaluations of Employee Voice Behavior," *Journal of Applied Psychology* 97, no. 1 [2012]: 159–182). Howell and colleagues (T. M. Howell et al., "Who Gets Credit for Input? Demographic and Structural Status Cues in Voice Recognition," *Journal of Applied Psychology* 100, no. 6 [2015]: 1765–1784) found that credit union employees who spoke up with improvement-oriented information received higher performance evaluations and recognition from their supervisors.

20. A courageous act may bolster the actor's sense of individual agency, self-confidence, and self-respect; see J. Boyd and K. Ross, "The Courage Tapes: A Positive Approach to Life's Challenges," *Journal of Systemic Therapies* 13, no. 1 (1994): 64–69; C. A. Castro, *Military Courage, Military Life: The Psychology of Serving in Peace and Combat* 4 (2006): 60–78.

21. D. L. Finfgeld, "Courage in Middle-Aged Adults with Long-Term Health Concerns," *Canadian Journal of Nursing Research Archive* 30, no. 1 (1998): 153–169; K. Ryan, D. K. Oestreich, and G. A. Orr, *The Courageous Messenger: How to Successfully Speak Up at Work* (San Francisco: Jossey-Bass, 1996).

22. The notion that courageous action can be contagious has been discussed for hundreds of years. The eighteenth-century philosopher Dave Hume, for example, noted that "observing courage tends to cause it to spread among the observers" (quoted in *The Psychology of Courage: Modern Research on and Ancient Virtue*, ed. C. L. S. Pury and S. J. Lopez [New York: American Psychological Association, 2010], 16).

Much more recently, Rachman found in his systematic studies of courageous acts in the military that modeling has a major influence on subsequent action by others: for many soldiers the most critical determinant of their own ability to cope in situations of extreme stress was the model provided by their leader (S. J. Rachman, *Fear and Courage* [San Francisco: W. H. Freeman and Company, 1978]). Many others have likewise noted the contagious nature of courage; see, for example, P. Bocchiaro, P. G. Zimbardo, and P. A. Van Lange, "To Defy or Not to Defy: An Experimental Study of the Dynamics of Disobedience and Whistle-Blowing," *Social Influence* 7, no. 1 [2012]: 35–50.)

23. R. Biswas-Diener, *The Courage Quotient: How Science Can Make You Braver* (San Francisco: Jossey-Bass, 2012), 9.

24. 204 MBA and executive MBA students.

Chapter 3

1. J. R. Barker, "Tightening the Iron Cage: Concertive Control in Self-Managing Teams," *Administrative Science Quarterly* 38, no. 3 (1993): 408–437.

2. K. D. Williams, "Ostracism," *Annual Review of Psychology* 58 (2007): 425–452.

3. For a review, see J. R. Detert and E. A. Bruno, "Workplace Courage: Review, Synthesis, and Future Agenda for a Complex Construct," *Academy of Management Annals* 11, no. 2 (2017): 593–639; see also G. Scarre, *On Courage* (London, New York: Routledge, 2012).

4. N. Bienefeld and G. Grote, "Silence That May Kill: When Aircrew Members Don't Speak Up and Why," *Aviation Psychology and Applied Human Factors* 2, no. 1 (2012): 1–10.

5. L. M. Janes and J. M. Olson, "Jeer Pressure: The Behavioral Effects of Observing Ridicule of Others," *Personality and Social Psychology Bulletin* 26, no. 4 (2000): 474–485.

6. S. C. Rudert et al., "When Silence Is Not Golden: Why Acknowledgment Matters Even When Being Excluded," *Personality and Social Psychology Bulletin* 43, no. 5 (2017): 678–692.

7. J. D. Margolis and A. Molinsky, "Navigating the Bind of Necessary Evils: Psychological Engagement and the Production of Interpersonally Sensitive Behavior," *Academy of Management Journal* 51, no. 5 (2008): 847–872.

8. L. K. Trevino and B. Victor, "Peer Reporting of Unethical Behavior: A Social Context Perspective," *Academy of Management Journal* 35, no. 1 (1992): 38–64.

9. D. Stone and S. Heen, *Thanks for the Feedback: The Art and Science of Receiving Feedback Well* (New York: Penguin, 2015), 5.

10. M. London, *Job Feedback: Giving, Seeking, and Using Feedback for Performance Improvement* (London: Psychology Press, 2003).

11. Adi Ignatius and Howard Schultz, "The HBR Interview: 'We Had to Own the Mistakes,'" *Harvard Business Review*, July–August 2010, https://hbr.org/2010/07/the-hbr-interview-we-had-to-own-the-mistakes.

12. A. Karras, *Even Big Guys Cry* (New York: Signet, 1978).

13. Robin J. Ely, Debra Meyerson, and Martin N. Davidson, "Rethinking Political Correctness," *Harvard Business Review*, September 2006, https://hbr.org/2006/09/rethinking-political-correctness.

14. A. Headd, A. Nucci, and R. Boden, "What Matters More: Business Exit Rates or Business Survival Rates?" (Washington, DC: United States Census Bureau, 2010), https://www.census.gov/library/publications/2010/adrm/ces/what-matters-more.html.

15. A. Hardy, "Does It Take Courage to Start a Business?" (master's thesis, Clemson University, 2016).

16. P. R. Clance, *The Imposter Phenomenon: Overcoming the Fear That Haunts Your Success* (Atlanta: Peachtree, 1985).

17. V. Romo, "Oklahoma Sheriff and Deputies Resign Over 'Dangerous' Jail," *NPR Radio*, March 21, 2019, https://www.npr.org/2019/03/21/705331915/oklahoma-sheriff-and-deputies-resign-over-dangerous-jail.

18. S. Garcia, "Oklahoma Sheriff and Deputies Resign Over 'Dangerous' Jail Conditions, *New York Times*, March 20, 2019, https://www.nytimes.com/2019/03/20/us/nowata-county-jail.html.

19. Romo, "Oklahoma Sheriff and Deputies Resign Over 'Dangerous' Jail."

20. 2013 National Business Ethics Survey, https://magazine.ethisphere.com/wp-content/uploads/2013NBESExecSummary.pdf.

21. Leora F. Eisenstadt and Jennifer M. Pacella, "Whistleblowers Need Not Apply," *American Business Law Journal* 55, no. 4 (2018): 665–719.

22. T. Miethe, *Whistleblowing at Work: Tough Choices in Exposing Fraud, Waste, and Abuse on the Job* (New York: Routledge, 2019).

23. 2013 National Business Ethics Survey.

24. T. Higgins and N. Summers, "GM Recalls: How General Motors Silenced a Whistle-Blower," *Bloomberg*, June 19, 2014, https://www.bloomberg.com/news/articles/2014-06-18/gm-recalls-whistle-blower-was-ignored-mary-barra-faces-congress.

25. A. S. Kesselheim, D. M. Studdert, and M. M. Mello, "Whistle-Blowers' Experiences in Fraud Litigation Against Pharmaceutical Companies," *New England Journal of Medicine* 362, no. 19 (2010): 1832–1839.

26. K. Ohnishi et al., "The Process of Whistleblowing in a Japanese Psychiatric Hospital," *Nursing Ethics* 15, no. 5 (2008): 631–642.

27. For instance, while observers acknowledge that peer reporters (of unethical behavior) are highly ethical, they also tend to evaluate them as unlikeable

(L. K. Trevino and B. Victor, "Peer Reporting of Unethical Behavior: A Social Context Perspective," *Academy of Management Journal* 35, no. 1 [1992]: 38–64). For related work on the rejection of moral rebels, see B. Monin, P. J. Sawyer, and M. J. Marquez, "The Rejection of Moral Rebels: Resenting Those Who Do the Right Thing," *Journal of Personality and Social Psychology* 95, no. 1 (2008): 76–93.

28. In the speaking-up and voice literatures, scholars have found resistance to workplace bullying to have mixed results. For example, Lutgen-Sandvik found that employees often failed to stop the bullying, especially when taking action by themselves. This resulted in the victims commonly quitting or transferring from their position (P. Lutgen-Sandvik, "Take This Job and . . . Quitting and Other Forms of Resistance to Workplace Bullying," *Communication Monographs* 73, no. 4 [2006]: 406-433).

29. A. Friedersdorf, "The Cowardice of Covering for Too-Violent Cops," *The Atlantic*, April 24, 2018, https://www.theatlantic.com/politics/archive/2018/04/the-cowardice-of-covering-for-too-violent-cops/557603/.

30. S. Dewan and S. F. Kovaleski, "Thousands of Complaints Do Little to Change Police Ways," *New York Times*, updated June 8, 2020, https://www.nytimes.com/2020/05/30/us/derek-chauvin-george-floyd.html.

31. B. Pennington, "In Man's Game, Mark Herzlich Is Standing Up for Women," *New York Times*, October 24, 2015, https://www.nytimes.com/2015/10/25/sports/football/in-mans-game-mark-herzlich-is-standing-up-for-women.html.

32. On espoused versus in-use values, see Chris Argyris, "Teaching Smart People How to Learn," *Harvard Business Review*, May–June 1991, https://hbr.org/1991/05/teaching-smart-people-how-to-learn. On aspirational versus core values, see Patrick M. Leoncioni, "Make Your Values Mean Something," *Harvard Business Review*, July 2002, https://hbr.org/2002/07/make-your-values-mean-something.

Chapter 4

1. S. J. Rachman, "Courage: A Psychological Perspective," in *The Psychology of Courage: Modern Research on an Ancient Virtue*, ed. C. L. S. Pury and S. J. Lopez (Washington, DC: American Psychological Association, 2010), chapter 5.

2. K. Gray, "Moral Transformation: Good and Evil Turn the Weak into the Mighty," *Social Psychological and Personality Science* 1, no. 3 (2010): 253–258.

3. D. K. Goodwin, *Leadership in Turbulent Times* (New York: Simon & Schuster, 2018), 129.

4. Goodwin, *Leadership in Turbulent Times*, 130.

5. A. Ericsson and R. Pool, *Peak: Secrets from the New Science of Expertise* (Boston: Houghton Mifflin Harcourt, 2016).

6. J. F. Stone, *Meditation for Healing: Particular Meditations for Particular Results* (Albuquerque, NM: Good Karma Publishing, 1995).

7. https://onbeing.org/programs/john-lewis-love-in-action/#transcript; https://scopeblog.stanford.edu/2020/07/22/remembering-rep-john-lewis-a-civil-rights-icons-words-to-stanford-students/.

8. J. E. LeDoux, *Anxious: Using the Brain to Understand and Treat Fear and Anxiety* (New York: Penguin, 2015), 261–262.

9. J. M. Strayhorn, *Anxiety Reduction and Courage Skills* (Wexford, PA: Psychological Skills Press, 2012), 43.

10. M. S. Peck, *Further along the Road Less Traveled: The Unending Journey towards Spiritual Growth* (New York: Simon & Schuster, 1998).

11. Strayhorn, *Anxiety Reduction and Courage Skills*.

12. I. Chaleff, *The Courageous Follower: Standing Up to and for Our Leaders.* (San Francisco: Berrett-Koehler, 2009).

13. https://citatis.com/a18429/31b134/.

14. Ibid.

15. A. Carey and J. Hoffman, "Lessons in the Delicate Art of Confronting Offensive Speech," *New York Times*, October 12, 2016, https://www.nytimes.com/2016/10/13/science/donald-trump-billy-bush-offensive-speech.html.

16. A. Bandura, *Self-Efficacy: The Exercise of Control* (New York: W. H. Freeman, 1997).

17. A. B. Caza and L. P. Milton, "Resilience at Work: Building Capacity in the Face of Adversity," in *Oxford Handbook of Positive Organizational Scholarship*, ed. K. S. Cameron and G. M. Spreitzer (New York: Oxford University Press, 2012), 895–908.

18. For more on the need for courage in the auditing profession, see https://www.iia.nl/SiteFiles/Moral%20Courage%20and%20Internal%20Auditors-bw-web.pdf.

19. K. E. Weick, "Small Wins: Redefining the Scale of Social Problems," *American Psychologist* 39, no. 1 (1984): 40–49.

Chapter 5

1. E. P. Hollander, "Conformity, Status and Idiosyncrasy Credit," *Psychological Review* 65, no. 2 (1958): 117–127.

2. A. Cuddy, P. Glick, and A. Beninger, "The Dynamics of Warmth and Competence Judgments, and Their Outcomes in Organizations," in *Research in Organizational Behavior*, vol. 31 (Amsterdam: Elsevier, 2011), 73–98.

3. For more on the distinction between power and influence, see R. M. Emerson, "Power Dependence Relations," *American Sociological Review* 27 (1962): 30–41; and R. B. Cialdini and N. J. Goldstein, "Social Influence: Compliance and Conformity," *Annual Review of Psychology* 55 (2004): 591–621.

4. For a review of and citations related to these nonverbal tactics for creating immediate warmth judgments, see Cuddy, Glick, and Beninger, "The Dynamics of Warmth and Competence Judgments," 88.

5. D. E. Meyerson, *Rocking the Boat: How Tempered Radicals Effect Change without Making Trouble* (Boston: Harvard Business Review Press, 2008).

6. Jay Conger, "The Necessary Art of Persuasion," *Harvard Business Review*, May–June 1998, https://hbr.org/1998/05/the-necessary-art-of-persuasion.

7. Author interview, December 15, 2015.

8. For example, Wickert and DeBakker, in their study of how those who pitch corporate social responsibility in ways that overcome resistance, found that influence is a cumulative process that requires time to build relationships and demonstrate credibility (C. Wickert and F. De Bakker, "Pitching for Social Change: Toward a Relational Approach to Selling and Buying Social Issues," *Academy of Management Discoveries* 4, no. 1 [2018]: 50–73). Likewise, Vadera and colleagues argued that networking/coalition or alliance building prior to engaging in constructive deviance is likely to reduce the degree to which subsequent acts get one labeled a troublemaker and/or ignored (A. K. Vadera, M. G. Pratt, and P. Mishra, "Constructive Deviance in Organizations: Integrating and Moving Forward," *Journal of Management* 39, no. 5 [2013]: 1221–1276).

9. For a discussion of the components of emotional intelligence and science-based recommendations for how to best assess these abilities, see J. D.

Mayer, D. R. Caruso, and P. Salovey, "Selecting a Measure of Emotional Intelligence: The Case for Ability Scales," in *The Handbook of Emotional Intelligence: Theory, Development, Assessment, and Application at Home, School, and in the Workplace*, ed. R. Bar-On and J. D. A. Parker (San Francisco: Jossey-Bass, 2000), 320–342.

10. J. P. Near and M. P. Miceli, "Effective-Whistle Blowing," *Academy of Management Review* 20, no. 3 (1995): 679–708.

11. J. Sprague and G. L. Ruud, "Boat-Rocking in the High-Technology Culture," *American Behavioral Scientist* 32, no. 2 (1988): 169–193; Meyerson, *Rocking the Boat*.

12. Linda Hill and Suzy Wetlaufer, "Leadership When There Is No One to Ask: An Interview with Eni's Franco Bernabé," *Harvard Business Review*, July–August 1998, https://hbr.org/1998/07/leadership-when-there-is-no-one-to-ask-an-interview-with-enis-franco-bernabe.

13. M. Rowe, L. Wilcox, and H. Gadlin, "Dealing with—or Reporting—'Unacceptable' Behavior," *Journal of the International Ombudsman Association* 2, no. 1 (2009): 52–64.

14. I. Chaleff, *The Courageous Follower: Standing Up to and for Our Leaders* (San Francisco: Berrett-Koehler Publishers, 2009), 21.

Chapter 6

1. A. H. Redmoon, "No Peaceful Warriors!" *Gnosis* 21 (1999).

2. D. Brooks, "The Moral Bucket List," opinion, *New York Times*, April 11, 2015, https://www.nytimes.com/2015/04/12/opinion/sunday/david-brooks-the-moral-bucket-list.html.

3. M. Rowe, L. Wilcox, and H. Gadlin, "Dealing with—or Reporting—'Unacceptable' Behavior," *Journal of the International Ombudsman Association* 2, no. 1 (2009): 52–64.

4. M. P. Glazer and P. M. Glazer, *The Whistleblowers: Exposing Corruption in Government and Industry* (New York: Basic Books, 1989).

5. S. Simola, "Understanding Moral Courage through a Feminist and Developmental Ethic of Care," *Journal of Business Ethics* 130, no. 1 (2015): 29–44.

6. J. L. Badaracco, *Defining Moments: When Managers Must Choose between Right and Right* (Boston: Harvard Business Review Press, 2016).

7. Adam Bryant, "Executive Women, Finding (and Owning) Their Voice," *New York Times*, November 13, 2014, https://www.nytimes.com/interactive/2014/11/16/business/corner-office-women-executives-owning-their-voice.html.

8. V. R. Newkirk, "Sometimes There Are More Important Goals Than Civility," *The Atlantic*, December 5, 2016, https://www.theatlantic.com/politics/archive/2016/12/discussing-racism-white-voters/509528/.

9. "Howard Schultz: Starbucks' First Mate," *Entrepreneur.com*, October 10, 2008, https://www.entrepreneur.com/article/197692.

10. B. George, "Why It's Hard to Do What's Right; Today's CEOs Are Being Swayed by Every Voice—Except Their Own," *Fortune*, September 29, 2003, http://archive.fortune.com/magazines/fortune/fortune_archive/2003/09/29/349894/index.htm.

11. G. D. Vitaglione and M. A. Barnett, "Assessing a New Dimension of Empathy: Empathic Anger as a Predictor of Helping and Punishing Desires," *Motivation and Emotion* 27, no. 4 (2003): 301–325.

12. C. D. Batson et al., "Anger at Unfairness: Is It Moral Outrage?" *European Journal of Social Psychology* 37, no. 6 (2007): 1272–1285.

13. Dale R. Olen, *Reducing Anger: Harnessing Passion and Fury to Work for You, Not Against Others* (New York: Joda Communications Ltd., 1993).

14. B. L. Fredrickson, "What Good Are Positive Emotions?" *Review of General Psychology* 2, no. 3 (1998): 300–319.

15. D. E. Meyerson, *Rocking the Boat: How Tempered Radicals Effect Change without Making Trouble* (Boston: Harvard Business Review Press, 2008).

16. W. I. Miller, *The Mystery of Courage* (Cambridge, MA: Harvard University Press, 2002), 268.

17. Kathleen K. Reardon, "Courage as a Skill," *Harvard Business Review*, January 2007, https://hbr.org/2007/01/courage-as-a-skill?autocomplete=true.

18. E. H. Dodd et al., "Respected or Rejected: Perceptions of Women Who Confront Sexist Remarks," *Sex Roles* 45, nos. 7–8 (2001): 567–577.

19. A microaggression is defined as, "a statement, action, or incident regarded as an instance of indirect, subtle, or unintentional discrimination against members of a marginalized group such as a racial or ethnic minority" (https://www.lexico.com/en/definition/microaggression).

20. M. C. Gentile, *Giving Voice to Values: How to Speak Your Mind When You Know What's Right* (New Haven, CT: Yale University Press, 2010), chapter 7.

21. Meyerson, *Rocking the Boat*.

22. Lois Kelly and Carmen Medina, "5 Mistakes Employees Make When Challenging the Status Quo," hbr.org, November 24, 2016, https://hbr.org/2016/11/5-mistakes-employees-make-when-challenging-the-status-quo.

23. Susan J. Ashford and James R. Detert, "Get the Boss to Buy In," *Harvard Business Review*, January–February 2015, https://hbr.org/2015/01/get-the-boss-to-buy-in.

24. A. Downs, "Up and Down with Ecology: The Issue-Attention Cycle," *The Public Interest* 28 (1972): 38–50.

25. M. C. Nisbet and M. Huge, "Attention Cycles and Frames in the Plant Biotechnology Debate: Managing Power and Participation through the Press/Policy Connection," *Harvard International Journal of Press/Politics* 11, no. 2 (2006): 3–40.

26. D. K. Goodwin, *Leadership in Turbulent Times* (New York: Simon & Schuster, 2018), 233.

Chapter 7

1. For examples, see J. E. Dutton and S. J. Ashford, "Selling Issues to Top Management," *Academy of Management Review* 18, no. 3 (1993): 397–428; L. Van Dyne, L. L. Cummings, and J. M. Mclean Parks, "Extra-Role Behaviors: In Pursuit of Construct and Definitional Clarity (A Bridge over Muddied Waters)," *Research in Organizational Behavior* 17 (1995): 215–285; M. C. Gentile, *Giving Voice to Values: How to Speak Your Mind When You Know What's Right* (New Haven, CT: Yale University Press, 2010); and R. B. Cialdini, *Influence: The Psychology of Persuasion* (New York: Collins, 2007).

2. D. E. Meyerson, *Rocking the Boat: How Tempered Radicals Effect Change without Making Trouble* (Boston: Harvard Business Review Press, 2008). Note that if your issue involves multiple stakeholders, successfully tailoring to your targets' preferred way of seeing or thinking about the world takes even more skill. For example, Wickert and DeBakker have written about the skill it takes to tailor cor-

porate social responsibility (CSR) pitches to the emotional and functional needs of different audiences. What appeals to or scares lawyers about CSR, for instance, is often very different from what draws or compels the same company's salespeople (C. Wickert and F. De Bakker, "Pitching for Social Change: Toward a Relational Approach to Selling and Buying Social Issues," *Academy of Management Discoveries* 4, no. 1 [2018]: 50–73).

3. James R. Detert and Laura Morgan Roberts, "How to Call Out Racial Injustice at Work," hbr.org, July 16, 2020, https://hbr.org/2020/07/how-to-call-out-racial -injustice-at-work.

4. B. J. Drury, "Confronting for the Greater Good: Are Confrontations That Address the Broad Benefits of Prejudice Reduction Taken Seriously? (doctoral dissertation, University of Washington, 2013).

5. M. Rowe, L. Wilcox, and H. Gadlin, "Dealing with—or Reporting—'Unacceptable' Behavior," *Journal of the International Ombudsman Association* 2, no. 1 (2009): 52–64.

6. Cialdini, *Influence*, 173–174.

7. Gentile, *Giving Voice to Values*, chapter 7.

8. Specifically, as an example, take responses to the question posed in a June 2018 survey: "The actor proposed solutions rather than just pointing out the problem." The mean agreement rating (on a 7-point scale) for the question among the 127 respondents who shared and rated a courage act they'd observed with a positive outcome was 5.46; the mean agreement for the 98 respondents who shared and rated a courage act with a negative outcome was 4.39. These means are statistically highly likely to be different from each other ($p < .01$).

9. J. P. Near and M. P. Miceli, "Effective WhistleBlowing," *Academy of Management Review* 20, no. 3 (1995): 679–708.

10. Noel Tichy and Warren Bennis, "Making Judgment Calls," *Harvard Business Review*, October 2007, https://hbr.org/2007/10/making-judgment-calls.

11. J. E. Russo and P. J. Schoemaker, *Decision Traps: Ten Barriers to Brilliant Decision-Making and How to Overcome Them* (New York: Doubleday/Currency, 1989).

12. Jay Conger, "The Necessary Art of Persuasion," *Harvard Business Review*, May–June 1998, https://hbr.org/1998/05/the-necessary-art-of-persuasion.

13. Mary C. Gentile, *Giving Voice to Values: How to Speak Your Mind When You Know What's Right* (New Haven, CT: Yale University Press, 2010).

14. D. Stone, S. Heen, and B. Patton, *Difficult Conversations: How to Discuss What Matters Most* (New York: Penguin, 2010).

15. Meyerson, *Rocking the Boat*.

16. For more on promotion versus prevention focus, see E. T. Higgins, "Promotion and Prevention: Regulatory Focus as a Motivational Principle," *Advances in Experimental Social Psychology* 30 (1998), 1–46.

17. D. Mayer et al., "The Money or the Morals? When Moral Language Is More Effective for Selling Social Issues," *Journal of Applied Psychology* 104, no. 8 (2019): 1058.

Chapter 8

1. W. I. Miller, *The Mystery of Courage* (Cambridge, MA: Harvard University Press, 2002).

2. J. Kish-Gephart et al., "Silenced by Fear: Psychological, Social, and Evolutionary Drivers of Voice Behavior at Work," *Research in Organizational Behavior* 29 (2009): 163–193.

3. J. Haidt, "The Moral Emotions," in Richard J. Davidson, Klaus R. Scherer, and H. Hill Goldsmith, eds, *Handbook of Affective Sciences* (Oxford: Oxford University Press, 2003).

4. J. S. Lerner and L. Z. Tiedens, "Portrait of the Angry Decision Maker: How Appraisal Tendencies Shape Anger's Influence on Cognition," *Journal of Behavioral Decision Making* 19, no. 2 (2006): 115–137.

5. Robin J. Ely, Debra Meyerson, and Martin N. Davidson, "Rethinking Political Correctness," *Harvard Business Review*, September 2006, https://hbr.org/2006/09/rethinking-political-correctness.

6. J. E. LeDoux, *Anxious: Using the Brain to Understand and Treat Fear and Anxiety* (New York: Penguin, 2015).

7. D. D. Burns, *Feeling Good: The New Mood Therapy*, rev. edition (New York: Avon, 1999).

8. James R. Detert and Ethan Burris, "Don't Let Your Brain's Defense Mechanisms Thwart Effective Feedback," hbr.org, August 18, 2016, https://hbr.org/2016/08/dont-let-your-brains-defense-mechanisms-thwart-effective-feedback.

9. For more on this, see Dale Olen's excellent short book *Reducing Anger: Harnessing Passion and Fury to Work for You, Not against Others*, 2nd ed. (New York: Joda Communications Ltd., 1993).

10. Jay A. Conger, "The Necessary Art of Persuasion," *Harvard Business Review*, May–June 1998, https://hbr.org/1998/05/the-necessary-art-of-persuasion.

11. A. Ward et al., "Naive Realism in Everyday Life: Implications for Social Conflict and Misunderstanding," *Values and Knowledge* (1997): 103–135.

12. J. Tosi and B. Warmke, "Moral Grandstanding, *Philosophy & Public Affairs* 44, no. 3 (2016): 197–217.

13. C. Argyris and D. A. Schön, *Theory in Practice: Increasing Professional Effectiveness* (San Francisco: Jossey-Bass, 1974).

14. R. L. Daft and R. H. Lengel, "Organizational Information Requirements, Media Richness and Structural Design," *Management Science* 32, no. 5 (1986): 554–571.

15. A. Goman, *The Silent Language of Leaders* (San Francisco: Jossey-Bass, 2011).

Chapter 9

1. D. Well Stone and S. Heen, *Thanks for the Feedback: The Science and Art of Receiving Feedback Well* (New York: Penguin, 2014).

2. In my study comparing the outcomes of courageous acts, people who experienced positive outcomes were also significantly more likely to have followed up to address lingering negative emotions or hurt feelings they may have caused.

3. https://hbr.org/product/Leadership-for-Change--En/an/304062-PDF-ENG.

4. Reported in D. K. Goodwin, *Leadership in Turbulent Times* (New York: Simon & Schuster, 2018).

5. J. White, *Rejection* (Reading, MA: Addison-Wesley, 1982).

6. C. Dweck, *Mindset: The New Psychology of Success* (New York: Ballantine Books, 2006).

7. C. S. Dweck, "Motivational Processes Affecting Learning," *American Psychologist* 41 (1986): 1040–1048.

8. S. B. Sitkin, "Learning through Failure: The Strategy of Small Losses," *Research in Organizational Behavior* 14 (1992): 231–266; S. Ellis and I. Davidi,

"After-Event Reviews: Drawing Lessons from Successful and Failed Experience," *Journal of Applied Psychology* 90, no. 5 (2005): 857–871.

Chapter 10

1. S. J. Rachman, *Fear and Courage*, 2nd ed. (San Francisco: W.H. Freeman. 1990).

2. A. T. Beck, *Cognitive Therapy and the Emotional Disorders* (New York: Penguin: 1979).

3. A. Bandura, *Self-Efficacy: The Exercise of Control* (New York: Macmillan, 1997).

4. M. C. Gentile, *Giving Voice to Values: How to Speak Your Mind When You Know What's Right* (New Haven, CT: Yale University Press, 2010).

5. A. Argyris, *Overcoming Organizational Defenses: Facilitating Organizational Learning* (Boston: Allyn & Bacon, 1990).

6. Jenny W. Rudolph, Robert Simon, Peter Rivard, Ronald L. Dufresne, and Daniel B. Raemer, "Debriefing with Good Judgment: Combining Rigorous Feedback with Genuine Inquiry," *Anesthesiology Clinics* 25, no. 2 (2007): 361–376.

7. Personal correspondence with Deborah Kolb.

8. Lila MacLellan, "The CEO of AETNA Was Considering Suicide Before He Found Meditation," *Quartz*, June 4, 2018, https://qz.com/work/1294914/the-ceo-of -aetna-was-considering-suicide-before-he-found-meditation/.

9. R. Q. Wolever et al., "Effective and Viable Mind-Body Stress Reduction in the Workplace: A Randomized Controlled Trial," *Journal of Occupational Health Psychology* 17, no. 2 (2012): 246.

10. J. E. LeDoux, *Anxious: Using the Brain to Understand and Treat Fear and Anxiety* (New York: Penguin, 2015), 261–262.

11. J. E. Driskell, C. Copper, and A. Moran, "Does Mental Practice Enhance Performance?" *Journal of Applied Psychology* 79, no. 4 (1994): 481.

12. S. J. Rachman, *Fear and Courage*, 2nd ed. (New York: W. H. Freeman and Company, 1990), 312.

13. On the importance of creating safe spaces for this kind of learning, see N. H. Goud, "Courage: Its Nature and Development," *Journal of Humanistic Counseling, Education and Development* 44, no. 1 (2005): 102–116; J. E. Gilham and M. E. P. Seligman, "Footsteps on the Road to a Positive Psychology," *Behaviour Research and Therapy* 37 (1999): 163–173; and Rachman, *Fear and Courage*, 312.

14. In hundreds of studies, specific, challenging goals have been shown to lead to more improvement than your "best" goals. For a review, see E. A. Locke and G. P. Latham, *A Theory of Goal Setting and Task Performance* (Englewood Cliffs, NJ: Prentice-Hall, 1990).

15. For more on goal setting and motivation, see E. A. Locke and G. P. Latham, "Building a Practically Useful Theory of Goal Setting and Task Motivation: A 35-Year Odyssey," *American Psychologist* 57, no. 9 (2002): 705–717.

16. P. M. and P. Sheeran, "Implementation Intentions and Goal Achievement: A Meta-Analysis of Effects and Processes," *Advances in Experimental Social Psychology* 38 (2006): 69–119.

17. T. L. Webb et al., "Using Implementation Intentions to Overcome the Effects of Social Anxiety on Attention and Appraisals of Performance," *Personality and Social Psychology Bulletin* 36, no. 5 (2010): 612–627.

18. Locke and Latham, "Building a Practically Useful Theory of Goal Setting and Task Motivation."

19. W. I. Miller, *The Mystery of Courage* (Cambridge, MA: Harvard University Press, 2002), 131.

20. https://www.stickk.com/tour.

21. C. Kahneman and A. Tversky, "Choices, Values, and Frames," *American Psychologist* 39, no. 4 (1984): 341–350.

Chapter 11

1. C. A. Sanderson, *Why We Act: Turning Bystanders into Moral Rebels* (Cambridge MA: Belknap Press, 2020).

2. P. M. Lencioni, "Make Your Values Mean Something," *Harvard Business Review*, July 2002, https://hbr.org/2002/07/make-your-values-mean-something.

3. C. Peterson and M. E. Seligman, *Character Strengths and Virtues: A Handbook and Classification*, vol. 1 (Oxford: Oxford University Press, 2004).

4. S. Oliner and P. Oliner, *Altruistic Personality: Rescuers of Jews in Nazi Europe* (New York: Simon & Schuster, 1992); S. Milgram, *Obedience to Authority: An Experimental View* (New York: Harper, 1974); C. L. Pury and S. J. Lopez, *The Psychology of Courage: Modern Research on an Ancient Virtue* (Washington, DC: American Psychological Association, 2010).

5. P. Schilpzand, D. R. Hekman, and T. R. Mitchell, "An Inductively Generated Typology and Process Model of Workplace Courage," *Organization Science* 26, no. 1 (2015): 52–77.

6. S. J. Rachman, "Courage: A Psychological Perspective," in Pury and Lopez, *The Psychology of Courage*.

7. C. L. S. Pury, "Is Courage an Accolade or a Process? A Fundamental Question for Courage Research," in C. L. S. Pury and C. B. Starkey, *The Psychology of Courage: Modern Research on an Ancient Virtue* (2010), 67–87.

8. Nick Wagoner, transcript of Colin Kaepernick's comments about sitting during national anthem, espn.com, August 28, 2016, https://www.espn.com/blog/san-francisco-49ers/post/_/id/18957/transcript-of-colin-kaepernicks-comments-about-sitting-during-national-anthem.

9. R. Safian, "'I Knew I Would Get Fired': Sallie Krawcheck," *FastCompany*, October 14, 2014, https://www.fastcompany.com/3036587/i-knew-i-would-get-fired-sallie-krawcheck.

10. Andrew Ross Sorkin, "When Business Executives Become Reluctant Statesmen," Dealbook, *New York Times*, Oct 16, 2018, https://www.nytimes.com/2018/10/16/business/dealbook/saudi-arabia-journalist-business-executives.html.

11. R. Eisenberger et al., "Leader–Member Exchange and Affective Organizational Commitment: The Contribution of Supervisor's Organizational Embodiment," *Journal of Applied Psychology* 95, no. 6 (2010): 1085–1103.

12. R. W. Emerson, *Collected Works of Ralph Waldo Emerson, Volume VIII: Letters and Social Aims* (Boston: Harvard University Press, 2010).

13. See, for example, Hiscox at https://www.hiscox.com.

14. R. M. Kidder, *Moral Courage* (New York: Harper Collins, 2005).

15. For more on creating psychologically safe organizations, see A. C. Edmondson, *The Fearless Organization: Creating Psychological Safety in the Workplace for Learning, Innovation, and Growth* (Hoboken, NJ: John Wiley & Sons, 2018).

16. P. E. Slater and W. G. Bennis, "Democracy Is Inevitable," *Harvard Business Review*, March–April 1964.

17. See items 17 and 23 in: https://www.opm.gov/fevs/reports/governmentwide -reports/governmentwide-management-report/governmentwide-report/2018/2018 -governmentwide-management-report.pdf.

18. Zorana Ivcevic, Jochen I. Menges, and Anna Miller, "How Common Is Un-ethical Behavior in US Organizations?" hbr.org, March 20, 2020, https://hbr.org/ 2020/03/how-common-is-unethical-behavior-in-u-s-organizations.

19. This quote is commonly misattributed to Mark Twain but actually comes from H. Jackson Brown's mother; see H. J. Brown, Jr., *P.S. I Love You* (Nashville, TN: Rutledge Hill Press, 1990), 13.

20. Amy Gallo, "How to Speak Up About Ethical Issues at Work," hbr.org, June 4, 2015, https://hbr.org/2015/06/how-to-speak-up-about-ethical-issues-at -work.

21. J. Izzo, *The Five Secrets You Must Discover before You Die* (San Francisco: Berrett-Koehler, 2008).

INDEX

ACKNOWLEDGMENTS

My first thanks go to all who shared their stories with me—both those illustrating best practices worth emulating and those harder-to-share examples of blundered efforts that are vital to the development of a more valid and complete picture of workplace courage. Some individuals are named (using first and last name); most have their identity disguised (first name only) so that they can offer their experiences without potentially exposing themselves or the other people involved to new consequences. All of them were instrumental in my coming to understand what competent courage looks like and in inspiring me to share what I've learned. This book literally couldn't exist without them.

I also want to thank my "teachers"—those individuals who throughout my life led me to love learning and to choose the path I continue to pursue. My mom (Sue Detert) taught me the love of reading, learning, and hard work from a very young age; my dad's (Dick Detert) own career as a professor has led to decades of good advice. And my hostparents—Teiko and Takanori Sakaue—taught me lessons about life and love that helped make me what I am today. I have also been blessed to have so many caring teachers from kindergarten through graduate school. While they are too many to name individually, collectively they have saved and supported me my entire life. Similarly, I thank the innumerable authors whose works have comforted, inspired, and taught me. They say that books "come to you when you need them"; that has certainly been true for me.

I do want to thank by name several of my most meaningful teachers, mentors, and colleagues relative to this work. My PhD committee was truly instrumental—both during my doctoral studies and since—in shaping the scholar I have become. Mike Beer, Amy Edmondson,

Peter Marsden, and the late Chris Argyris were, and remain, invaluable sources of support and mentorship. The late Warren Bennis was similarly inspirational and instructional to me.

Thanks to Ethan Burris, my primary research partner for more than fifteen years now on the topic of speaking up, and to Elizabeth Long Lingo for the very first thinking we did together about workplace courage nearly two decades ago.

Thanks also to many at my three post-PhD academic homes. Thanks to Dave Harrison, Tim Pollock, and Linda Trevino for teaching me to do first-rate social science at Penn State and for their enduring support. Thanks to my colleagues (especially Mark Milstein), my doctoral students (especially Sean Martin and Nate Pettit), my undergraduate research team (Malik Saric, Jess Reif, and Beatrice Jin), and the support staff (Nancy Bell, Annie Johnston, and Terri Whitaker) at Cornell, where I did much of the research that supports this book. I also give specific acknowledgement to the late Lieutenant Colonel Jerry Rizzo, my partner in developing competent courage in emerging leaders at Cornell, and a man whose own life depicted the courage, character, and compassion we strove to inculcate in others.

At the University of Virginia, where I wrote this book, I am grateful to many associated with the Darden School of Business. Thank you to Kelly Bean for her support of the development of the Workplace Courage Acts Index (WCAI), to the Darden Research Committee for their support of this work, and to Ed Hess for offering unwavering support of me and keen insight about this work.

I am also grateful to Bobby Parmar, Connie Dunlop, Brianna Hare, and the rest of the team with whom I've developed the Experiential Leadership Development Lab, where we aspire to help individuals develop the kinds of competencies described in this book using state-of-the-art equipment and pedagogical approaches.

As at Cornell, I've been aided tremendously by a research support team at Darden. First among these partners is Evan Bruno, my codeveloper of the WCAI and coauthor on courage-related research. Britton Taubenfeld has also provided outstanding assistance, as have

Christina Black, Caitlin Boyer, Patsy Leonard, Cheryl McGough, and Hassan Ziauddin. I am also grateful to Laura Goodman and Michael Woodfolk for their introductions to many Darden alums, some of whose "defining moment" stories appear in disguised fashion in this book.

I have also been fortunate to have an incredible group of people supporting my work at *Harvard Business Review* for many years. I am grateful to Lisa Burrell for taking the first chance on me and for her partnership numerous times since. She and other editors, designers, and marketing and communication experts there have helped bring my work to a broader audience.

My editor for this book—Kevin Evers—has been all I could have hoped for and more. He's constructive, conscientious, and incredibly competent. His stated goal was to help take the book "from good to great" while always maintaining my values and voice. If we've achieved that, it's due to his outstanding work.

I also thank my agent, Giles Anderson, for sticking with me for more than five years before I finally produced the book we first discussed. His insights into the world of publishing, and his support throughout the entire process, were invaluable for a first-time book author. I'm also grateful to Annie Cull, Rose Convery, and Tom Ash for their amazing work in helping me with the specific process of developing a website and the much more general task of bringing coherence to the questions "Who is Jim?" and "What is his work about?"

Finally, I end with the thanks that also reflect this book's dedication—"To the Detert women." For twenty-five years, my wife, Natalie, has processed with me nearly every professional idea and experience I've had, often to the point where I'm sure she couldn't stomach it much longer. I don't have a "life coach" because I have a "wife coach"—a partner whose wisdom, emotional intelligence, and kindness are unparalleled. And for twenty-one and eighteen years, respectively, I've been the proud father of Laurel and Ellie, the brightest two lights my world has and ever will have. All three of these Detert women have read my work, listened to my presentations, and discussed my ideas and stories with me so often that they could have written a pretty similar version of this book without me! They've also supported me emotionally as I've tried to act courageously throughout the years and sometimes failed to do so skillfully—and therefore found myself licking my wounds at home. This book is for them, and because of them.

ABOUT THE AUTHOR

JAMES R. (JIM) DETERT is the John L. Colley Professor of Business Administration in the Leadership and Organizational Behavior area at the University of Virginia's Darden School of Business and a professor of public policy at the Batten School of Leadership and Public Policy. Educated at the University of Wisconsin (BBA), University of Minnesota (MBA), and Harvard University (MA and PhD), Detert has also been on the faculty at Cornell and Penn State.

Detert's research, teaching, and consulting work focus on courage, voice and silence, ethical decision-making and behavior, and other leadership-related topics. His work spans global high-technology and service-oriented industries as well as public sector institutions. His award-winning research has appeared in all of the leading management journals and has been regularly featured in various online and print media outlets, including *Harvard Business Review*.

Detert is also a passionate educator and curriculum designer, having taught thousands of students of all ages around the world in degree and nondegree formats. He has developed dozens of teaching cases and tools and built several novel courses using simulations, actors, and state-of-the-art technologies to provide high-intensity, high-impact experiential learning. For this work he has received multiple teacher-of-the-year awards in both MBA and executive MBA contexts.

For more about Jim, see www.jimdetert.com.